CONRADIANA
A Journal of Joseph Conrad Studies

| Volume 49 | Fall/Winter 2017 | Numbers 2–3 |

PREFACE

Preface: Robert Hampson's Contribution to Conrad Studies　　iii
JOHN G. PETERS

Introduction
KATHERINE ISOBEL BAXTER and YAEL LEVIN　　1

ARTICLES

Conradian Claustrophobia: Gender, Confinement, Emancipation　　9
JEREMY HAWTHORN

The Tropical Forests of Conrad and His British Contemporaries,
in the Context of Aristotle and T.H. Huxley　　27
BEN FELDERHOF

Underwater Conrad　　47
STEPHEN DONOVAN

Geography and Law in *Almayer's Folly*　　67
KATHERINE ISOBEL BAXTER

The Spatialization of Moral Judgement: Borders in Conrad's
"Amy Foster," *Heart of Darkness*, and *Under Western Eyes*　　85
YAEL LEVIN

The Inheritors, H. G. Wells, and Science Fiction:
The Dimensions of the Future　　103
LINDA DRYDEN

Conrad and George Eliot: Imagining Time, Space, and
Event in *Lord Jim* and *The Lifted Veil* 121
   NIC PANAGOPOULOS

Movement, Gesture, and Space in *Heart of Darkness* and *Lord Jim* 137
   SUSAN JONES

"Ba! ba! Ba!": Voicing Noise 157
   JOHAN ADAM WARODELL

A "Modern" Amongst the "Standards": Conrad in the Classroom 173
   PATRICIA PYE

REVIEW

JENNIFER JANECHEK on Katherine Isobel Baxter's
and Robert Hampson's *Conrad and Language* 189

Notes on Contributors 195

Preface

Robert Hampson's Contribution to Conrad Studies

JOHN G. PETERS

Robert Hampson is among the most prominent Conrad scholars in the world today. He is also among the most prolific. Along with numerous articles, book chapters, and edited works, Robert Hampson has written three monographs on Conrad, all making important contributions to the development of the history of commentary on Conrad's works.

I first encountered Hampson's work many years ago while reviewing a collection of essays on Conrad. In an otherwise pedestrian volume, Hampson's essay was among few that stood out from the rest. Invariably, that has been a pattern in my experience. I am always impressed by the quality and originality of Hampson's work. This fact is all the more impressive when one considers that Hampson often works in well-traveled areas of scholarship (such as Conrad and colonialism or Conrad's later career) and yet consistently contributes new and evocative insights to the critical conversations.

Hampson's first such work was his *Joseph Conrad: Betrayal and Identity* (1992). As early as Virginia Woolf's reviews of Conrad's later novels in the *Times Literary Supplement*, concern began to be expressed about the literary quality of Conrad's later works. Not until M.C. Bradbrook's *Joseph Conrad: Poland's English Genius* (1941), though, did scholars pick up this thought and elaborate on it. Bradbrook's study was followed by Albert Guerard's *Joseph Conrad* (1947), Douglas Hewitt's *Conrad: A Reassessment* (1952), and finally Thomas Moser's *Joseph Conrad: Achievement and Decline* (1957), which codified this "achievement and decline" theory concerning Conrad's career. This view of Conrad's works became the dominant view on Conrad criticism for twenty-five or more years, and still has many adherents. To be sure, Paul L. Wiley, in his *Conrad's Measure of Man* (1954), took issue with this theory, as did John A. Palmer in his *Joseph Conrad's Fiction: A Study in Literary Growth* (1968), but these were voices crying in the wilderness as it were. Beginning with Gary Geddes's *Conrad's Later Novels* (1980) and Daniel R. Schwarz's *Conrad: The Later Fiction* (1982), some scholars started to challenge the "achievement and decline" theory in earnest. Geddes and Schwarz, however, tend to respond to the "achievement and decline" theory by arguing that Conrad's later works still reflect his early ideas and strengths but in a different way. It was not until Hampson's *Joseph Conrad: Betrayal and Identity* (1992), though, that anyone argued that Conrad in fact shifted direction in his later writings and sought to do something different from what he had done previously. This critical turn would largely push the debate about Conrad's later work in a new direction, as those who followed Hampson, such as Susan Jones in her *Conrad and Women* (1999) and Katherine Isobel Baxter in her *Joseph Conrad and the Swan Song of Romance* (2010), ceased to argue necessarily for the literary quality or focus of Conrad's later works in light of his early works and instead argued for their value based upon other criteria.

Like *Joseph Conrad: Betrayal and Identity*, Hampson's next monograph, *Cross-Cultural Encounters in Joseph Conrad's Malay Fiction* (2000), also enters a well-established critical conversation. Even though commentary on Conrad's colonial fiction goes back at least as far as Florence Clemens's dissertation "Conrad's Malaysian Fiction" (1937), criticism on the colonial aspects of Conrad's works did not begin in earnest until Chinua Achebe's famous essay "An Image of Africa" (1977). Since that time, issues of colonialism and imperialism in Conrad's works have been consistently one of the most dominant strains of commentary even down to the present. Much of the discussion has tended to consider issues related to whether Conrad affirmed or rejected colonial practice and ideology, as we see, for example, in Benita Parry's *Conrad and Imperialism: Ideological Boundaries and Visionary Frontiers* (1983) or even Edward Said's *Culture and Imperialism* (1993). Hampson, however, focuses instead on the way in which the West perceives the East and more particularly how Conrad presents the West through its encounters with the East.

Finally, unlike his earlier monographs, Hampson's *Conrad's Secrets* (2012) does not enter an already-existing critical conversation but turns in a different direction to introduce something unique. At the same time, *Conrad's Secrets* follows a critical pattern of its time of engaging with critical topics that had previously received minimal if any attention, such as Peter Lancelot Mallios's *Our Conrad: Constituting American Modernity* (2010), Richard Niland's *Conrad and History* (2010), Stephen Donovan's *Joseph Conrad and Popular Culture* (2005), and Richard Hand's *The Theatre of Joseph Conrad: Reconstruction Fiction* (2005). Like these other books, Hampson's *Conrad's Secrets* enters a new area of scholarly emphasis. In this work, Hampson considers issues that would have been familiar to Conrad but are unfamiliar to the modern reader, in effect, secrets. More particularly, Hampson considers such topics as slave trading and gunrunning in *Almayer's Folly* (1895), *An Outcast of the Islands* (1896), and *The Rescue* (1920); speculative finance and scandals in *Chance* (1914); revolutionary politics in *The Secret Agent* (1907); and trade secrets and lies in *Heart of Darkness* (1899). In each case (and others as well), Hampson brings to light historical and cultural contexts that have been largely lost to the modern reader. As a result, *Conrad's Secrets*, like all of Hampson's other works, illuminates these works of literature and makes the world of Conrad scholarship better for his having been there.

John G. Peters

Introduction

KATHERINE ISOBEL BAXTER AND YAEL LEVIN

Conrad scholarship is forever widening its reach. Over the years scholars have turned their attention to questions of biography, composition, and publishing history, geography, politics, identity, sexuality, language, translation, adaptation, medicine, music, food, finance, and more. Among this cornucopia of scholarship certain key issues emerge, notably identity, international and transnational concerns, and the life of the man himself. It is striking that these themes are also those which shape the key publications of one of the field's leading scholars, Robert Hampson. From *Joseph Conrad: Betrayal and Identity* (1992), through *Cross-Cultural Encounters in Joseph Conrad's Malay Fiction* (2000) to *Conrad's Secrets* (2012), Hampson's critical work anticipates and shapes these issues in Conrad scholarship.

On February 17, 2018, a symposium was held at Senate House in London to celebrate Hampson's work on the occasion of his retirement from Royal Holloway. The symposium brought together colleagues, collaborators, and former doctoral students who worked with Hampson over the years. The articles collected here developed out of that event. Our broad theme was "Space and Geography in Conrad's Fiction" and, in keeping with the variety of approaches noted above, contributors brought to the theme a striking array of perspectives.

This critical range notwithstanding, the articles collected here all demonstrate the huge impact of what has commonly come to be designated the "spatial" turn on how we adopt and adapt our approaches to Conrad. This critical turn in literary studies can be traced back to the work of poststructuralists, social theorists, and geographers of the 1970's. Fredric Jameson's *Postmodernism, Or, The Cultural Logic of Late Capitalism* (1991) follows the shift heralded by such thinkers as Michel Foucault, Henri Lefebvre, and David Harvey in articulating the need to attend to this particular critical focus. For Jameson, the transition should be understood as a historical marker of critical change. He writes: "Our psychic experience, our cultural languages, are today dominated by categories of space rather than by categories of time, as in the preceding period of high modernism" (16). Space emerges as *the* dominant historical, cultural, and literary trope, superseding time. Moreover, in Jameson's reading, this transition traces a fault line between modernism and postmodernism.

The stakes of this critical shift are helpfully unpacked in Robert T. Tally, Jr.'s introduction to *The Routledge Handbook of Literature and Space*:

> Whereas it had once seemed that the nineteenth century had been dominated by a discourse of time, history, and teleological development and a modernist aesthetic of the early twentieth century enshrined the temporal dimension, especially with respect to individual psychology, and—apart from interest in mere setting, regionalism, or local color, perhaps—matters of geography, topography, or spatiality played a subordinate role in critical scholarship and teaching. In the great works of realism and modernism, at least in the most influential scholarship devoted to them, time maintained its supremacy, with both history and temporality dominating the discourse, while geography and a sense of place were in many cases relegated to secondary status. Whereas time represented narrative development and change, space was often viewed as mere background or an empty container in which the unfolding of events over some *durée* could take place. In recent literary and cultural studies, notably with the advent of postmodernism and postcolonial theory, but also in other interdisciplinary approaches to literature, space has reemerged as a principal concern. (1–2)

The significant reconceptualizations of space emerging in the latter half of the twentieth century offer methods to read against the time-centered modernist ethos. They stake out a new critical engagement with a new literary and cultural aesthetic.

More recently, scholarly efforts to widen the scope of traditional modernist studies helpfully intervene in what has come to be seen as an artificial epistemic divide between time-bound modernism and space-bound postmodernism. Rather than follow the rule of different methodologies for different literary moments, such studies draw from the insights of current writing on space in order to reconsider canonical modernist texts. Andrew Thacker's *Moving through Modernity: Space and Geography in Modernism* proceeds from the premise that "Jameson's distinction between a diachronic modernism and a synchronic postmodernism seems a little overstated" (2). Thacker argues that modernist writing has always been preoccupied with space, place and the way they might be fruitfully explored to renegotiate the interrelation between figurative uses of space and its material reality. Closer to home, Christopher Gogwilt's *The Invention of the West: Joseph Conrad and the Double Mapping of Empire* (1995) and more recently Con Coroneos's *Space, Conrad and Modernity* (2001) have both studied Conradian spaces against assumptions that modernism's preoccupation with time results in a neglect of its spatial other.

Such insights might themselves appear obvious to readers of Conrad whose modernist aesthetic is always spatial and whose very identity is the product of a constant tension between allegiances to places left and placed adopted. Still, there is too much evidence of the temporal dominance in his work to suggest that the historical significance of the dominant literary and historical trope of time is just a fiction made up by thinkers of the late twentieth century. In "The Romance of Travel" (later titled "Geographers and Some Explorers"), Conrad writes that "of all the sciences geography finds its origin in action, and what is more, in adventurous action of the kind that appeals to sedentary people who like to dream of arduous adventure in the manner of prisoners dreaming behind bars of all the hardships and hazards of liberty dear to the heart of man" ("Romance of Travel" xviii). Geography is liberating to the imagination—but it also unfolds in the form of an action. To associate space with action is to collapse it with time, a form of narrative movement that is produced by stringing together causally linked events. The maps that inspire Conrad in "The Romance of Travel" take him from place to place, but also from moment to moment in the recesses of the creative mind that strings together stories of adventure.

A familiar conflation of space and time emerges in Marlow's narration of the journey down river in *Heart of Darkness*. We recall that "going up that river was like traveling back to the earliest beginnings of the world, when vegetation rioted on the earth and the big trees were kings" (Conrad, *Youth* 92). The simile demonstrates how space disappears in considerations of time. The modernist bias evidenced here is also the product of a known colonialist commonplace. Barney Warf and Santa Arias explain that "Orientalist thought structured the Western geographical imagination such that distance from Europe became equated with increasingly more primitive stages of development" so that ultimately "historicism eclipse[d] space in the service of imperial thought" (3). In Bernard McGrane's words, "what was *beyond* Europe was rearranged into a series of stages that were held to be both *before* Europe and *leading to* it" (94).

A significant contribution to recent modernist scholarship has been made by interventions in such colonialist tropes to offer more inclusive and nuanced explorations of spaces and voices by refusing to read them as the clichés of colonial enterprise. What we gain is not merely the ability to see through former blind spots but also a new set of concepts that allow us to intervene productively in our very understanding of the relations between time and place, between figural and literal spaces. Modernist writing, Thacker argues, "is about living and experiencing 'new times', not in the abstracted location of literary history, but in specific spatial histories: rooms, cities, buildings, countries and landscapes" (13). The earlier artificial separation of time and space in critical studies effectively collapses in the rethinking of these interrelations. But rather than eclipsing one category for the other—space for time—these new approaches allow us to think the two together. Much as Mikhail Bakhtin's chronotope facilitates a thinking of time *with* space rather than *against* it, Henri Lefebvre's exploration of social space, Foucault's heterotopia and Michel de Certeau's distinction between tour and map, offer methods to distinguish between space and place and to inform our considerations of the same with an attention to history and context.

Following Thacker's premise and Coroneos's reconsideration of Conradian space, the present volume proceeds from a rejection of the artificial fault-line between modernism and postmodernism and the separation of the dominant literary tropes of time and space on which it stands. Instead it takes inspiration from a range of critical theories and disciplines, from structuralism to post-structuralism, from law to dance. In *Teaching Space, Place, and Literature* (2018), Tally further underlines the urgency of reconceptualizing space by tracing far-reaching changes in the way we think, perceive and attend to the world today. The spatial turn, he argues, "has led to distinctive new approaches to literature, including geocriticism, geopoetics, literary geography, and spatially oriented critical theory," engendering "corresponding changes to the ways in which literature is taught and studied" (2).

The articles included here reflect Tally's observation and shed new light on Conrad's work by turning to new ways of thinking about and evaluating literature. Jeremy Hawthorn's article, "Conradian Claustrophobia: Gender, Confinement, Emancipation," examines the intersection of gender and space in Conrad's short and long fiction. Hawthorn attends in particular to the experience of spatial confinement across a range of works from "The Inn of the Two Witches" to *The Arrow of Gold* to show how Conrad uses "constrictive physical spaces to explore gender stereotypes." The study of gender in Conrad's oeuvre is, by now, a well-established area of scholarship. Hawthorn's contribution moves us beyond observations about straightforwardly socially gendered spaces to consider the affective gendering of space that confinement makes visible.

Ben Felderhof's "The Tropical Forests of Conrad and His British Contemporaries, in the Context of Aristotle and T.H. Huxley" moves us into different terrain. Felderhof argues that at the turn of the century the introduction and anglicization of the term "jungle" from Sanskrit marks the return into intellectual and aesthetic thinking of the classical concept of *hyle*—"unordered matter." This application of "jungle" to what today we would call "tropical forests" gave authors like Conrad the ability to invoke a set of associations that extended far beyond the legal and ecological domain in which the word had originally operated.

Steven Donovan makes a similar observation about a very different environment in the following article, "Underwater Conrad." Donovan argues provocatively that Conrad's capacity as a nautical writer comes less from his own maritime experience than from his lifelong maritime reading, which led to a desire to "reimagine the sea as a *literary* object." Through illuminating comparisons with Verne, Donovan shows how the alien environment that Verne conjures in his submarine fiction creates a space apart from the commerce of much other Victorian sea narratives, where enchantment emerges once again as a possibility for the novel.

In "Geography and Law in *Almayer's Folly*," Katherine Baxter returns us to the historical context. She examines the legal indeterminacies of British and Dutch colonial rule in Borneo in which Conrad's first novel is set. Taking Conrad's "suppressed" "Author's Note" as her starting point, she demonstrates how attending to the details of law in the novel enables us to recognise the contribution Conrad sought to make to contemporary debates about colonialism through his early fiction.

Yael Levin's "The Spatialization of Moral Judgment: Borders in Conrad's 'Amy Foster,' *Heart of Darkness* and *Under Western Eyes*" returns to some of the questions raised in Baxter's article through an aesthetic-moral framework. It traces the significant but frequently elided distinctions between international and transnational identities to which Hampson has also gestured in the past. These distinctions help us to discern how spatial affiliations and coordinates serve as "scaffolding for moral judgment" in Conrad's fiction. The analysis extends beyond characterization to suggest that diegetic stratification, i.e., narratological space, functions in a parallel fashion. The moral worth of characters can be assessed by the manner in which they are circumscribed within the diegesis or outside it, whether their positions are fixed or changing.

Linda Dryden also attends to disorientations of space in "*The Inheritors*, H.G. Wells and Science Fiction: The Dimensions of the Future." Here, too, moral judgment is key in a discussion that traces the entanglements of ethics, futurity, and dimensional imagination through not only the works but also the friendships of Wells, Conrad, and Ford. Dryden demonstrates how *The Inheri-*

tors reflects ideas that captured the attention of all three writers at the turn of the century, whilst inspiring very different responses. Dryden reads *The Inheritors* as Conrad's and Ford's imaginative rebuttal of Wells's more outrageous predictions about the future.

Following on from Dryden's interest in spatial imagination, ethics, and futurity, in "Conrad and George Eliot: Imagining Time, Space, and Event in *Lord Jim* and *The Lifted Veil*" Nic Panagopoulos considers the chronotopic implications of the motif of the lifted veil. Comparing the motif in Eliot and Conrad, Panagopoulos demonstrates how both novelists frustrate the usual expectations of revelation that the lifted veil suggests. In both novels, in as much as anything is revealed at all, it is neither illuminating nor salvific. Nonetheless, the veil and its lifting provide Eliot and Conrad with a suggestive "figure for artistic representation itself" and "an antidote to both the barren materialism and the disembodied idealism of modernity."

Susan Jones turns our attention to bodily gesture in "Movement, Gesture, and Space in *Heart of Darkness* and *Lord Jim*." Drawing on Gabriele Brandstetter's *The Poetics of Dance* (1995; English trans. 2015), Jones shows how Conrad repeatedly deploys physical movements in space to dramatize the limits of verbal communication that his protagonists experience. Jones's argument thus picks up on the attention to the relationship between affect and space that we find in Hawthorn's "Conradian Claustrophobia."

The question of spatialized gesture and the limits of communication is tested further in Johan Adam Warodell's "'Ba! ba! Ba!': Voicing Noise." Considering Conrad's typographical representation of non-linguistic expression, Warodell traces the various expressive sounds of Conrad's speakers as they splutter, trail off, and sometimes explode with feelings that test the limits of language. By attending to these sometimes idiosyncratic transcriptions of the noises of speech, Warodell demonstrates how we might extend Conrad's reputation from author of the spoken word to an author of human expression beyond language.

Patricia Pye's "A 'Modern' amongst the 'Standards': Conrad in the Classroom" concludes this special issue. Pye invites us to consider not the spaces of Conrad's fiction but rather the spaces of his reception. Through close examination of how Conrad was framed for the classroom, and his own contributions to that framing, Pye shows the important but previously hidden impact of curriculum design to his reception in the first decades of the twentieth century. Her analysis demonstrates that it was as much in the space of the classroom as in the pages of the *Athenaeum* that Conrad's virtues as a master of the English language were first propounded.

WORKS CITED

Brandstetter, Gabrielle. *Poetics of Dance: Body, Image, and Space in the Historical Avant-Gardes*. Translated by Elena Polzer, with Mark Franko, Oxford University Press, 2015.

Conrad, Joseph. *Youth, Heart of Darkness and the End of the Tether*. Dent, 1965.

———. "The Romance of Travel." *Countries of the World*. Edited by J.A. Hammerton, Harmondsworth, 1924, pp. xviii–xxviii.

Coroneos, Con. *Space, Conrad, and Modernity*. Oxford University Press, 2002.

GoGwilt, Christopher. *The Invention of the West: Joseph Conrad and the Double Mapping of Empire*. Stanford University Press, 1995.

Hampson, Robert. *Joseph Conrad: Betrayal and Identity*. Palgrave Macmillan, 1992.

———. *Cross-Cultural Encounters in Joseph Conrad's Malay Fiction*. Palgrave Macmillan, 2000.

———. *Conrad's Secrets*. Palgrave Macmillan, 2012.

Jameson, Fredric. *Postmodernism, Or, The Cultural Logic of Late Capitalism*. Duke University Press, 2003.

McGrane, Bernard. *Beyond Anthropology: Society and the Other*. Columbia University Press, 1989.

Tally Jr., Robert T., ed. *The Routledge Handbook of Literature and Space*. Routledge, 2018.

———. *Teaching Space, Place, and Literature*. Routledge, 2018.

Thacker, Andrew. *Moving through Modernity: Space and Geography in Modernism*. Manchester University Press, 2003.

Warf, Barney, and Arias, Santa, eds. *The Spatial Turn: Interdisciplinary Perspectives*. Routledge, 2009.

Conradian Claustrophobia:
Gender, Confinement, Emancipation

JEREMY HAWTHORN

NORWEGIAN UNIVERSITY OF SCIENCE AND TECHNOLOGY

ABSTRACT

This article discusses the ways in which space is gendered in a number of Conrad's fictions, with a particular focus on those spaces experienced as metaphorically or literally claustrophobic and stifling. First two shorter works in which men face entrapment are discussed: "The Inn of the Two Witches" and "Amy Foster." The article then builds on the treatment of Alice's imprisonment in "A Smile of Fortune" to consider two works that focus on a woman who feels stifled and entrapped in physical and cultural spaces: "To-morrow" and *The Arrow of Gold*. The movement through these works does not follow the chronology of their composition, but rather focuses on the varying ways in which Conrad uses constrictive physical spaces to explore gender stereotypes.

KEYWORDS

Joseph Conrad, claustrophobia, gender, imperialism, femme fatale, women

> O my America! my new-found-land,
> My kingdom, safeliest when with one man manned,
> My mine of precious stones, my empery,
> How blest am I in this discovering thee!
> —John Donne, "To His Mistress Going to Bed"

These lines from John Donne's "To His Mistress Going to Bed" involve a convoluted blending of imperialist exploitation and male sexual conquest, one that presents the woman as a newly discovered territory waiting and willing to offer riches to a male conqueror. If the woman is a new-found land then by implication the new-found land is female, and the invading male is free to take or leave what he wants from it. Joseph Conrad regularly depicts space as gendered, but gendered in what are arguably more complex, contradictory, and cross-hatched patterns than in Donne's poem. In Conrad's fiction, a new-found land is more likely to offer danger than opportunity to the European intruder. Territories in Conrad's fiction do not present themselves in the same way to all who inhabit or enter them. A given territory will be experienced differently by men and by women, by the European invader and by the non-European inhabitant.

Conrad was writing at a time when there were fewer and fewer new-found lands to be invaded by the European male, a time, too, when European women were not only resisting being treated as territories to be explored and exploited but were also claiming a right to that freedom of movement enjoyed by men. But space was still gendered in ways unfamiliar to a present-day reader. On board cargo ships there were few women, and in "Youth" the presence of the captain's wife on a ship is seen by the sailors as unnatural and a hindrance to the carrying out of their duties. In "A Smile of Fortune," the captain whose child has died in the presence of his wife at sea exclaims: "By God it isn't fair!" and he tells the captain-narrator: "Don't you ever marry unless you can chuck the sea first" (Conrad, "Smile" 27). Robert Hampson has argued that in *Chance*, "the discovery that Captain Anthony has a wife on board ship is not so much surprising as scandalous," given "the homosocial world of sailors, which is explicitly presented in opposition to the life of 'the shore gang' with their 'wives and children'" (*Secrets* 106). Even the memory of a shore liaison can pollute the atmosphere on board ship, as the captain-narrator of *The Shadow-Line* learns through his mate's account of the descent into madness of the captain's besotted predecessor.

But if on board ship there were no, or few, women, on shore women were waiting. In new-found lands they might offer the prospect of conquest and exploitation, but also the danger of traps and entanglements of various kinds. A return to land-life in Europe for the male wanderer was a return to a world containing not just one but two sexes, one in which male bonding gave way to the need to negotiate relationships with both men and women. Men might possess the final trump card—flight—but playing this card did not necessarily have the desired effect. At the end of *Lord Jim*, Jewel sums up her relationship with Jim to Marlow: "She recognized me at once, and as soon as I had stopped looking down at her: 'He has left me,' she said quietly; 'you always leave us—for your own ends'" (Conrad, *Lord Jim* 262). These are words that could equally well have been uttered by the female protagonists of "A Smile of Fortune," "To-Morrow," and "The Return," but the men to whom they can be applied, like Jim, are not always satisfied with what the pursuit of their own ends leaves them with.

* * *

The stereotypical pattern in which the naively innocent man is crushed to death by a woman or set of women is seen in its starkest, pared-down, and shockingly literal form in "The Inn of the Two Witches," in the tale-within-a-tale reported in the "litter of loose pages" found by the frame narrator in the box of used books he purchases. The events recounted in these pages take place in 1813 and involve a couple of sailors who are put ashore from a sloop-of-war on the north coast of Spain. One of these—Tom Corbin or Cuba Tom—has a mission inland, and the writer of the memoir, Edgar Byrne, accompanies him ashore and watches him depart on his mission. To begin with, it might seem as if the year, the mission, and the foreign territory will introduce a miniature version of the conquering European male in a territory waiting to be subdued. Indeed, when the two sailors progress through the village, "women stared from the doors of houses" while the men "pressed behind the two Englishmen staring like those islanders discovered by Captain Cook in the South Seas" ("Inn" 112). Given Captain Cook's eventual fate in Hawaii this comment has a proleptic quality, but in Conrad's tale it is not the local male population that will take a life. This is a European village, not a ship or an undiscovered territory, and almost immediately Byrne encounters a more dangerous, female, threat. After having been told many times that no mule is available, Byrne is given information by "a diminutive Spaniard":

> "*Señor!*" he said without any preliminaries. "Caution! It is a positive fact that one-eyed Bernardino, my brother-in-law, has at this moment a mule in his stable. And why he who is not clever has a mule there? Because he is a rogue; a man without conscience. Because I had to give up the *macho* to him to secure for myself a roof to sleep under and a mouthful of *olla* to keep my soul in this insignificant body of mine, yet, *señor*, it contains a heart many times bigger than the mean thing which beats in the breast of that brute connection of mine of which I am ashamed, though I opposed that marriage with all my power. Well the misguided woman suffered enough. She had her purgatory on this earth—God rest her soul." (115)

Here "*macho*" is clearly used to refer to the "mule," but the primary meaning of the word in Spanish is "masculinity," and the speaker's implied loss of his masculinity prefigures Tom Corbin's loss of his life at the hands of the two "witches." Their chosen method of murder is the ultimate loss of free space: Tom is suffocated in a mechanical bed while he is sleeping. Imagining that he can hear Tom warning him, and believing that his companion is still in the bed, "Byrne ran to the bed and attempted to lift up, to push off the horrible lid smothering the body" (132).

Michael Greaney sees the words of the diminutive Spaniard "as the text's sidelong commentary on its story of survival through emasculation, a story in which 'giving up the macho'—being too scared to sleep—is the only way to stay alive" (9). Moreover, Greaney suggests that for Byrne:

> an unexpected side-effect of survival is an altered sense of his own gender identity: he is feminized by the experience of sleeplessness, behaving "like a silly girl" during his night of jittery paranoia in the fatal bedroom. Byrne's loss of masculine self-possession notably contributes to the story's gently subversive treatment of the culture of machismo. (9)

I am not so sure of "gently subversive." This is a story in which three women conspire to kill two fit and active men. With the first, they succeed, while the second is symbolically emasculated. Their chosen method involves constriction and smothering. As the tale progresses, the sailors have less and less space within which to move, while finding themselves more and more exposed to the power of women, a process that parallels the loss of unexplored space for white men in the world at large at the time Conrad is writing, when the whole surface of the globe is depicted as threatened with European domestication. As Conrad declared in his essay "Travel," written to serve as preface for his young friend Richard Curle's book *Into the East: Notes on Burma and Malaya* (1923), presently "there will be no backyard left in the heart of Central Africa that has not been peeped into by some person more or less commissioned for the purpose" (*Last Essays* 68).

The word "breath" occurs six times in "The Inn of the Two Witches," providing the reader with a constant reminder that we must breathe to live. The young woman driven from the door of the Inn by Byrne on his entry, recovering her equilibrium, "drew a hissing breath through her set teeth" ("Inn" 120), and it is she who shows Byrne to his bedroom: "'You sleep here, señor,' she murmured in a voice light like a child's breath, offering him the lamp" (124). As for her aged companions, "The sorceress with the spoon ceased stirring the mess in the pot, the very trembling of the other's head stopped for the space of a breath" (121). After he discovers Tom Corbin's body, with no obvious injuries, Byrne concludes: "So Tom had died striking against something which could be hit and yet could kill one without leaving a wound—by a breath," and that the "thing which could deal death in a breath was outside that bolted door" (129–30). When finally Byrne witnesses the descent of the bed canopy and realizes that he is the intended victim, in a sort of reenacted bodily sympathy, he "stood up, gasped for breath, and let out a cry of rage and dismay" (131). In this story, for men, breathing is always under threat, always in danger of being curtailed by smothering female containment. In Greaney's summary, "the image of sealedness connotes not blissful insulation from the cares of the waking world but rather claustrophobic entrapment in a deadly plot" (8). If Greaney is correct that the story subverts the culture of machismo, it must be added that it also underwrites the clichéd masculinist view of women as trappers and destroyers of men.

In an article on three of Conrad's full-length novels, Janice Ho also makes reference to claustrophobia:

> The view of the world as vast and immense—a view fuelled by exploration and imperialism from the fifteenth century onwards—was unsustainable by the end of the nineteenth century when the late Victorians felt not a "sense of expansiveness" but its opposite: a sense of constriction, that the world was too small. Such spatial claustrophobia is attributable to first, major achievements in the science of cartography; and second, unprecedented advances in the fields of transportation and telecommunications—two phenomena that reflect, more broadly, the processes of modernization. Conrad's novels, I suggest, must be located within this historical context. (2)

What, if any, connection is there between Greaney's perception of a gender-dependent claustrophobia called forth in both Byrne and Conrad's reader by the activities of the two "witches," and Ho's much more universal sense of spatial claustrophobia brought on by advances in transportation and telecommunications? "The Inn of the Two Witches" is set at a time before the world facing the European male began to be experienced as too small, but it reflects a sense of stifling containment that is very much of a later period. In this story, the claustrophobia resultant upon what Ho calls "modernization" (which must include not just technology but also imperialism, colonialism, the globalizing force of capitalism, and the growing movement for female emancipation) is displaced on to an older, pre-modern association of women and domestic space with imprisonment, constriction, and suffocation—metaphorical and literal.

While the presence of three malevolent women may carry with it a clear echo of *Macbeth*, only two of them conform to the pattern of that play's "weird sisters." The third is different:

> The orphan crouching on the corner of the hearth had been looking at Byrne. He thought that she was more like a child of Satan kept there by these two weird harridans for the love of the Devil. Her eyes were a little oblique, her mouth rather thick but admirably formed; her dark face had a wild beauty, voluptuous and untamed. As to the character of her steadfast gaze attached upon him with a sensuously savage attention, "to know what it was like," says Mr Byrne, "you have only to observe a hungry cat watching a bird in a cage or a mouse inside a trap." (Conrad, "Inn" 122)

While the final sentence may recall the parrot-ingesting cat in "Amy Foster," of which more below, the description of the orphan brings to mind not the dull Amy but the young Alice in Conrad's "A Smile of Fortune"—also a sort of orphan and also perceived by the young captain as a threat, albeit a threat of a different sort. If the wild beauty of the murderous orphan is "voluptuous and untamed," the enclosed space of the walled garden that contains Alice, the captain notes even before he has met her, is "a brilliantly coloured solitude, drowsing in a warm, voluptuous silence" ("Smile" 44). In Conrad's fiction, the word "voluptuous" rings alarm bells—if not for the male character who experiences the alluring promise of pleasure offered by that which is sensually inviting, then certainly in its proleptic note of warning to the reader. The orphan's thick mouth and dark face may, too, hint at a racial otherness picked up by the term "gipsy" later on.

As the captain gets to know Alice, he is "seduced by the moody expression of her face, by her obstinate silences, her rare, scornful words; by the perpetual pout of her closed lips, the black depths of her fixed gaze turned slowly upon me as if in contemptuous provocation, only to be averted next moment with an exasperating indifference" (55). The orphan's "steadfast gaze," like Alice's "fixed gaze," indicates a female power and self-direction by which the man involved feels challenged. If the orphan's eyes are oblique like a cat's, Alice has "long eyes, a narrowed gleam of liquid white and intense motionless black, with their gaze so empty of thought and so absorbed in their fixity that she seemed to be staring at her own lonely image, in some far off mirror hidden from my sight amongst the trees" (60). While the orphan's gaze at Byrne is clearly that of the predator sizing up a potential meal, Alice's gaze is harder for the captain and the reader to interpret. At times it seems to signal a desire to be rescued from her paradisal but suffocating prison, at other times it seems characterized by an "exasperating indifference" that frustrates and excites the captain. After leaving Alice and the island, the captain appears to experience both loss and relief, and the story does not aid the reader in choosing between these responses. But what of Alice? Here the weight of the narrative encourages the reader to see the captain's departure as tragic in its implications for her. "The Inn of the Two Witches," in contrast, does not encourage the reader to feel any sympathy for the orphan's fate (although, given that she is guilty of murder, this is perhaps understandable).

Byrne notices that the orphan's "soiled white stockings [are] full of holes" ("Inn" 124); Alice also wears "white cotton stockings" ("Smile" 48), and when her father picks up her discarded footwear it becomes apparent that it "was not really a slipper, but a low shoe of blue glazed kid, rubbed and shabby. It had straps to go over the instep but the girl only thrust her feet in carelessly in her slovenly manner" (67). Soiling, shabbiness, wear ("rubbed") all serve to underline Alice's indifference to what others, including the captain, think of her, an indifference by which he is challenged and aroused. If Byrne is "certain she [the orphan] was a casual gipsy admitted there for some reason or other" ("Inn" 123), for the captain Alice is "like a spell-bound creature with the forehead of a goddess crowned by the dishevelled, magnificent hair of a gipsy tramp" ("Smile" 57). The combination of goddess and tramp suggests impossibility as potential partner: Alice is simultaneously in a different and higher sphere from the captain, and socially unacceptable because of what the captain perceives as a racial otherness and class inferiority. If one of the cultural stereotypes associated with the Roma people ("gipsies") was and remains that of mobility—forever moving from place to place rather than settling down to life in a fixed dwelling—the entrapment experienced by Alice must be perceived as doubly ironic and tragic.

What is striking about "A Smile of Fortune" is the story's insistence upon the fact that both the narrator-captain and Alice are victims. The story's title is ironic: the captain's masculine ability to love and then to sail away is exposed as one that leaves him sad and reduced, while Alice's fate is much more tragic as she remains trapped in the stifling imprisonment of tropical garden and gender role.

***

In "Amy Foster," Doctor Kennedy is old enough to have ventured into geographical interiors while there still were lands to be discovered and before the world became too small. Kennedy, the tale's frame narrator informs the reader,

> had begun life as surgeon in the Navy, and afterwards had been the companion of a famous traveller, in the days when there were continents with

unexplored interiors. His papers on the fauna and flora made him known to scientific societies. And now he had come to a country practice—from choice. The penetrating power of his mind, acting like a corrosive fluid, had destroyed his ambition, I fancy. ("Amy Foster" 106)

This description has the effect of erasing from history those "natives" who lived undiscovered in these interiors—indeed, the passage leaves the reader in doubt as to whether or not there were any human beings in the territories in which Kennedy studied his flora and fauna. Back in England, however, it is people, rather than plants, that have become the subjects of the doctor's investigation. He and the frame narrator appear both to be without wives: the latter reports that "a good many years ago, on my return from abroad, he invited me to stay with him" (106). The two men may themselves have avoided (or survived) direct involvement with women,[1] but they are witnesses to the destruction of one described as an adventurous, vivacious, and free male spirit—the castaway Yanko—by the young Amy Foster and her culture. Many commentaries on the story focus on the sullen, unadventurous, and generally stuck-in-the-mud quality of the people of the town, presented in sharp contrast to Yanko's lightness and freedom. Kennedy tells the narrator that Yanko was "so different from the mankind around that, with his freedom of movement, his soft—a little startled, glance, his olive complexion and graceful bearing, his humanity suggested to me the nature of a woodland creature" (111). However it is worth noting that Amy is at one with the "mankind" around her. The narrator's first encounter with her provides sufficient time "to see her dull face, red, not with a mantling blush, but as if her flat cheeks had been vigorously slapped, and to take in the squat figure, the scanty, dusty brown hair drawn into a tight knot at the back of the head" (107). If Yanko is associated with movement and grace, even Amy's hair suggests restriction and a denial of naturalness. The narrator and Kennedy seem at one in their positive depiction of Yanko and negative view of Amy, and it is hardly overreading to detect in this agreement a homosocial perception on their part of Amy as unworthy of Yanko: unable to appreciate or even detect his physical and spiritual beauty in a manner in which the two significantly single men do.

"Amy Foster" is packed with images of entrapment and imprisonment. When first cast ashore after being shipwrecked, Yanko "struggled instinctively like an animal under a net" (112), and after the birth of his son it seems to Kennedy "as if the net of fate had been drawn closer round him already" (137), while "with his panting breast and lustrous eyes he reminded me again of a wild creature under the net; of a bird caught in a snare" (141). From the moment Yanko is seen heading towards New Barns Farm, "he is plainly in the toils of his obscure and touching destiny" (119), a formulation in which Conrad makes use of the semi-archaic meaning of "toils": a net or series of nets used to capture birds.

All of these images of entrapment lead the reader to view Yanko as not just a victim of a sullen, turgid, and ignorant culture, but also as the free male spirit who—like Byrne—wanders into a feminine space that suffocates him. However while Byrne is threatened with asphyxia right from the moment that he enters the inn with its murderous females, Yanko's initial experience of Amy is a positive one. Early on in the story she performs a liberating function for him: she resists the prejudice of the community, treats Yanko as she treats the injured animals she tends, and offers him a refuge from the dull unimaginative lifelessness of the village. But her early inability to save Mrs. Smith's gray parrot from the cat prefigures her inability to save Yanko from the hostility or neglect of an alien culture with which she eventually aligns herself, and this inability, the narrative suggests, stems from her unwillingness to resist the pull of her native culture once she is responsible for bringing her son into the community. With a child of her own, she can no longer mother Yanko, and once the mothering relationship is unavailable, Yanko is cast out of the community and alienated from Amy's care.

Richard Ruppel has argued that the primary narrator and Dr. Kennedy "create a homosocial world that is highly critical of women and that is intensely sympathetic to the doomed protagonist, who is in every way more attractive than the other characters and especially the *femme fatale*" (82). One might respond that Amy is surely the Conradian female character who least conforms to the conventional stereotype of the *femme fatale*, but against this it can be countered that in many of Conrad's earlier works, for the sailor or explorer who is set ashore, all women are potentially fatal. In her book *The Fabrication of the Late-Victorian Femme Fatale: The Kiss of Death*, Rebecca Stott has argued that in Conrad's Malay fiction and *Heart of Darkness*, "the native women are framed and held by the jungle but are also inseparable from it; they are like carnivorous jungle plants—*fleurs de mal*—alluring and deadly" (128). Writing about *Lord Jim*, she notes: "Jewel clings to Jim ('Thou art mine!') and must be cut away from him before he can escape from her embrace. This clinging, caressing, cloying quality of the jungle and of the native women is likened to the great jungle vines which cling to the giant trees, felling them by erotic strangulation" (138). Amy is hardly guilty of erotic strangulation, and yet her responsibility for the emasculation and death of Yanko bears a strong resemblance to Aïssa's involvement in the death of Willems in *An Outcast of the Islands*, although Willems, unlike Yanko, shares responsibility for his eventual fate. The sympathy of the two men, and the reader, is in this story directed towards Yanko, not Amy.

***

The narrative's direction of sympathy in "To-morrow" is, in contrast, towards the imprisoned woman, not the man threatened with entrapment. In this story the focus on a woman's experience of spatial and cultural immurement is given a more focused, and arguably a more sympathetic, portrayal than it is in "A Smile of Fortune." Bessie Carvil is incarcerated in the domestic space dominated by her blind father and responds with hope to the possibility of escape when the rootless wanderer Harry appears. Unlike the male victims considered previously, Harry perceives the proffered alliance with Bessie—like the home offered by his mad father—as a trap. Instead of the bird cage, the metaphor used to describe domestic incarceration in this story makes use of another animal prison. Harry describes the houses in which his father and the Carvils live (and in which he grew up) as rabbit hutches, and makes it clear that he hates containment of any sort.

> "Where do you come from?" she asked.
> "Right away from a jolly good spree," he said, "by the London train—see? Ough! I hate being shut up in a train. I don't mind a house so much."
> "Ah," she said; "that's lucky."
> "Because in a house you can at any time open the blamed door and walk away straight before you."
> "And never come back?"
> "Not for sixteen years at least," he laughed. "To a rabbit hutch, and get a confounded old shovel . . ."
> "A ship is not so very big," she taunted.
> "No, but the sea is great." (Conrad, "To-morrow" 267–68)

There is a long list of Conradian male characters who are terrified of being locked up. In *Lord Jim*, Gentleman Brown is more scared of prison than of execution, and the first-person narrator of the jointly written "The Nature of a Crime" is prepared to take his own life to avoid prison. It is true that the swindler De Barral, in *Chance*, considers prison to be preferable to life at sea, but he is not a seaman, and the fact that "the sea is great" seems for Conrad's sailors enough to outweigh the fact that a ship is small. The narrator of "Freya of the Seven Isles" asks the rhetorical question: "Who was it who likened a ship to a prison?" and responds: "May I be ignominiously hanged at a yard-arm if that's true" (129). Conrad and his character are probably thinking of

Samuel Johnson, who is reported by James Boswell both in the *Life of Johnson* and in his account of their journey to the Western Isles of Scotland to have made the comparison. Here is the latter mention:

> I yesterday expressed my wonder that John Hay, one of our guides, who had been pressed aboard a man of war, did not chuse to continue longer than nine months, after which time he got off.—*Johnson*. "Why, Sir, no man will be a sailor, who has contrivance enough to get himself into a jail; for, being in a ship is being in a jail, with the chance of being drowned." (Boswell 151)

A ship, or a ship's cabin, is perhaps unlike a prison because the sea is great, but another possible reason is that there are unlikely to be many women on board ship, and this may be what prompts the spirited disagreement of the narrator of "Freya of the Seven Isles."[2] Nathalie Martinière has argued that the "function of cabins in ships (either the forecastle or the captain's cabin) is quite different from the function of rooms in a house" (27): it is only in exceptional circumstances that a cabin contains women.

In "To-morrow" the familiar pattern of the wanderer being offered but rejecting the chance of rest in a domestic space is complicated by two mirror-images. To start with, the domestic tyrants—Captain Hagberd and Bessie's father—are not female but male, and it is not just Harry who wants to escape domesticity, but also Bessie. The divergence from the norm is underlined in the text: Captain Hagberd observes to Bessie that "Girls, of course, don't require so much—h'm—h'm. They don't run away from home, my dear" (Conrad, "To-morrow" 253).[3] In terms of gender politics, Captain Hagberd has bucked the norm, feminizing himself and his house. As his son tells Bessie, the Captain "was always one of your domestic characters" (265). He was, moreover, an unwilling and very half-hearted sailor, siding with Samuel Johnson rather than his son Harry on the subject of the ship as prison: "'People did not know what they let their boys in for when they let them go to sea,' he expounded to Bessie. 'As soon make convicts of them at once'" (249).

> Captain Hagberd had been one of those sailors that pursue their calling within sight of land. One of the many children of a bankrupt farmer, he had been apprenticed hurriedly to a coasting skipper, and had remained on the coast all his sea life. It must have been a hard one at first: he had never taken to it; his affection turned to the land, with its innumerable houses, with its quiet lives gathered round its firesides. Many sailors feel and profess a rational dislike for the sea, but his was a profound and emotional animosity—as

if the love of the stabler element had been bred into him through many generations. (249)

While Harry is a wanderer who hates confinement—"I want either hard work, or an all-fired racket, or more space than there is in the whole of England"—and is "confoundedly afraid of being locked up even in mistake," his father and Bessie "never talked without a fence or a railing between them" (263, 267, 256). The descriptions of Hagberd shopping, objecting to Bessie's hanging her washing on the fence, buying furniture, using a needle and thread, and becoming more and more attached to the security of his house, all bespeak that which, at the time Conrad is writing, would be considered stereotypically female behavior and attitudes. And when Harry is injured, it is not by a *femme fatale* but by his own (feminized) father, who throws a shovel at him, thereby symbolically rejecting a tool associated with male labor. Moreover, while the village barber declares that he would not be caught going crazy over any of his eight children clearing out, Captain Hagberd is obsessed with getting his son to settle down with Bessie in his own house.

In the late-nineteenth and early-twentieth century, the writer most scandalously associated with a female rejection of domestic imprisonment was perhaps Henrik Ibsen, and especially through his play *A Doll's House*. Two of Conrad's shorter fictions finish in a way that seems deliberately to reverse the celebrated ending of *A Doll's House*: instead of the imprisoned woman leaving the confines of an intolerable domestic incarceration, it is, in "The Return" and "The Tale," the man who makes his exit and leaves the woman in the domestic space. The former tale ends with the three-word paragraph "He never returned," while "The Tale," as Robert Hampson points out, "contains another variation upon that famous ending" (*Secrets* 203). The Commanding Officer, after having disengaged himself from the woman, "pressed her hands to his lips, and went out" (Conrad, "The Tale" 81). In yet another possible rejoinder to Ibsen's work, at the end of "To-morrow" it is the woman who reenters the house and returns to a more extreme version of the domestic tyranny depicted in Ibsen's play, following a briefly glimpsed but illusory vision of freedom with a rootless sailor. The link to Ibsen is important, because it underlines the fact that the reader's sympathy is directed towards the imprisoned Bessie (and Alice), rather than their being presented as the symbolic jailors of men. This direction of sympathy towards imprisoned young women is explored in greater depth in the final work I wish now to consider: *The Arrow of Gold*.

* * *

> This, his first great adventure, as he calls it, begins in Marseilles. It ends there, too. Yet it might have happened anywhere. This does not mean that the people concerned could have come together in pure space. The locality had a definite importance. (*Arrow* 4)

Space in *The Arrow of Gold* is never "pure," never neutral when it comes to the divisions in humanity—not least those involving power and gender. It might be countered that it is never pure anywhere, and certainly not in any of Conrad's works of fiction, but in this late novel the precise impurity of each space occupied by Monsieur George has, as we are told here in the first of the two notes that sandwich George's story, a definite importance. On the opening page of the first note, and the novel, the woman whose letter is said to have prompted George's account writes to him, telling him that not only did he select his own road, but, "to us, left behind, it always looked as if you had struck out into a pathless desert" (3). For Hampson, whose insightful criticism of the novel has played a key role in countering the view that it represents Conrad in full decline, this comment indicates that George "has found an identity that is outside those of his own society" (*Betrayal* 253). George's geographical movements do indeed indicate changes sought—and accomplished—in his own identity. And yet "the locality had a definite importance." Perhaps, indeed, the noun should be in plural form, for the different localities—countries, areas on land and at sea, towns, buildings and, crucially, rooms—in which both George and Doña Rita find themselves—serve in the novel as metonyms for the characters' evolving identities. Although his female correspondent thinks that George has set out into a pathless desert, and George associates the voice called out by Dominic with "the immense space of the sea" (Conrad, *Arrow* 128), George's encounters with Rita take place repeatedly in closed spaces circumscribed by walls and secured by locks and barriers. *The Arrow of Gold* shares with "To-morrow," "The Return," and "A Smile of Fortune" a probing concern with the issue of female imprisonment and claustrophobia, and can in many ways be seen as the most profound investigation into this topic in Conrad's *oeuvre*. If in "The Inn of the Two Witches" it is the men who find breathing difficult in the presence of women, here it is a woman who feels deprived of air:

> "I am perfectly aware that Monsieur George is here, and that he has been breathing a very different atmosphere from what he gets in this room. Don't you find this room extremely confined?" she asked me.
> The room was very large but it is a fact that I felt oppressed at that moment. This mysterious quarrel between those two people, revealing

something more close in their intercourse than I had ever before suspected, made me so profoundly unhappy that I didn't even attempt to answer. And she continued:

"More space. More air. Give me air, air." She seized the embroidered edges of her blue robe under her white throat and made as if to tear them apart, to fling it open on her breast, recklessly, before our eyes. We both remained perfectly still. Her hands dropped nervelessly by her side. "I envy you, Monsieur George. If I am to go under I should prefer to be drowned in the sea with the wind on my face. What luck, to feel nothing less than all the world closing over one's head!" (147–48)

The sentiment is familiar, but here it is not one that is expressed by the male sailor, as it is in "To-morrow," but by a woman whose inability to move freely in space both results from and expresses an inability to escape a stifling gender role. If Tom Corbin is literally suffocated, Rita finds her imprisonment in the role of female object of desire (for no fewer than four different men in the novel) tantamount to being smothered. To claim that this suggests that Rita is masculinized would be at best a half-truth. At one level her declared identification with the masculine territory of the sea and her rejection of the feminine domain of the domestic room certainly does indicate her desperate need to escape a conventional gender identification. But this is a half-truth precisely because it would suggest merely a simple exchange of one limited gender identity for another. Rita is a more complex and challenging character than this: recalling the topical New Woman figure from the turn of the century, she wants not to be a man, but to be a woman with the privileges that hitherto have been the exclusive possession of men: self-determination, freedom of movement (with geographical freedom to roam expressing symbolically a yearning for social and cultural freedom), and above all room to define herself away from the claustrophobic pressures of conventional society.

In the final scene between Rita and Monsieur George, she implores him no fewer than three times, "Take me out of this house." Like Bessie Carvil, she experiences her domestic situation as an incarceration, and her declaration that she cannot breathe in the house has progressed from expressing a metaphorical association to reporting a literal sensation. Monsieur George, however, in response to her dramatic demand for more air and her wish to die at sea, merely fantasizes a new form of ship-borne enclosure for her. When Rita declares that she wishes George would take her away, he imagines the astonishment with which her presence on board ship would have been met with by the hardened sailor Dominic, and then inserts her into this new fantasy, a fantasy set in a new confined space, before recognizing it for what it is:

But what a charming, gentle, gay, and fearless companion she would have made! I believed in her fearlessness in any adventure that would interest her. It would be a new occasion for me, a new viewpoint for that faculty of admiration she had awakened in me at sight—at first sight—before she opened her lips—before she ever turned her eyes on me. She would have to wear some sort of sailor costume, a blue woollen shirt open at the throat . . . . Dominic's hooded cloak would envelop her amply, and her face under the black hood would have a luminous quality, adolescent charm, and an enigmatic expression. The confined space of the little vessel's quarterdeck would lend itself to her cross-legged attitudes, and the blue sea would balance gently her characteristic immobility that seemed to hide thoughts as old and profound as itself. As restless, too—perhaps.

But the picture I had in my eye, coloured and simple like an illustration to a nursery-book tale of two venturesome children's escapade, was what fascinated me most. Indeed I felt that we two were like children under the gaze of a man of the world—who lived by his sword. (149)

Whereas Rita's desire to have the whole world close over her head is, in spite of its death-wish element, a vision of liberation, George's fantasy of Rita in sailor costume sitting cross-legged in a new "confined space" is merely a change of venue for female imprisonment—and in his final sense that he has just spun himself a nursery book tale, George appears to recognize this.

If one way to escape the burden of being a man is to regress to being a child, another is to insert oneself into an fantasized female identity through indulgence in a sort of masochistic feminization, as George also does. I have written at length about this elsewhere, drawing attention to the inescapable echoes of Sacher-Masoch's *Venus in Furs* in the long late scene in the house of Rita's sister Therese (*Sexuality* 138–43), but I would like to stress that the feminization of George seems in no way an extension of his identity in the manner of Rita's repeated desire to escape the confines of her allotted gender role, but rather a surrender to and luxuriation in an extreme version of a stereotypical feminine role. It is, in brief, a fantasy, not (as in Rita's case) a desire for a changed life in the real world. One quotation will have to suffice to make this point:

I had the time to lay my infinite adoration at her feet whose white insteps gleamed below the dark edge of the fur out of quilted blue silk bedroom slippers, embroidered with small pearls. I had never seen them before; I mean the slippers. The gleam of the insteps, too, for that matter. I lost myself in a feeling of deep content, something like a foretaste of a time of felicity which must be quiet or it couldn't be eternal. I had never tasted such perfect quietness before. It was not of this earth. I had gone far beyond. It was as if I had reached the ultimate wisdom beyond all dreams and all passions. She was That which is to be contemplated to all Infinity. (Conrad, *Arrow* 288)

If Rita wishes for "nothing less than all the world," even if it is closing over her head, Monsieur George wants something "not of this earth": infinite adoration at Rita's feet, something eternal, ultimate wisdom, contemplated to all Infinity—the absolutes match the extraterrestrial nature of his unreal fantasy. While Rita wants, in today's cant phrase, to get a life, George is tempted by a masochistic fantasy of subservience to an otherworldly woman. In the locked room from which Rita is desperate to escape, George has lost himself in a feeling of deep content. Rita wants a fully human life, while George reduces her to a non-human absolute, the capitalized "That."

***

Our metaphors often render complex cultural and social experiences and situations understandable by associating them with primal physical experiences. Being unable to move, or unable to breathe—these are physical experiences associated with sensations that date back to some of our earliest and most terrifying pre-verbal sensations, and with reactions that are programmed into us by our genes: pre-rational and outside of our control. Trapped in relationships and social roles that are restrictive and smothering, we are thrown back on comparisons with some of our most negative infantile experiences. As we grow older, spaces often have a double significance: the enclosed space is both refuge and prison, the unenclosed space offers both freedom and abandonment, movement and isolation. As Nathalie Martinière puts it, "Conrad's fiction shows a struggle between two simultaneous types of desire: a desire for supportive togetherness, and a desire to assert the pre-eminence of the self, regardless of the community's best interests" (24). For men, asserting the pre-eminence of the self could mean withdrawing to the private cabin, as Martinière notes, but it often involves leaving the enclosed space: in Conrad's time the (rapidly diminishing) territory unexplored by Europeans often appeared to offer the possibility of escape from domestic entrapment. The house, the room, the bed could all contain men and women, but leaving them was easier for a man than for a woman, and so they became obvious symbols of potential incarceration, of unwanted enclosure, especially of men by women and the domestic. In the works I have considered above, Conrad's treatment of the gender stereotypes associated with domestic spaces and geographical territories is often double-edged. Women are sometimes *femmes fatales*, but sometimes individuals as trapped in and stifled by their situations and their gender roles as are the men with whom they interact. The liberation of women requires and enables a parallel liberation of men from a "machismo" that is as stifling for them as is domestic imprisonment for women.

NOTES

1. Richard Ruppel describes Dr. Kennedy as a bachelor (82), but his marital status is not made explicit in the tale.
2. Until the nineteenth century, no prison in Britain apart from Bridewell's was sexually segregated, and one long-term inmate of Newgate, John Bernardi, locked up for having made an attempt on King William's life, got married and fathered ten children during his twenty-eight years inside. If you were looking for a homosocial environment in Johnson's day, prison was not the place to find it. My thanks to Lucy Powell for this information.
3. I have argued elsewhere that James Joyce's "Eveline" was almost certainly influenced by Conrad's "To-morrow." Both stories certainly bear witness to the fact that girls at the time of writing "don't run away from home." See Hawthorn, "The Richness of Meanness."

WORKS CITED

Boswell, James. *The Journal of a Tour to the Hebrides With Samuel Johnson, Ll.D.* Charles Dilly, 1785.
Conrad, Joseph. "Amy Foster." *Typhoon and Other Stories*. J.M. Dent, 1950.
———. *The Arrow of Gold: A Story Between Two Notes*. J.M. Dent, 1947.
———. *Chance: A Tale in Two Parts*. J.M. Dent, 1949.
———. "Freya of the Seven Isles." *'Twixt Land and Sea*. Cambridge University Press, 2008.
———. "The Inn of the Two Witches." *Within the Tides*. Cambridge University Press, 2012.
———. *Last Essays*. Cambridge University Press, 2010.
———. *Lord Jim: A Tale*. Cambridge University Press, 2012.
———. "A Smile of Fortune." *'Twixt Land and Sea*. Cambridge University Press, 2008.
———. "The Tale." *Tales of Hearsay*. J.M. Dent, 1955.
———. "To-morrow." *Typhoon and Other Stories*. J.M. Dent, 1950.
Donne, John. *The Variorum Edition of the Poetry of John Donne*. Vol. 2, edited by Gary A. Stringer, Indiana University Press, 2000.
Greaney, Michael. "Terribly Strange Beds: Conrad, Sleep, and Modernism." *The Conradian*, vol. 37, no. 1, 2012, pp. 1–20.
Hampson, Robert. *Conrad's Secrets*. Palgrave Macmillan, 2012.
———. *Joseph Conrad: Betrayal and Identity*. Macmillan Press, 1992.
Hawthorn, Jeremy. "The Richness of Meanness: Joseph Conrad's 'To-morrow' and James

Joyce's 'Eveline,'" *Literary Sinews: Essays in Honour of Bjørn Tysdahl*, edited by Jakob Lothe, Juan Christian Pellicer, and Tore Rem, Novus Forlag, 2003, pp. 107–20.

———. *Sexuality and the Erotic in the Fiction of Joseph Conrad*. Continuum, 2007.

Ho, Janice. "The Spatial Imagination and Literary Form of Conrad's Colonial Fictions." *Journal of Modern Literature*, vol. 30, no. 4, 2007, pp. 1–19.

Martinière, Nathalie. "Symbolic Space and Narrative Focus: The Cabin in Conrad's Sea Stories." *The Conradian*, vol. 27, no. 1, 2002, pp. 24–38.

Ruppel, Richard. *Homosexuality in the Life and Work of Joseph Conrad: Love Between the Lines*. Routledge, 2008.

Stott, Rebecca. *The Fabrication of the Late-Victorian Femme Fatale: The Kiss of Death*. Macmillan Press, 1992.

The Tropical Forests of Conrad and His British Contemporaries, in the Context of Aristotle and T.H. Huxley

BEN FELDERHOF

ABSTRACT

This article seeks to explain the prevalence and significance of tropical forest settings and symbolism in the fiction of Joseph Conrad and other authors. It follows up the argument made by Corinne J. Saunders in *The Forest of Medieval Romance* (1993) that literary forests were once used to explore the concept of unordered matter and to integrate it into the Christian worldview. The contention of this article is that Darwinian ideas and waning religious belief in late-nineteenth-century Britain prompted renewed anxieties about chaotic nature, and thus a revival of the convention of the tangled wilderness. While many Victorian-Edwardian authors conjure fallen but redeemable jungles as a way of staving off the materialism of natural selection and justifying the purposive alternative of Lamarckian evolutionary theory, Conrad's forest is more unorthodox, ambiguous, and far less encouraging.

KEYWORDS

tropical forest, jungle, evolution, Thomas Henry Huxley, *hyle*, H.G. Wells, Rudyard Kipling

In the summer of 2010, I was travelling alone, down the western coast of Sumatra. For about a thousand miles between Aceh and the Sunda Strait a single-carriage highway runs beside the Indian Ocean, twisting through the dark green vegetation which stretches almost unbroken to a parallel road a hundred miles inland. The minibus drivers who ply the route press on all night. With only the radio's mournful-sounding *nasyids*[1] and the sighs of oblivious customers for company, they contend with mopeds and onrushing lorries for passage. During such times, I would stare into the jagged blackness half in awe, half in fear at what it concealed. Like Marlow in *Heart of Darkness*, I had "heard enough" about the tropical forest. For me, it *did* bring plenty of images with it from British fiction: Mowgli and the wolf pack in *The Jungle Books* (1894–95) of Rudyard Kipling,[2] or Prendick and the Beast Folk in *The Island of Doctor Moreau* (1896) by H.G. Wells; the ethereal Rima in W.H. Hudson's *Green Mansions* (1904), or the ignoble ape-men in *The Lost World* (1912) by Arthur Conan Doyle; the rapacity of Case in Robert Louis Stevenson's "The Beach of Falesá" (1893); the benevolent rule of Jim, or the murderous cult of Kurtz. When I listed these tales in my head, what struck me was the brevity of the time span in which they had been published: just over two decades before the Great War. What were the reasons for this explosion of fiction set in tropical forests? What was it about the landscape that the authors found so inspiring or disturbing, as we still do to this day?

The obvious explanation is that during the nineteenth century the British were increasingly brought into contact with the tropical forest, whether through field sports in India and Ceylon;[3] botanical and ecological surveys of the Amazon;[4] African exploration and missionary work;[5] or the cultivation of Pará rubber in Malaya and beyond.[6] Non-fictional accounts, imparting wonders, riches, and atrocities, flowed back to the homeland and a voracious audience. For some authors of popular fiction, the tropical forest was merely a fashionable and profitable backdrop for their pro-imperial tales of derring-do.

All the same, I would like to outline another, more profound explanation for the proliferation of a "jungle motif" during the 1890s; one related to the decline of Christianity and the re-emergence of materialism, beliefs (or lack thereof) which have frequently been associated in the literature of Christian Europe with tangled wastelands. For thousands of years, in fact, the organic landscape has been used in literature to represent and investigate the essential state of the universe and humanity. For materialists, who believe that no immaterial causes are required to explain the evolution of the cosmos, the archetypal landscape is a haphazard, morally neutral scene of creation and destruction. Their idealist counterparts represent the divinely conceived forms constituting pure reality as a well-ordered city or garden. Due to the corrupting influence of matter, the idyll may temporarily degenerate, but order will always ultimately be restored. The image of nature as either amoral or fallen receded during the Enlightenment, but with the advent of Darwin's theory of natural selection, there arose once again the threat (in the eyes of the typical mid-nineteenth-century idealist) of contingency and meaninglessness,[7] to be countered in the traditional manner. In this context, the jungles of fin-de-siècle fiction are not so much thrilling novelty as the revival of an ancient literary convention, encapsulating something important about the *Zeitgeist* and the beliefs of the authors.

HYLE

Aristotle seems to have been the first to refer to unordered matter as ὕλη (*hyle*), which could also be translated as "forest," "undergrowth," or "timber" (Liddell and Scott). But he was undoubtedly influenced by various pre-existing conventions, such as Plato's primordial receptacle ὑποδοχή (*hypodoche*), likened in the *Timaeus* to χώρα (*khora*) (52a), the territory beyond the city limits (Liddell and Scott). Both the Aristotelian and Platonic concepts owe something to the swarm of atoms in the void postulated by Leucippus and Democritus, and the primeval substratum named "the boundless" by the Milesian Anaximander in the sixth century BCE (Novack 93, 138–41). And all must have been inspired by the ancient Greek creation myth that began with the silent and misty gap of χάος (*khaos*), attended by Night, Darkness, and Hell; from which sprang *Gaia*, "the Earth."[8] This lineage explains the correspondence in literature between wild spaces and not only primal matter but also the underworld and regeneration.[9]

Aristotle diverged from pre-Socratic atomism in distinguishing between unstable matter and eternally constant "forms" or "ideas." In the *Metaphysics*, he argued that every sensually perceptible substance is a combination of *hyle* and form ("all nature has matter"), just as a human comprises body and soul (995a, 1037a). The relationship is akin to that between sleep and wakefulness (1048b), or slave and master. *Hyle* is unruly, "the cause of the accidental" (1027a), but rightfully subordinate to the orderly spiritual axis. After Aristotle, the association between chaotic matter and the uncultivated forest was perpetuated by the Romans, who translated ὕλη into Latin as *silva*.[10] And early Christian symbolism would take it even further, contrasting the fallen wilderness with the garden regulated by *Logos*— "word," "reason," "narrative," "law" —associated in the Gospel of John 1:1–5 with God, life, and light. The *errorem sylvarum* ("the deception of the forest") was a common metaphor for the temptation to sin. In his *Confessions*, St. Augustine writes, "In this vast forest, filled with snares and dangers, see how many I have cut away and thrust out of my heart. [. . .] O God of my salvation" (10.35). And in his Christian interpretation of *The Aeneid*, Servius equates the Avernus forest of book 6 with the enticements of earthly life through which the hero must travel to find the golden bough of spiritual perfection: "for by the forests, shadows and dark places are signified, where lust and unbridled passion rule" (qtd. in Saunders 21).

During the Middle Ages and Renaissance, authors continued to discuss the interwoven questions of cosmogony, religion, and metaphysics through literary forest quests and imagery,[11] and, in spite or because of heretical eruptions, to depict in general a Manichean universe in which savage wildernesses denote a fall from the harmony of the original garden.[12] However, I do not think the same simplification applies from the late-seventeenth century onwards, when European philosophy reacted to thinkers like Descartes and Hobbes (the latter of whom saw chaos and savagery as the fundamental state of nature) by envisioning existence as not only divinely regulated and unchanged from its inception, but designed exclusively for mankind's happiness. The historian Norman Hampson describes this period as "a truce between science and religion," when scientists abandoned the quest for metaphysical implications in nature, Christians "turned their attention away from original sin," and "the Deists agreed that the heavens declared the glory of God" (85). Even Diderot, who was at the centre of the more radical materialist ideas which circulated among French intellectuals during the second half of the eighteenth century, declared in his *Interprétation de la nature* (1754) that chaos was an impossibility (N. Hampson 91).

Just as the image of the universe as sometimes hostile and unruly passed out of fashion during these years, so in British literature did tangled forest wildernesses.[13] Simultaneously, many of the country's real woodlands were converted into functional, mono-cultural plantations, and their medieval associations with disorder, bestial savagery, and illicit passions faded. Therefore, when Darwin's heirs wanted to express a more gothic image of nature as tumultuous, they turned instead to the domestic forest's tropical equivalent, a landscape already (erroneously) connected in readers' minds with impenetrable undergrowth by the accounts of mid-Victorian explorers and their use of a loan-word recently imported from the Indian subcontinent. "Jungle" had been a Hindu legal term for land that had lain uncultivated for at least five years (*Code of Gentoo Laws* 15, 190), but the British applied it more generally to any area of tangled vegetation and later as a synonym for the tropical forest as a whole. It was nothing less than the rebirth of *hyle* in Western culture.

RE-OCCUPATION

John Glendening has claimed that the dominant theme in British intellectual life at the end of the nineteenth century was "entanglement," and not the orderly complexity of the Enlightenment and Darwin's "entangled bank," but the disorder of materialism's relativistic value system (15). He says that previously oppositional concepts like "human" and "animal," or "modern civilisation" and "primitive savagery," became confused. The misinterpretation of Darwin, to infer that self-interested creatures would generally prevail at the expense of the selfless, even threatened to entangle "good" and "evil" (16–17, 19). As evidence, Glendening draws on such works of fiction as *The Island of Doctor Moreau* and *Heart of Darkness*, in which "the forces of chaos generally overmatch order [. . .] entanglement as snarl outweighs entanglement as network" (20). The trend in public discourse during this period may have led towards skepticism and a vision of nature as amoral, but I would query whether it was the overriding image before 1914. The ideological territory that Christianity ceded during the second half of the nineteenth century was not immediately seized by atheism. To begin with, the pioneers of scientific naturalism, like T.H. Huxley, explicitly did not identify themselves as materialists, but as "agnostics."[14] The way in which they used religious language and imagery to reiterate the "uniformity of nature" was both a deliberate continuation of theistic science and an attack upon it.[15] What's more, in the final decades of the century, they faced a resurgence of teleology, manifested in neo-Lamarckian evolutionary theory, social Darwinism, the "New Imperialism," and spiritualism (only the first of which I shall discuss here). There was no "Darwinian revolution" in the 1860s whereby materialism suddenly became the predominant outlook in the country. Instead, subsequent decades were characterized by cultivation of the gap where Christian beliefs had once stood, a process called *Umbesetzung* (or "re-occupation") by Hans Blumenberg (1983).

Numerous authors of fictional jungles reproduced in miniature the age's crisis of faith, either through profound doubt or outright rejection of Christianity, and most sought consolation in other beliefs.[16] Their tropical forests are often chaotic places where the binary oppositions of idealism meld, but they tend fundamentally to support of a vision of nature with underlying moral purpose. The primary setting of Kipling's *Jungle Books* may at times be an ambiguous site, where the energy of being is entwined with the quietude of death, but, as when the wolves kill their aging leader and a new one is born, "to be killed in his turn," violent struggle and the elimination of life are always the means to an ultimate good, the perpetuation of life (19). This is especially obvious during the springtime, when even the plants must "put away the hanging-on, over-surviving raffle of half-green things which the gentle winter has suffered to live" (309). The fatal quarrels of animals, which look to the naïve observer like outbursts of destruction, are all part of the process by which the jungle is renewed. In contrast to the irrationality of Conrad's forest,[17] Kipling's is more straightforwardly "full of words that sound like one thing but mean another" (307–8). It is, in effect, a paradise imperfectly regained through laws based on struggle, segregation, and the fear of natural mankind.[18]

Of all Conrad's fellow jungle writers, H.G. Wells had arguably the knottiest relationship with faith, exhibiting at times the sombre attitude of an atomist for whom chaos is the *status quo* of existence, but never abjuring altogether the possibility of a perfect world. He was at his most impious in early scientific romances like *The Island of Doctor Moreau*, in which the "green confusion" of the forest does indeed resemble an amoral universe ruled by chance and prone to lurches into formlessness (Glendening 39–40):

> I pushed on. Colour vanished from the world, the tree tops rose against the luminous blue sky in inky silhouette, and all below that outline melted into formless blackness. Presently the trees grew thinner, and the shrubby undergrowth more abundant. Then there was a desolate space covered with white sand, and then another expanse of tangled bushes. (Wells, *Island* 44)

There, Prendick becomes "perplexed" (45), a word related to the Latin *perplexus*, meaning "entangled" (Glendening 56). Elsewhere, however, Wells suggests that perplexity is not inevitable. During the early years of the twentieth century, when he appears to have retreated somewhat from secularism, Wells produced *Tono-Bungay*, a story so bleak for the most part that the narrator claims a far better name for it would be *Waste* (*Tono-Bungay* 381). George Ponderevo shows all the signs of being an irremediable materialist, who does not "believe in anything at all" and feels that life is generally fortuitous and futile (51, 10, 348). Without constant and autonomous standards, he is beset by entanglement and unable to make sense of the world. He says, "The perplexing thing about life is the irresolute complexity of reality, of things and relations alike. Nothing is simple. Every wrong done has a certain justice in it, and every good deed has dregs of evil" (195–96). Appropriately, the essential episode of George's life is a journey into the jungle of a West African island, where the ambiguity of all existence is distilled into a single, incomprehensible image (325). Life is disclosed as a "strange by-play of matter" culminating only in barrenness and decay, represented by two small heaps of a radioactive substance called "quap" (329–30). The shocking implications of the absence of a final cause are made plain when George murders an innocent native as though it were "a matter-of-fact transaction," like the packing of a portmanteau (335). And yet it is precisely through his experience on Mordet Island that George learns some mode of belief is necessary. It isn't the Christian God, but eventually he finds an absolute to cut through the confusion of life: "Sometimes I call this reality Science, sometimes I call it Truth. But it is something we draw by pain and effort out of the heart of life, that we disentangle and make clear" (388).

Apart from the ambivalence of Wells, Conrad was unusual for a British author before the Great War in that he appeared to be more resigned to the materialist perspective than intent on countering it. Outwardly, he could adopt an attitude of unconcern. Reflecting in one letter to R.B. Cunninghame Graham on humanity "condemned to perish from cold" in "a universe made of drops of fire and clods of mud," he writes that, "If you take it to heart it becomes an unendurable tragedy" (Conrad, *Letters to Cunninghame Graham* 65). Instead of taking it to heart, Conrad claims that the pointless, "remorseless process is sometimes amusing." He might have been able to believe in the promises of Christianity, Polish nationalism, and benevolent imperialism in an earlier age, but their values had since been distorted into empty words and false hopes. Again he wrote to Cunninghame Graham, reiterating the futility of his idealism: "You with your ideals of sincerity, courage and truth are strangely out of place in this epoch of material preoccupations" (*Selected Letters* 90). Judging by his fiction, however, Conrad must also have felt some dismay at the prospect of a purposeless cosmos, in which man is no more than an insignificant brute.

Many of Conrad's novels and stories deal with attempts to mold nature according to various aspects of teleology (supernatural, racial, imperial, heroic, etc.), and to discern something meaningful in the narrative of existence. His characters' forest quests are superficially in keeping with the conventional approach to such questions, but the answers they yield are less conventional and far from encouraging: "Nothing." That is the sum of Almayer's existence in Sambir (*Outcast* 244); it is the verdict pronounced by the white man on Arsat's search for meaning in "The Lagoon" (167), and by Davidson in response to the "Samburan mystery" in *Victory* (350). Unlike the redeemed woodlands of some of his contemporaries,[19] Conrad's forests serve to undermine any hope of progress towards a heavenly *telos*. A "conquering darkness" positively "oozes" and "flows" from between the trees, ambushing and "devouring" light, and obliterating all form ("Lagoon" 156). The plants dismember and decompose the human body and man-made structures, like Cornelius's trading post, Kurtz's inner station, and the abandoned sheds of the Tropical Belt Coal Company. His jungle is engaged in the task of turning the world into one great wasteland, and it will be "victorious."

The tropical forest in Conrad is not always imposing, uncaring, and destructive. It can be a temporarily dreamlike venue for mutual infatuations, ambitious schemes, and enthralling rhetoric, but any suggestion of intention in nature is nullified by contrary indications (e.g., the "contemptuous" or "scornful pity" of the trees [*Outcast* 59, 125]), so that it should be read as an erroneous projection of the individual mind. In Conrad's forests, beliefs of all kinds are ultimately shown to be illusions, and characters are introduced to the world as the skeptic is able to see it. However, this awakening is not a joyful liberation.[20] Those of Conrad's characters who attain disillusionment, like Marlow, are overtaken by the "too dark" truth and by feelings of loneliness and despair; conversely, the Intended's idolatrous worship of Kurtz is "that great and saving illusion that shone with an unearthly glow in the darkness" (*Youth* 121, 123).

While Conrad differed from most other authors of the time in using the jungle motif to represent an exclusively material universe, it is doubtful that he viewed total disenchantment and the abandonment of man-made values as desirable, but rather anticipated Hermann Hesse in recognizing "die grossen Weltgegensätze zugleich als Notwendigkeit und als Illusion" ("the great opposites of the world at once as both necessary and illusion") (126). Conrad was in fact conscious that the world could be a bewilderingly difficult place to negotiate without the comforting fallacies of order and hierarchy. He once compared himself to "a man who has lost his gods. My efforts seem unrelated to anything in heaven and everything under heaven is impalpable to the touch like shapes of mist" (Conrad, *Letters from Joseph Conrad* 155). Along with the dense vegetation and rotting riverbanks, spells of cloud and fog make Conrad's forests apposite representations of a chaotic universe by blurring objects and values. It is the place where Kurtz realizes "'there was nothing on earth to prevent him killing whom he jolly well pleased'" (*Youth* 102), just as Gentleman Jones is a cold-blooded killer because he behaves "as if the world were still one great, wild jungle without law" (*Victory* 104). Ironically, given his professed disdain for idealism, it is arguable that Conrad's jungle stories did far more than those of his contemporaries who sought to compensate for waning Christian beliefs to vilify the "might is right" philosophy that had crept into the discourse of the age via the field of evolutionary biology.

NEO-LAMARCKISM

Contrary to popular belief, the theory of natural selection was not widely and swiftly accepted following the 1859 publication of *On the Origin of Species*.[21] In reality, most Victorians were loath to believe that the apparent order of the organic world was the result of chance, competition, and the annihilation of the weak, rather than a purposeful intelligence or law of progress. It wasn't until the beginning of the twentieth century that natural selection emerged as the dominant evolutionary model in Britain, with alternative ideas remaining prevalent until the 1930s. The intervening period has been called "the eclipse of Darwinism."[22]

The scientific establishment preferred the evolutionary theory of French biologist Jean-Baptiste de Monet, Chevalier de Lamarck, sometimes referred to as the "inheritance of acquired characteristics." Formulated at the beginning of the century, but revived by Herbert Spencer, this model supposed that nature is a ladder that species steadily ascend because of an inherent urge to become ever-more complex. Greater sophistication is achieved by individuals consciously adapting their behavior, leading to changes in the organs used or disused, which are then passed on to their offspring. Lamarckism was a more acceptably teleological alternative to the materialism of natural selection. Darwin himself concluded that, although ostensibly violent, nature was hierarchical and progressive in essence: "Thus, from the war of nature, from famine and death, the most exalted object which we are capable of conceiving, namely, the production of the higher animals, directly follows" (490). Although he drew reluctantly upon Lamarck in the 1859 edition of On the Origin of Species to placate his critics, the process of "use and disuse" became increasingly prominent in later editions and subsequent works.[23]

In 1885, the term "neo-Lamarckism" was coined to encompass the slew of hypotheses that sought a place for intention in nature, including Samuel Butler's vision of a supernatural "Life Force" acting through organisms to drive their development, and which constituted the predominant evolutionary doctrine at that time.[24] Doubts as to whether environmental conditions affect an organism's genotype did not take hold until the 1890s. The notion of hard heredity began to reassert itself, championed by "neo-Darwinists," like August Weismann.[25] Another was T.H. Huxley, who was skeptical of the late-Spencerian vision of natural struggle as a progressive force that should not be impeded by humankind.

For Huxley, uninhibited nature was amoral and as likely to "work towards degradation" as enhanced complexity (L. Huxley, *Life* 284). However, in the *Prolegomena* of his "Evolution and Ethics" (1893), the imagery he uses to illustrate this "cosmic process" is reminiscent of the Christian antipathy for riotous and degenerative *hyle*. He imagines the unchecked "state of nature" as the British landscape before the arrival of the Romans, when the vegetation "was as different from the present Flora of the Sussex downs, as that of Central Africa now is" (Huxley, *Collected Essays* 3).[26] In opposition to this jungle scene, he posits "a state of art" produced and maintained through the constant application to nature of human intelligence and energy. This is of course represented as a garden, a patch of soil "cut off from the rest by a wall," where the native vegetation is extirpated and replaced by a "colony of strange plants." Within, the herbage is carefully regulated to ensure that competition does not assert itself, as it does in the luxuriant jungle. Where Huxley's philosophy differs from Christianity is the ephemerality of the garden, dependent not on God, but man. The mortal horticulturalist cannot forever ward off "the victory of the cosmic powers," and in his absence the walls will decay, pests invade, and native weeds choke their rivals (10).

The tropical forest was likewise a popular trope in discussions of evolutionary theory by fin de siècle British novelists, most of whom subscribed to one or another form of Lamarckism.[27] W.H. Hudson felt a visceral aversion to the theory of natural selection from the moment he first read *The Origin of Species* as a youth,[28] referring to it as "the giant tree in whose shadow [. . .] perhaps all men must come and sit with [Darwin] forever" (qtd. in Tomalin 90). He was much closer to Samuel Butler's supernatural Lamarckism in believing that the adaptation of the individual "is accomplished through a super-abundance of vital energy, and urge to realize one's potentialities, and, particularly among the more advanced forms of life, the guidance of the intelligence."[29] Hudson's *Green Mansions* is an exploration of the apparent inconsistency between nature's artistry and cruelty, as well as the author's own need to intuit some higher purpose in life.[30] In keeping a beautiful but deadly forest-realm in order, the nymph-like Rima seems to Abel the embodiment of that deity or principle which bestows evolutionary gifts (Hudson, *Green Mansions* 199). Having ignored the intrinsic volatility of nature, Abel's delusion that a highly evolved native girl constitutes the height of supernatural creation is shattered when a tribe of Indians cause Rima to fall to her death (275). Following this crushing disillusionment, the forest becomes a darker, more chthonic location, full of hostile, creeping beasts, which are more mechanical than alive (289), and whose calls are like the wailing of the dead (286–87). Only after a prolonged spell in this Darwinian hell does he reach a philosophical compromise that rejects religion but retains a place for the soul (314).

It is evident from *The Lost World* that Arthur Conan Doyle's evolutionary perspective emphasized the importance of struggle as a condition for adaptation and progress. The novel deals with two locations where this law of nature has been disrupted, one European and one tropical. The clement conditions in modern London have nurtured a bovine population, while seismic activity has isolated the jungly plateau of Maple White Land and its inhabitants, allowing creatures to survive "which would otherwise disappear" (Doyle 42). Only recently has a tribe of Indians found its way up to this land "under the stress of famine or of conquest," where it became engaged in a bitter contest with beasts and anthropoid apes (165). The evolutionary mechanism implied by Doyle is Lamarckian. The narrative asserts that plants "which have never been known to climb elsewhere learn the art as an escape from that sombre shadow" of the forest floor (75). And the hero, Professor Challenger, has no time for the "fallacy" of Weismann's neo-Darwinism (16), speculating that the newly-discovered dinosaurs will soon die out due to the stupidity which makes it "impossible for them to adapt themselves to changing conditions" (145).

There is little in Conrad's jungle stories, besides some of Marlow's opinions, to suggest that Conrad credited progressionism and the inheritance of acquired characteristics.[31] In communicating that evolution is a tumultuous, trial and error affair, in which reason and morality are utterly extraneous, Conrad's forests display the influence of "Evolution and Ethics." As Glendening points out, their luxuriance recalls the moment in Huxley's figurative landscape at which peaceful utopia, having resulted in Malthusian profusion, collapses in a flurry of death and destruction (146). Feeble demonstrations of harmony and beauty belie a warlike reality, such as the perfumes which distract from plants noiselessly stampeding over each other (Conrad, *Almayer* 55); the moribund trees upon whose remains feast assertive and garishly colored parasites (117); or, the "thin twitter" of a bird "in the great silence full of struggle and death" (*Outcast* 257). In "The End of the Tether," a collapsed riverbank reveals a horrifying subterranean scene, "a mass of roots intertwined as if wrestling underground; and in the air, the interlaced boughs, bound and loaded with creepers, carried on the struggle for life" (193). In this violent tussle to survive and reproduce, the values of life, love, and energy are not arrayed in triumphant opposition to death, loneliness, and stasis, but are complicit. The scents, calls, and colors of the forest serve to thwart awareness and understanding of a deeper, deathly truth.

I have said that Conrad's forest is a venue for disillusionment, but the initial effect of this environment on European intruders is bewilderment. To the two traders in "An Outpost of Progress," the wilderness is "rendered more strange, more incomprehensible by the mysterious glimpses of the vigorous life it contained" (79). It throbs with life, and yet is "like a great emptiness" disclosing "nothing intelligible" (81). Similarly, Karain's arboreal dominion is "full of a life that went on stealthily with a troubling effect of solitude; of a life that seemed unaccountably empty of anything that would stir the thought" ("Karain" 14).

To appreciate the role that the jungle plays in the complex journey of Willems from possessing an idealized conception of nature towards awareness of a darker, more "Darwinian" reality, it is necessary to scrutinize the seemingly idyllic situation which we encounter at the beginning of *An Outcast of the Islands*. By allegedly adhering to a "straight and narrow path," the "confidential clerk" has gained a house with a perfumed and shady garden, where he lords it over his wife's family in the manner of Jehovah, feared and venerated: "They lived now by the grace of his will" (14). He obviously has a high opinion of his own willpower (appropriately so, given his name), because he believes he can deviate fleetingly from his putatively virtuous conduct without interfering "with the very nature of things" (13). These details could be the makings of a quite conventional, almost biblical morality tale. However, there is enough in the opening pages to hint that "the very nature of things," including of Willems himself, is different from how he imagines it to be. Repetition of the word "delight," in conjunction with the horticultural image, perhaps recalls the corruption of the "Garden of Earthly Delights" and casts doubt on the authenticity of his essential righteousness, as does the admission that the path of his "peculiar honesty" has for many years been "a faint and ill-defined track" skirting a "dangerous wilderness" (27).

Our incongruous first impressions of Willems help to explain the much later verdict that his "fall" can be attributed to "his continence" and "a blind belief in himself" (263), while much of the intervening narrative implies his lack of exactly that "power of resistance" endorsed by Marlow in *Lord Jim* (*Lord Jim* 38). Many of the reasons for his eventual demise stem from an obstinate refusal to accept his true nature as a hollow figure driven by ignoble urges (White 137), which he obfuscates with an increasingly unsustainable self-belief based on his race and the fiction that he has "always led a virtuous life" (Conrad, *Outcast* 211). He does not enter the forests of Sambir as part of a quest for self-knowledge and redemption, but to "hide his discouragement and weariness" (59).

On a suitably ill-defined track, Willems encounters Aïssa, who in many respects is depicted as the embodiment of the deceptive, corrupting jungle, but not so much in contrast to the European man as his mirror-image. Both are overpowered by erotic desire for one another, and yet they necessarily remain wedded to different cultural identities and racial prejudices, hence the need to isolate the other from their compatriots. For Willems, the idea that he has simultaneously "unveiled" Aïssa and tropical nature is clearly important in maintaining the illusion of his mastery. For as long as he believes the veil is rent, the forest takes on the tenuous appearance of a *locus amoenus*, although the narration reminds us that tropical life "seems to be all grace of colour and form, all brilliance, all smiles, but is only the blossoming of the dead; whose mystery holds the promise of joy and beauty, yet contains nothing but poison and decay" (62). This is why the "little matter" of Aïssa subsequently donning her traditional garb, contrary to his bidding, acts upon Willems "like a disclosure of some great disaster": "It increased his contempt for himself as the slave of a passion he had always derided, as the man unable to assert his will" (106).

Abnormally for a hero and *femme fatale* in imperial romance, the relationship between Willems and Aïssa is one of mutual surrender and mutual conquest. But the reason it cannot last is that, on the one hand, Willems fools himself that he is akin to an Ovidian god pursuing his mortal quarry (60), while in reality impatiently seeking enslavement and oblivion (62, 66, 118); on the other hand, Aïssa appears to submit coyly, but her expression is "of one charmed by a delightful dream, with the slight exaltation of intoxicating triumph lurking in its dawning tenderness" (67). As he struggles to conceal from himself the fact of his inner vacuity, Willems falls back on the notion that Aïssa, the diabolical personification of the jungle, has overrun and taken possession of his soul (R. Hampson 58).

When the mutual enchantment is broken, the horrors of neo-Darwinian nature are more obvious to both lovers. Aïssa finds herself misled, astray from the path on which she first met Willems, and in a quite different psychical forest:

> She followed as well as she could. Yet at times—very often lately—she had felt lost like one strayed in the thickets of tangled undergrowth in the great forest—pushing on till he can go no further, and held at last in the maze of branches and creepers, seeing nothing but thick leaves, tough green twigs, obstinate tendrils, clinging parasites; seeing all the interlaced confusion of those many things close before his eyes—yet unable to see the ground on which he stands. She was like one lost in a wilderness impenetrable and heavy, in a wilderness devoid of hope but full of surprises; one held captive amongst the restlessness of unseen forces that are silent and destructive, dangerous and indifferent, incomprehensible and strong. (Conrad, *Outcast* 196–97)

Willems also becomes aware of "death looking at him from everywhere," but he is unable to comprehend the jungle fully because he persists in viewing life and death as separate and antagonistic:

> He saw the horrible form among the big trees, in the network of creepers, in the fantastic outlines of leaves, of the great indented leaves that seemed to be so many enormous hands with big broad palms, with stiff fingers outspread to lay hold of him; hands gently stirring, or hands arrested in a frightful immobility, with a stillness attentive and watching for the opportunity to take him, to enlace him, to strangle him, to hold him till he died; hands that would hold him dead, that would never let go, that would cling to his body forever till it perished—disappeared in their frantic and tenacious grasp.
> And yet the world was full of life. (261)

In such surroundings, Willems ought to grasp that those qualities commonly thought ideal are not ends in themselves, but the means to expedite a mindless and hideous routine. Readers may expect a moment of irreversible recognition, having been told that "the dark forests" contain the "bones of the wise," those who have strayed like Willems from the monotonous road of virtue (158). Eventually, Willems appears to cross the threshold of understanding, leading to the admission that "'I am a lost man'" (267).

> The air was full of sweet scent, of the scent charming, penetrating and violent like the impulse of love. He looked into that great dark place odorous with the breath of life, with the mystery of existence, renewed, fecund, indestructible; and he felt afraid of his solitude, of the solitude of his body, of the loneliness of his soul in the presence of this unconscious and ardent struggle; of this lofty indifference; of this merciless and mysterious purpose, perpetuating strife and death through the march of ages. (265)

However, at the very last, he proves himself utterly incapable of resisting the teleological illusion and the promise of a "hopeful future." Failing to realize that he has been shot, he purports to understand "the triumphant delight of sunshine and of life," before immediately being overtaken by darkness and death (282).

CONCLUSION

I have attempted to demonstrate that, consciously or unconsciously, various authors before the Great War were fascinated by the image of the jungle due in part to the literary tradition which identified wooded wildernesses with chaotic *hyle* and godlessness, in contrast with the garden ideal. They lived in a period when the reassuring consensus around universal and human nature as purposive was being undermined at an unprecedented rate by scientific discovery and religious doubt, but which also witnessed numerous attempts to shore up crumbling beliefs with various teleological substitutes. Most of the authors were engaged in this process of "re-occupation" and conjure a fallen world by emphasizing certain aspects of the forest: hellish darkness; predatory animals; dense, tangled vegetation, which not only impedes progress but actively encroaches on and disintegrates existing structures. What better way to resist the menace of materialism and demonstrate that order would triumph than depicting the transformation of a chaotic jungle into paradise, by neo-Lamarckian evolution, the British Empire, and the human spirit? Conrad was less intent on doing so. Although he did not advocate nihilism, he was unusual in consistently using forest conventions to subvert idealism and lay bare the hypocrisy of modern dogmas. Conrad's forests do not progress towards perfection, in spite of some misleading indications, but only devolve further into irrationality.

The question of Conrad's influence on an ensuing generation of writers fascinated by the tropical forest is a topic for another discussion, but it would not be presumptuous to claim that British modernism, with its pessimism, ironic style, preoccupation with disintegration, disenchantment with imperialism, and vision of humanity as risibly pathetic in the face of nature, owes more to Conrad's jungle stories than to those of any of his contemporaries. In this respect, it may be said that his representation of the tropical forest grew out of ancient tradition, and yet was simultaneously *avant-garde*.

NOTES

1. Islamic chants or ballads.

2. Although Kipling's jungles do not tend to exhibit the perennial humidity, dense canopy, and darkness that typify rainforest, and the real locations upon which they are supposedly based lie near to, and sometimes north of, the Tropic of Cancer, his inclusion here is based on the fact that it is not unusual among geographers to include within the definition of "tropical forest" those "seasonal" or "monsoon forests" marked by a dry season of several months. For example, Whitmore 10, and Forsyth and Miyata 7.

3. For example, Walter Campbell's *The Old Forest Ranger* (1842); James Willyams Grylls's *The Out-Station; or, Jaunts in the Jungle* (1847); Henry Shakespear's *The Wild Sports of India* (1860); and William Gordon Cumming's *Wild Men and Wild Beasts: Scenes in Camp and Jungle* (1871).

4. See H.W. Bates's *In the Heart of the Amazon Forest* (1859); Clements Markham's *Travels in Peru and India* (1862); Frederick Boyle's *A Ride across a Continent* (1868); and Henry Wickham's *Rough Notes of a Journey through the Wilderness* (1872).

5. Examples include Richard Burton's *The Lake Regions of Central Africa* (1860); William Winwood Reade's *Savage Africa* (1864); David Livingstone's *The Last Journals* (1874); and Henry Morton Stanley's *Through the Dark Continent* (1878) and *In Darkest Africa* (1890).

6. See, for example, Alfred Russel Wallace's *The Malay Archipelago* (1869); John McNair's *Perak and the Malays* (1878); Isabella Bird's *The Golden Chersonese and the Way Thither* (1883); and Frank Swettenham's *Malay Sketches* (1895).

7. I am not advocating a connection between contingency and "meaninglessness," but it has certainly been a charge levelled against atheistic materialism. If the universe is entirely accidental, not created by a purposeful intelligence or governed by immutable laws, then any significance or justice which we intuit in its unfolding must be a man-made fiction. It may be desirable or necessary to create such tales to fill the void, but their narrators are fallible and meanings elusive.

8. See, for example, Hesiod's *Theogony*: "Chaos was born first and after her came Gaia/the broad-breasted" (lns. 133–34); and Aristophanes's *The Birds*: "There was Chaos at first, and Darkness [*Erebus*], and Night, and Tartarus vast and dismal" (lns. 693–95).

9. An early personification of this association is that chthonic son of an earth goddess, deity of dismemberment, fertility, and forests, Dionysus. It is later evident in Milton's description of Chaos in *Paradise Lost* as both "The dark unbottom'd infinite Abyss" (2.405) and a "wild expanse," "damp and dark" (2.1014, 10.283), through which Satan wanders "Alone, and without guide, half lost" (2.975). It is "The Womb of nature, and perhaps her Grave" (2.911), in contrast with the walled and shining city of Heaven (2.1035–38).

10. In Virgil's *Aeneid*, there is an early example of idealist cosmogony, when a *locus terribilis*, wooded and wild, is transformed into a gardenlike *locus amoenus* ("pleasant place"). In books 7 and 8, Aeneas and his band of followers travel up the Tiber into a marvellous forest, which he recognizes as the future site of his city. Evander, the builder of a pre-existing citadel, tells the hero that Latium was once the refuge of Saturn in the aftermath of his overthrow by Jupiter. Evander describes how the forest of that time became a new Arcadia when Saturn gave laws to the savage inhabitants—fauns, nymphs and men born of tough trees—and ruled over them until this idyll was replaced by a meaner age of greed and war (8.306–96).

11. According to Kellie Robertson, in the Middle Ages, vernacular literature was the "generically appropriate vehicle" for discussions regarding matter: "science happened in poetry and vice versa" (110–11).

12. For example, in Dante Alighieri's *The Divine Comedy*, the progress of the poet towards redemption is plotted via two wooded settings: the *selva oscura* ("dark forest"), where Dante is disorientated, having lost the "straight way," and the *selva antica*, "dense, alive with green, divine" (*Purgatorio* 28:1–6).

13. See, for example, Alexander Pope's "Windsor Forest," in which earth and water are now "Not *Chaos* like together crush'd and bruis'd, / But as the world, harmoniously confus'd: / Where order in variety we see, / And where, tho' all things differ, all agree" (lns. 13–16).

14. Huxley claimed to have coined the term "agnostic" in 1869. He described materialism and spiritualism as "opposite poles of the same absurdity" (qtd. in L. Huxley, *Life* 262), but said that "the 'bosh' of heterodoxy is more offensive to me than that of orthodoxy, because heterodoxy professes to be guided by reason and science, and orthodoxy does not" ("Agnosticism" 5).

15. According to Matthew Stanley, Huxley co-opted the symbolism of religion and the practices of theistic science to "sanctify his own reformism" and smooth the transition to naturalistic science (26, 243, 248). The "uniformity of nature," the notion that the principles which "govern" the universe do not vary with place and time, had for some time been used to verify the existence of a Divine Author. For Huxley, however, the fact that nothing happens by chance or without cause also precluded any miraculous supernatural interventions, and was, in his hands, "a bludgeon to drive theism out of science" (34, 62).

16. In 1873, aged twenty-two, R.L. Stevenson informed his distraught parents that he no longer believed in Christianity (Harman 79). Seven years later, around the time of his twenty-first birthday, Arthur Conan Doyle declared himself to be an agnostic (Booth 59). H.G. Wells claimed that his estrangement from Christianity took place at the age of eleven (1877–78), after he dreamt of God torturing a sinner in hell (*Experiment* 67). However, loss of faith tended to stoke feelings of anxiety in Conrad's jungle-writing peers, not liberation.

17. Conrad's forests are not unique in Victorian-Edwardian fiction in exhibiting dichotomous traits: for example, the "excessive shrieking" and "excessive silence" which renders the

landscape so unintelligible to Marlow in *Heart of Darkness* (62, 68). What is arguably exceptional about the Conradian forest is that perplexity may not be a transitory state, followed by the revelation of a hidden *logos* (as it is in Mowgli's case and the typical forest quest of romance).

18. It may seem inappropriate to refer to Kipling's jungle as any kind of "paradise regained" given the deadly violence inflicted by the animals upon each other and upon the local human population. However, these episodes serve to underline the importance of "the Law," and the positive consequences of learning and transcending it. Kipling's Law of the Jungle is a ruthless code which permits bloodshed in all but a few circumstances ("'thou canst kill everything that thou art strong enough to kill, [except bulls]'" (*Jungle Book* 20); "'Is there anything in the jungle too little to be killed? No.'" (32), and indeed is criticized by Bagheera for being too crude (23). Despite ultimately prioritizing the survival of the collective over the interests of the individual, Kipling's Law is consistent with the callous ethics of late-nineteenth-century social Darwinism. Nonetheless, it is preferable to the senselessness which ensues at those times and places where the Law is not adequately observed: for example, by Mowgli in his pupillage, before he has vanquished Shere Khan and returned the village to nature. It is only after (in terms of the tales' chronology, rather than their order) Mowgli assumes mankind's rightful position as the fearsome overlord of the jungle, that the landscape comes to resemble more closely the springtime greenwood of literary tradition (281, 309–14).

19. I have already indicated that Kipling's *Jungle Books* contain a forest redeemed by a combination of British governance and natural mankind. After the heroes of Doyle's *The Lost World* have helped the Indians to vanquish ape-men and marauding dinosaurs, they are able to enjoy the lovely summer evenings, lying "in good comradeship among the long grasses by the wood [. . .] while above us the boughs of the bushes were heavy with luscious fruit, and below us strange and lovely flowers peeped at us from among the herbage" (181). Even at the end of Hudson's *Green Mansions* the earth recovers "its everlasting freshness and beauty" (314).

20. See Conrad to Cunninghame Graham, January 31, 1889: "What makes mankind tragic is not that they are the victim of nature, it is that they are conscious of it. To be part of the animal kingdom under the conditions of this earth is very well—but as soon as you know of your slavery, the pain, the anger, the strife—the tragedy begins" (*Selected Letters* 93).

21. Peter J. Bowler cites the examples of evolutionary historians Michael Ruse (*The Darwinian Revolution*, 1979) and Thomas Kuhn (*The Structure of Scientific Revolutions*, 1962) (24).

22. The term was coined by Julian Huxley in *Evolution: The Modern Synthesis* (1942) and used by Bowler as the title of a 1983 book.

23. Darwin was initially ill-disposed towards the concept of acquired characteristics and especially towards self-directed adaptation, which he found absurd in the case of plants. However, in the Introduction to the 1859 edition of *Origin*, he conceded that "Natural Selection has been the main but not the exclusive means of modification" (6). His attitude to Lamarckism only softened with time and in response to problems thrown up during the 1860s by William Thomson and Fleeming Jenkin, among others, so that by the early 1870s Darwin's stance was unquestionably Lamarckian. This theoretical ambiguity helped to encourage multiple and conflicting interpretations of his works.

24. Professor A.S. Packard was the first to use the terms "neo-Lamarckian" and "neo-Lamarckianism" in the introduction to his 1885, *Standard Natural History*, according to Lester Frank Ward (53).

25. Arguably, neo-Darwinism originated with Darwin's cousin Francis Galton in *Hereditary Genius* (1869) and "A Theory of Heredity" (1875). However, the most staunchly dogmatic champion of hard heredity was Weismann, whose first lectures and essays rubbishing every evolutionary theory apart from natural selection appeared in 1883 and were translated into English in 1889. His ideas created a climate in which Mendel's law of heredity, neglected since the 1860s, could be rediscovered in 1900.

26. Huxley's mention of Central Africa is an indirect reference to Henry Morton Stanley's disastrous expedition up the Congo River to rescue the Emin Pasha: the subject of his 1890 book *In Darkest Africa*, which contributed to the establishment of the jungle as a symbol for an untamed and degenerative nature that "heroic" European mankind must penetrate, resist, and conquer. The more direct allusion is to William Booth's *In Darkest England and the Way Out* (also 1890). In comparing Roman or pre-Roman Britain to modern-day central Africa, Huxley was treading an already well-worn path. It had been customary to view the tropics as resembling the climate of primeval Europe since the French paleobotanist Adolphe Brongniart's *Histoire des végétaux fossils* (1828–37), but the advent of "developmentalist" anthropology in the 1860s and 1870s led to the incorporation of the human populations of these landscapes into the analogy. Ancient Europe and modern Africa were seen as occupying the same lowly rung on a single evolutionary ladder, far below the civilized Europe of the present.

27. Stevenson was an admirer of Herbert Spencer, of whom he said that "no more persuasive rabbi exists" (Harman 72). Kipling's Lamarckian thinking is particularly on show in "The Tomb of His Ancestors" and also in *The Jungle Books* when Mowgli severs the tail of the red dhole, taunting him with the prospect that "there will now be many litters of little tailless red dogs, yea, with raw red stumps that sting when the sand is hot" (296). Wells was influenced by Huxley and therefore opposed to "biological optimism" during the 1890s, but he was more agreeable in his early and later years to the possibility that evolution is purposeful.

28. Hudson was challenged at the age of eighteen by his brother, Edwin, to familiarize himself with Darwin's theory of natural selection. Hudson describes his outraged reaction in *The Book of a Naturalist* (214), which undoubtedly comprised anguish at the prospect of oblivion after death (see also *Far Away and Long Ago* 305), heightened by the recent loss in October 1859 of his pious mother. Only after a second reading, and many years of consideration, was he willing to accept at least some aspects of evolution.

29. Richard E. Haymaker, quoted in Miller (78). Even until his death in 1922, when such a viewpoint had become unfashionable, Hudson continued to praise Butler as the man who had "smashed the Darwin idol and finally compelled the angels of science to creep cautiously in where the jeered fool had rushed" (Hudson, qtd. in Miller 79).

30. According to Ruth Tomalin, the theme of *Green Mansions* is "rooted in the old struggle between Darwin and the Book of Genesis. Abel finds that he cannot go back and live innocently in Eden. There is no such place for man" (198).

31. I am unable to agree with Redmond O'Hanlon's claim that Conrad's "guiding biological conceptions are late Darwinian, Lamarckian; he believes, as did most of his scientist-

contemporaries [. . .] in the inheritance of acquired characteristics, in the lasting effects of use and disuse, of habit, as well as of natural and sexual selection" (11).

WORKS CITED

Aristophanes. *The Birds*. Translated by Benjamin B. Rogers, George Bell and Sons, 1906.
Aristotle. *Metaphysics*. Translated by Hugh Lawson-Tancred, Penguin Books, 2004.
Blumenberg, Hans. *Die Legitimität der Neuzeit*. Translated by Robert M. Wallace, Massachusetts Institute of Technology Press, 1983.
Booth, Martin. *The Doctor, The Detective, and Arthur Conan Doyle: A Biography*. Hodder and Stoughton, 1997.
Bowler, Peter J. *Evolution: The History of an Idea*. University of California Press, 2003.
A Code of Gentoo Laws or, Ordinations of the Pundits. Translated by Nathaniel B. Halhed, 1776.
Conrad, Joseph. *Almayer's Folly*. Cambridge University Press, 1994.
———. *Joseph Conrad's Letters to Cunninghame Graham*. Edited by C.T. Watts, Cambridge University Press, 1969.
———. "Karain." *Tales of Unrest*, Cambridge University Press, 2012.
———. "The Lagoon." *Tales of Unrest*, Cambridge University Press, 2012.
———. *Letters from Joseph Conrad, 1895-1924*. Edited by Edward Garnett, The Bobbs-Merrill Co., 1924.
———. *Lord Jim*. 1st ed., Cambridge University Press, 2012.
———. *An Outcast of the Islands*. Cambridge University Press, 2016.
———. "An Outpost of Progress." *Tales of Unrest*, Cambridge University Press, 2012.
———. *The Selected Letters of Joseph Conrad*. Edited by Laurence Davies, Cambridge University Press, 2015.
———. *Victory*. Cambridge University Press, 2016.
———. *Youth, Heart of Darkness, The End of the Tether*. Cambridge University Press, 2010.
Dante Alighieri. *The Divine Comedy*. Translated by Charles Eliot Norton, William Benton, 1952.
Darwin, Charles. *On the Origin of Species by Means of Natural Selection*. John Murray, 1859.
Doyle, Arthur Conan. *The Lost World and Other Thrilling Tales*. Penguin Books, 2001.
Forsyth, Adrian, and Miyata, Kenneth. *Tropical Nature*. Charles Scribner's Sons, 1984.
Glendening, John. *The Evolutionary Imagination in Late-Victorian Novels: "An Entangled Bank."* Ashgate, 2007.
Hampson, Norman. *The Enlightenment: An Evaluation of its Assumptions, Attitudes and Values*. Penguin Books, 1968.
Hampson, Robert. *Joseph Conrad: Betrayal and Identity*. St. Martin's Press, 1992.
Harman, Claire. *Robert Louis Stevenson: A Biography*. Harper Perennial, 2006.
Hesiod. *Theogony*. Translated by A. Athanassakis, The Johns Hopkins University Press, 1983.
Hesse, Hermann. *Sämtliche Werke in 20 Bänden, Band 11*. Suhrkamp, 2001.
Hudson, William Henry. *The Book of a Naturalist*. Hodder and Stoughton, 1919.
———. *Far Away and Long Ago: A Childhood in Argentina*. Eland, 1982.
———. *Green Mansions: A Romance of the Tropical Forest*. Dover Publications, 1989.

Huxley, Leonard, ed. *Life and Letters of Thomas Henry Huxley*. 2 vols., D. Appleton and Co., 1901.
Huxley, Thomas Henry. "Agnosticism, a Symposium." *Agnostic Annual* 1, 1884.
———. *Collected Essays, Vol. IX*. D. Appleton and Co., 1911.
Kipling, Rudyard. "A Conference of the Powers" and "In the *Rukh*." *Many Inventions*, House of Stratus, 2001.
———. *The Jungle Books*. Penguin Books, 1994.
———. "The Tomb of His Ancestors." *The Day's Work*, Macmillan and Co., 1898.
Liddell, H.G., and Scott, R. *A Greek-English Lexicon*. Clarendon Press, 1940.
Miller, David. *W.H. Hudson and the Elusive Paradise*. Macmillan, 1990.
Milton, John. *Paradise Lost*. Penguin Books, 1989.
Novack, George. *The Origins of Materialism: The Evolution of a Scientific View of the World*. Pathfinder, 1965.
O'Hanlon, Redmond. *Joseph Conrad and Charles Darwin: The Influence of Scientific Thought on Conrad's Fiction*. Salamander, 1984.
Plato. *Timaeus*. Translated by W.R.M. Lamb, William Heinemann, 1925.
Robertson, Kellie. "Medieval Materialism: A Manifesto." *Exemplaria*, vol. 22, no. 2, Summer 2010, pp. 99–118.
Saunders, Corinne J. *The Forest of Medieval Romance*. D.S. Brewer, 1993.
St Augustine. *The Confessions*. Translated by John K. Ryan, Image Books, 2014.
Stanley, Matthew. *Huxley's Church and Maxwell's Demon: From Theistic Science to Naturalistic Science*. University of Chicago Press, 2015.
Stevenson, Robert Louis. "The Beach of Falesá." *South Sea Tales*, Oxford University Press, 1996.
Tomalin, Ruth. *W.H. Hudson: A Biography*. Faber and Faber, 1982.
Virgil. *The Aeneid: Books VII–X*. Translated by A.A. Irwin Nesbitt, W.B. Clive and Co., 1900.
Ward, Lester Frank. "Neo-Darwinism and Neo-Lamarckism (1891)." Kessinger Legacy Reprint.
Wells, H. G. *Experiment in Autobiography, Vol. I*. Faber and Faber, 1934.
———. *The Island of Doctor Moreau*. Penguin Books, 2005.
———. *Tono-Bungay*. Penguin Books, 2005.
White, Andrea. *Joseph Conrad and the Adventure Tradition*. Cambridge University Press, 1993.
Whitmore, T.C. *An Introduction to Tropical Rain Forests*. Clarendon Press, 1990.

Underwater Conrad

STEPHEN DONOVAN

UPPSALA UNIVERSITY

ABSTRACT

This article seeks to challenge current understandings of Conrad's status as a maritime writer by considering his many treatments of the sea not as fictionalized versions of his personal experiences as a sailor but as a sustained attempt to reimagine the sea as a *literary* object. As the earliest reviews of *Typhoon* attest, contemporaries regarded Conrad's evocation of the sea as unparalleled in both its strangeness and its verisimilitude. This conundrum, I propose, derives from Conrad's desire to recover for literature a maritime space which, as he saw it, had become disenchanted (in Weber's sense) by its mediation in early twentieth-century culture. Indeed, *Typhoon*, it is argued, was inspired by and in key respects modelled upon Jules Verne's *Twenty Thousand Leagues Under the Sea* (1870), a novel that had been readily available to Conrad in its Polish serialization in Warsaw's *Gazeta Polska* in 1870–71.

KEYWORDS

Joseph Conrad, *Typhoon,* the sea, Jules Verne, *Twenty Thousand Leagues under the Sea*

> An island is but the top of a mountain.
> —Conrad, *Victory* (1915)

The name Joseph Conrad evokes very different things these days. For readers of *Almayer's Folly, An Outcast of the Islands, The Rescue,* and *Victory,* Conrad is a chronicler of frontier life in the Dutch East Indies. For students of *Heart of Darkness*, "An Outpost of Progress," and *The Inheritors*, he is either a mouthpiece or a critic of colonial and racist attitudes. For readers of *Nostromo*, *The Secret Agent*, *Under Western Eyes*, and *Chance*, Conrad is a sharp-eyed satirist of nationalism, terrorism, autocracy, and capitalism. As for the happy few who have read *The Arrow of Gold*, *The Rover*, or *Suspense*, it's frankly anyone's guess.

In Conrad's lifetime, matters were more straightforward. For contemporaries, as *McClure's Magazine* boasted in November 1907, he was quite simply "the greatest living writer of sea stories." By the early 1900s, *The Nigger of the "Narcissus,"* "Youth," *Lord Jim*, *Typhoon*, *The Mirror of the Sea*, and a large body of essays and short fiction had established him as the English-speaking world's foremost novelist and commentator on maritime affairs. Reviewers repeatedly evoked this status in terms of global mastery: "Conrad, like Britannia, rules the waves" (*CR* 1:329); "Joseph Conrad's premiership in his own domain of the sea is now [. . .] generally admitted" (Our London Letter). The synonymy of Conrad's name with pre-eminence in this genre was confirmed by the *New York Times*'s announcement of his death, "JOSEPH CONRAD DIES, WRITER OF THE SEA" ("Joseph Conrad"), invoking an honorific that Conrad had bestowed on his own precursor and hero, Frederick Marryat, in "Tales of the Sea" (1898) (46). That Conrad's greatest achievement had been to capture the reality and wonder of life on the ocean waves was also emphasized by early critical assessments such as Ruth Stauffer's *Joseph Conrad: His Romantic Realism*:

> As a writer of the sea he stands supreme:—the sea in serene weather, in dead calm, in tempest and in wind. He makes us know the cold, the heat, the color, the light of the sea; night and the stars, dawn and the clouds are there; the space and the majesty of the sea, its loneliness and its unfathomable mystery are there. We perceive it always through the eyes of the men whom it tosses to and fro as midgets in its power, but whose indomitable human spirit it cannot crush. (60)

Indeed, Stauffer's evaluation met with the approval of her subject, who included her among those "critics [who] have perceived my intention" (*CL* 8:37).

Conrad's identification with the sea was central to his public image as circulated in newspapers, magazines, publicity materials, and popular ephemera. Editors seized upon photographs of Conrad on board ship to illustrate serializations, interviews, and feature articles, and, when these were not to be had, commissioned artists to imagine him in maritime costumes ranging from a sou'wester to a rating's togs.[1] Publishers, too, sought to exploit the inherent drama of Conrad's first profession, as when Doubleday issued a promotional pamphlet sporting a silhouette which it captioned, somewhat fancifully, "Joseph Conrad at the helm of a U-boat patrol during the war" (Davies). When the United States military during World War II inaugurated a series of classic novels, the Armed Services Edition, it logically chose Conrad titles set at sea: *Lord Jim*, *The Shadow Line*, and *The Mirror of the Sea*.[2] As contemporaries never wearied of pointing out, Conrad had sailed the Mediterranean, been shipwrecked in the Java Sea, and battled storms at the Cape of Good Hope. Readers, they explained, might know the sea only as fiction but Conrad had experienced it for himself, a lived reality that accounted for the unmatched vividness of his writing. This perspective is evident in a whimsical anecdote related by Christopher Morley about reading *The Nigger of the "Narcissus"* on a commuter train. As Morley came to Conrad's description of a monstrous wave rolling towards the ship, the train carriage seemed to pitch, causing him to drop his book and call to a fellow-passenger in panic: "God, she's going over!" ("MacIntyre" 8).

To complicate the relationship between these two seas—one real, the other literary—is the overarching aim of this essay, which is premised on the idea that because Conrad first encountered the maritime world as a literary object we need to identify the salient features of that *literary* sea in order to fully understand his writing and public identity. Long before Conrad first glimpsed the sea itself, at Odessa in 1867, he had encountered it extensively in works of fiction, including some translated by his father. They included the adventure stories of Frederick Marryat and James Fenimore Cooper as well as Victor Hugo's *The Toilers of the Sea* (1866), a novel that Apollo had translated in 1866 and that Conrad famously recalled as "my first introduction to the sea in literature" (*Reminiscences* 72).[3] He was also a keen reader of the thrilling accounts of sea voyages and shipwrecks in Polish periodicals, particularly the illustrated Cracow travel magazine *Wędrowiec* (Najder 42-4). Taking this biographical detail as its point of departure, my essay proposes a thought experiment: to reimagine Conrad's maritime career not as the experiential basis for his maritime writing but rather as an interlude between his two literary interactions with the sea, the first as reader, the second as author. Instead of seeing Conrad's novels and stories as fictional reworkings of real maritime events, let us consider them as maritime literary events, albeit events which derived both their imaginative power and their public authority from the author's first-hand insights. Lastly, let us suppose that Conrad went to sea not to escape Russian conscription, not to realize a boyish dream of adventure, and not to find a source of income but to acquire the materials with which to reinvent the sea in English literature.

Counterfactual though it may be, this thought experiment promises to bring a fresh perspective to bear on Conrad's maritime writings, particularly their setting, a term here designating less the geographical location of his stories, which have already been identified with varying degrees of precision, than their literary setting: the imaginative maritime spaces in which they unfold. Differentiating between physical and imaginative place is crucial because the sea as a body of water has few distinguishing features and ostensibly no topography, settlements, or boundaries, whether natural or national.[4] Like a mirror, Conrad's preferred locution for the sea, it is also incapable of preserving any lasting vestige of human presence. Thus Conrad recalls in *The Mirror of the Sea* how a disabled vessel suddenly disappeared from view barely a few minutes after the rescue of its crew:

> By a strange optical delusion the whole sea appeared to rise upon her in one overwhelming heave of its silky surface, where in one spot a smother of foam broke out ferociously. [. . .] Far away, where the brig had been, an angry white stain undulating on the surface of steely-gray waters, shot with gleams of green, diminished swiftly, without a hiss, like a patch of pure snow melting in the sun. (244)

In *Nostromo*, likewise, we are told how "the brilliant Don Martin Decoud, weighted by the bars of the San Tomé silver, disappeared without a trace, swallowed up in the immense indifference of things" (501).

As these passages imply, the sea exists as an object of imaginative projection to a quite different degree than, say, the Alps, the Sahara, or the Tuilleries, none of which could have substituted for the space of the sea in the parting words of his father's friend Stefan Buszczyński to a young Conrad in 1883: "Remember, wherever you may sail, you are always sailing towards Poland!" (*CL* 1:7–8). This imaginative or conceptual aspect profoundly determined the sea of Conrad's fiction as well as the reception of his maritime fiction: the reviewer who noted approvingly that "it may be said of Conrad that in the great universe of English fiction he has created a little world of his own, and has peopled it with the children of his fancy" (*CR* 2:90); the publishers who promoted Conrad as the creator of a maritime world all his own ("*his* glamorous seas" trilled advertisements for Doubleday's Kent Edition [Carabine, *Lives* 199, emphasis added]); and the audiences in the United States who welcomed the efforts of Henry Louis Mencken and Alfred Knopf to situate American experiences at the heart of Conrad's sea fiction.[5] In each of these statements we discern the contours of an imagined literary sea that is not reducible to—indeed, is often incompatible with—actual maritime space. It follows, then, that the literary sea in Conrad's writings neither allows of easy definition nor lends itself to the needs of twenty-first-century tourism or retail in the mode of Joyce's Dublin or Stevenson's Edinburgh. Conrad's high seas are a place where social relations are disrupted and inverted, a space of secrecy and fatal misapprehension that is disconcerting, transformative, uncanny, and sublime. It is utopian in the word's original sense of a no-place. Conrad, in short, restores the literary sea to a state that is best described with one of his favorite words: *enchantment*.

To grasp why the literary sea should have needed such recuperation in the first place, we need to consider the reverse process, disenchantment. In Max Weber's influential coinage, disenchantment (*Entzauberung*) describes a process of scientific rationalization that strips the world of its capacity to convey an experience of wonder and sensory plenitude. As Weber declared in 1917: "Precisely the ultimate and most sublime values have withdrawn from public life. They have retreated either into the abstract realm of mystical life or into the fraternal feelings of personal relations between individuals" (30). No reader of Conrad needs telling where to look for evidence of this development since his maritime writings are saturated with complaints about the baleful impact of modernity: the transatlantic liners resembling hotels of thin steel plate; the new navigational principle of ramming everything in one's path; and the journalists who misuse nautical terminology and sensationalize disaster at sea.[6] For Conrad, maritime modernity marks the threefold victory of technology, commodities, and the cash nexus, whose embodiment and agent is his bête noire, the steamship. For him, passage on steamships transformed individuals into detached and insensate observers. Steamships domesticated and mechanized the sea in a grotesque parody of the maritime amusements on show at circuses, fairgrounds, and international exhibitions, including simulacra of ocean travel such as Hengler's Circus's hydraulic aquatic spectacle "Ye Ocean Wave from the Paris Exhibition: A Realistic Sail on the Sea," which opened at the London Palladium in 1889 and ran for a decade. Steamships provided not experience but its pale shadow.

Conrad was far from alone in regarding the literary sea as in need of re-enchantment. Throughout this period maritime writers sought to radically reimagine the sea in a host of ways: the exotic romances of Robert Louis Stevenson and Pierre Loti; the naturalisms of Rudyard Kipling, Stephen Crane, W.W. Jacobs, and Morgan Robertson; and the modernisms of James Hanley, Richard Hughes, and Ernest Hemingway. Critics have also detailed at length Conrad's debt to specific maritime tales, notably Crane's "The Open Boat" (1897) and Stevenson's *The Ebb-Tide* (1894). At the same time, Conrad took pains to distance himself from maritime genre writers such as Morley Roberts and William Clark Russell, whom he saw as irredeemably debased by commercialism and conventionality. His own efforts to forge a new idiom in fiction, he declared to William Blackwood, belonged to a more revolutionary aesthetic lineage: "I am *modern*, and I would rather recall Wagner the musician and Rodin the Sculptor [. . .] and Whistler the painter who made Ruskin the critic foam at the mouth" (*CL* 2:418). This sentiment evidently guided Conrad's own tastes in maritime art, which tended towards symbolism and abstraction. He was deeply gratified that the *Pall Mall Magazine*'s serialization of *Typhoon* in 1902 had featured illustrations by Maurice Greiffenhagen that "combine[d] [. . .] the effect of his own most distinguished personal vision with an absolute fidelity to the inspiration of the writer" (Conrad, *Typhoon* 51–2), and he later exerted himself to secure the marine Modernist John Everett as illustrator for *The Mirror of the Sea*.[7] In these artists' experiments with the resources of pictorial form, Conrad seems to have recognized an impulse similar to that which drove his own project of reinventing literary maritime space.

To the aforementioned list of maritime writers who launched Conrad on this course of radical innovation may now be added a new name: Jules Verne. Conrad's efforts to re-enchant the sea of English literature owe a largely unacknowledged debt to Verne, one of the most popular authors of the late nineteenth century and someone whose influence beyond France in Conrad's formative years is not easily overestimated. Verne ushered in an entirely new way of thinking about the sea with *Twenty Thousand Leagues Under the Sea* (1870), a novel that opened up the underwater realm to literary as well as pictorial representation for the very first time. Those to whom this claim sounds hyperbolic should reflect on the fact that the pictorial tradition of Western art prior to 1870 contains virtually no images of the underwater world. To all intents and purposes, before *Twenty Thousand Leagues* it simply did not exist.[8]

Critics have often remarked upon the unusual breadth of Conrad's reading of popular texts, ranging from numbers of *The Boy's Own* to a treasured volume of Max Adler's comic sketches *Out of the Hurly-Burly* (1874). These ecumenical tastes had been formed during his adolescence, when, as he recalled to *The Teachers World* in 1923, "I was a voracious reader" ("Famous Stories"). [9] Even so, his own writings have rarely been considered in relation to those of Verne, an undisputed giant of nineteenth-century popular fiction. The oversight is particularly striking given the testimony of Marguerite Poradowska, who knew Conrad well as a child, that he "always loved reading Jules Verne's travels" (Stape and Knowles 9).[10] To be sure, Gustav Morf has speculated that Conrad may have read Verne's *A Fifteen-Year-Old Captain* (1870) (69), and Richard Berrong has proposed that an echo of *Journey to the Centre of the*

Earth (1864) can be heard in Marlow's oft-quoted statement in *Heart of Darkness* (1899), "I felt as though, instead of going to the centre of a continent, I were about to set off for the centre of the earth" (31, n.). Yet the only critic to have compared Conrad and Verne in any detail is Graham Huggan, who has identified a number of thematic parallels between *Twenty Thousand Leagues* and *The Nigger of the "Narcissus"* (1897), including the way in which both the *Nautilus* and the *Narcissus* are defined by geographical placelessness, their multinational crews travelling through not so much a physical landscape as what Huggan calls a "moral topography" (*Novelist* 9).[11]

Although Huggan does not ask where or when Conrad encountered *Twenty Thousand Leagues*, there is good reason for thinking that he first read it not in French but in Polish. The novel was serialized in full in Warsaw's *Gazeta Polska* in autumn 1870 and spring 1871 while Conrad was living with his grandmother in Cracow, and was published as a book by the newspaper's own press shortly thereafter.[12] For Conrad to have encountered *Twenty Thousand Leagues* in Polish, barely a year after the death of his father, would have been doubly ironic because Verne had initially conceived of Captain Nemo as a Pole and, indeed, specifically as a hero of the 1861 January Uprising in which Apollo Korzeniowski had played a leading role and for which he, too, had been forced into exile. The original idea for the book, Verne explained to his publisher, Pierre-Jules Hetzel, had been "a Polish nobleman whose daughters have been raped, wife killed with an axe, father killed with a knout, a Pole whose friends all die in Siberia and whose nationality will soon disappear from Europe under the Russian tyranny" (qtd. in Verne 437). In his reply, Hetzel fretted about the cost of offending Russian readers and insisted that his client anonymize Nemo's nationality. All Verne could do was surreptitiously adorn Nemo's bedroom with a portrait of Poland's national hero Tadeusz Kościuszko alongside those of other independence heroes such as George Washington, Daniel O'Connell, Markos Botsaris, and Daniele Manin, although even this paragraph was excised from both the serial version in *Gazeta Polska* and the first English translations. Even so, Nemo's tragic heroism would always hold a special appeal for those at the receiving end of colonial oppression. The Indian literary critic Swati Dasgupta describes her parents recalling their excitement in India between the world wars when reading *The Mysterious Island* (1874), a sequel in which Verne resurrected Nemo as a Hindu insurgent against British imperialism (225). Despite Hetzel's suppressions, it would thus have been natural for a Pole in Conrad's position to identify with the heroic submarine captain of *Twenty Thousand Leagues*, a defiant exile whose nationality is both an enigma and the unexplained cause of his unending persecution.

Even more important than Nemo's residual association with Conrad's native country is the significance of *Twenty Thousand Leagues* for the maritime writing tradition. Verne's novel revealed just how spectacularly the literary sea could be re-enchanted without recourse to the supernatural or even the need for directly verifiable experience.[13] For conventional sailors like Conrad, of course, such experience was acquired above the waves, for which reason his narratives ostensibly have nothing in common with the legion of landlubber imitators who followed Verne into the ocean depths.[14] It is just possible that Verne's extended descriptions of underwater mountains and active volcanoes, most famously in the submariners' exploration of Atlantis in chapter 9 of *Twenty Thousand Leagues*, obliquely inform Conrad's epigrammatic observation in *Victory*, "An island is but the top of a mountain" (1), or the musings of *Youth*'s semi-autobiographical narrator when hurled into the air by an explosion: "What is it?—Some accident—Submarine volcano?" (25) Yet in the vast majority of Conrad's maritime writings, fiction and non-fiction alike, the epithet which he most frequently applies to the sea is that of reflective, impenetrable, and unfathomable *surface*:

> He had almost forgotten why he was there, and dreamily he could see all his past life on the smooth and boundless surface that glittered before his eyes. (*Folly* 141)

> The sheet of paper portraying the depths of the sea presented a shiny surface under the light of a bull's-eye lamp lashed to a stanchion, a surface as level and smooth as the glimmering surface of the waters. (*Lord Jim* 57)

> I stepped to the side swiftly, and on the shadowy water I could see nothing except a faint phosphorescent flash revealing the glassy smoothness of the sleeping surface. ("Secret Sharer" 32)

> On the unruffled surface of the straits the brig floated tranquil and upright as if bolted solidly, keel to keel, with its own image reflected in the unframed and immense mirror of the sea. (*Rescue* 5)

In accordance with this perspective, Conrad's references to submarines in his wartime essays, "Poland Revisited" (1915) and "Tradition" (1918), and his short story "The Tale" (1917), are all negative, as might be expected given the resentment of submarines in Britain prompted by Germany's adoption of unrestricted submarine warfare.[15] As he reflects ominously in "Flight" (1917), an account of landing on the North Sea in a biplane: "It strikes me as I write that, when next time I leave the surface of this globe, it won't be to soar bodily above it in the air. Quite the contrary. And I am not thinking of a submarine either" (*Notes* 164).

Thinking about submarines may have left Conrad cold, but Verne would nonetheless have represented for him a very special source of inspiration, a writer who had transformed the literary sea into a space capable of confounding his contemporaries' most fundamental ideas about the natural world. And the work in which Conrad goes furthest in seeking to emulate that achievement is *Typhoon*, a novella that forms the cornerstone of his own maritime oeuvre. *Typhoon* is Conrad's *Twenty Thousand Leagues Under the Sea*. What makes this tale of a steamship in a storm so extraordinary as to justify comparison with a novel that uncovered an undreamt-of maritime kingdom? Clearly not its plot, which is hardly more complicated than the sketch for a short story from which it evolved. The answer lies rather in its formal complexity: the multiple points of view, the temporal flashbacks, the emphasis upon the operations of consciousness, the ironic narrative voice, and, above all else, the stylistic Modernism that undergirds Conrad's rendering of a storm at sea. Like Verne, Conrad set himself the task of rendering strange the seemingly known environment of the sea. To this end he drew, consciously or unconsciously, upon the settings and narrative devices of *Twenty Thousand Leagues*, above all in his own novella's climactic scenes.

The earliest responses to *Typhoon* offer plentiful evidence of the revolutionary nature of Conrad's depiction of the sea. The vast majority of reviewers took the *Athenaeum*'s view that "Anything more thorough and convincing of its kind we have never read" (*CR* 2:32). *Typhoon*, they declared, was "tremendous," "quite breathlessly absorbing," "of almost overwhelming power," "tremendous—no less," "an extraordinary piece of writing," "a sonata of ships and storms and breaking waves," and "the most amazing description of the utter madness of the sea when tormented by a force almost as great as itself that we have ever read" (*CR* 2:37, 88, 86, 35, 59, 17, 22). Reviewers likewise concurred upon the "magnificent originality" of the tale, which they pronounced "magnificent almost to the point of uniqueness," "hardly [. . .] matched, even in his works," and "introduc[ing] something new into our fiction" (*CR* 2:42, 87, 24, 56). Reviewer after reviewer affirmed the opinion of *T.P.'s Weekly* that Conrad's storm "seems to stand out from the storms of other narratives" (*CR* 2:44): "No storm at sea has ever been described with such force and elaboration"; "The most elaborate storm-piece [. . .] in English literature"; "absolutely unsurpassed by any writers of the sea who have preceded him"; and "[a] more interesting sea sketch than 'Typhoon' we have never known" (*CR* 2:93–4, 74, 84). Indeed, these reviewers' insistence that Conrad had succeeded in evoking a spectacle previously thought unimaginable may explain why in 1935 the Royal

National Institute of Blind People chose Conrad's novella as the first of its "talking book" audio recordings.[16]

The extraordinarily kinetic quality of *Typhoon*'s storm did not fail to impress even those reviewers who found its story banal. In an era of mechanical maritime simulation—cinema films, fairground attractions, and theatrical spectacles—Conrad's virtuoso description had triumphantly reclaimed the sea for literary narrative by means of language capable of eliciting physical sensation in the reader:

There is [. . .] the descriptive power of some wild and terrific upheaval of a tornado in which the very language seems to speak, giving the sense almost of physical noise. (*CR* 2:20)

[T]o read his book, which leaps at this point into a splendid, sonorous fortissimo, as though all the stops of the full organ had been pulled at once, is the best substitute a landsman may have for the overwhelming sensation of a great storm at sea. (*CR* 2:68)

So vivid is the description that you feel you are actually on board the steamer *Nan-Shan* and that you cling to her bulwarks so as not to be blown into the raging waters. (*CR* 2:71–2)

The reader goes on breathlessly from hour to hour on the trip, bracing himself as do the actors to meet the awful shock of waves and wind, the sickening rise and plunge of the ship, to dodge the flying débris and the oncoming rush of brine. (*CR* 2:78)

His sentences buffet you about, and leave you with the feeling that you have gone through the typhoon yourself. (*CR* 2:81)

Conrad has the knack of word-painting so effectively that the reader feels himself bouncing and pounding in the tempestuous path of the typhoon. (*CR* 2:88)

Reviewers nonetheless struggled to explain precisely how *Typhoon* had achieved this feat. The *New York Tribune* proposed imagining its author as "a kind of conductor, through which the terror and the beauty of a great storm passed to the printed page as if by some magical process of translation" (*CR* 2:63), while *The Independent* extravagantly declared: "If ever a man whipped a hurricane into sentences, congealed a typhoon into drops of ink, that man is

Joseph Conrad" (*CR* 2:85). Whatever the means, they overwhelmingly agreed that *Typhoon* had become an instant landmark of maritime literature. As the reviewer for the *Brooklyn Daily Eagle* concluded: "Although numberless authors have expended all their imagination and all their force and craft of diction in an endeavor to really picture the nightmare of a typhoon it is possible that Mr. Conrad's 'Typhoon' will stand as the classic in this sort of realism" (*CR* 2:60).

Not only did *Typhoon*, as these comments imply, mark a threshold or turning-point in the representation of the sea in language, it also struck many observers as having departed from the conventions of realist fiction in some fundamental aspect. Conrad, the *Daily News* explained, "splashes great lumps of colour on his canvas, tortures and twists the language till it cries like some creature in pain" in order to achieve "the descriptive power of some wild and terrific upheaval of a tornado in which the very language seems to speak" (*CR* 2:19–20). This view was echoed by New York's *Commercial Advertiser*, which pronounced the novella "in some ways an even more remarkable literary approach to a prose epic of a storm at sea than the English language will permit" (*CR* 2:78). In seeking to pin down what the *Forum* called *Typhoon*'s "peculiar kind of impressionism" (*CR* 2:89), reviewers repeatedly held up passages which they saw as exemplifying Conrad's peculiarly overdetermined style:

It was something formidable and swift, like the sudden smashing of a vial of wrath. (*CR* 2:20, 37, 89)

At its setting the sun had a diminished diameter and an expiring, brown, rayless glow, as if millions of centuries elapsing since the morning had brought it near its end. (*CR* 2:61)

The ring of dense vapors gyrating madly around the calm of the center encompassed the ship like a motionless and unbroken wall of a blackness inconceivably sinister. (*CR* 2:68)

A faint burst of lightning quivered all round, as if flashed into a cavern—into a black and secret chamber of the sea, with a floor of foaming crests. (*CR* 2:68, 93)

One way to understand *Typhoon*, then, is as a Modernist rewriting of *Twenty Thousand Leagues*. Where Verne had taken to an extreme the materialist underpinnings of classical realism—inventories of dimensions and prices, cartographic and geographic descriptions, and zoological and oceanographic taxonomies—Conrad inducted readers into *Typhoon*'s own "secret chamber of the sea" (*Typhoon* 40) by means of a disorienting new idiom of maritime language. Supporting this view is the fact that *Typhoon* exhibits a number of narrative and stylistic parallels with Verne's novel which have hitherto gone unnoticed. One occurs when Verne's and Conrad's protagonists must subdue a writhing, multi-eyed beast which threatens to overwhelm their vessel:

> Then our rage boiled over against the monsters. We were no longer in control of ourselves. Ten or twelve squid had invaded the platform and sides of the *Nautilus*. We were sliding around in the midst of the truncated serpents, tossing about on the platform in waves of blood and black ink. It was as if the viscous tentacles were coming back to life again like Hydra's heads. Ned Land's harpoons plunged repeatedly into the glaucous eyes of the squid, destroying them with each blow. But my brave companion was suddenly knocked down by the tentacles of a monster he could not avoid. (*Leagues* 347)

> They charged in, stamping on breasts, on fingers, on faces, catching their feet in heaps of clothing, kicking broken wood; but before they could get hold of him Jukes emerged waist deep in a multitude of clawing hands. In the instant he had been lost to view, all the buttons of his jacket had gone, its back had got split up to the collar, his waistcoat had been torn open. The central struggling mass of Chinamen went over to the roll, dark, indistinct, helpless, with a wild gleam of many eyes in the dim light of the lamps. (*Typhoon* 77)

In each instance, readers behold the spectacle of an epic battle in which crewmen prevail against a nightmarish adversary whose unnerving eyes follow them in the darkness: for Verne, a shoal of gigantic cephalopods; for Conrad, an orientalized, subhuman collectivity of "Celestials" (77). Both pairs of adversaries are likewise initially kept apart by a steel door, with the crucial difference that Verne's squid are trying to get in, Conrad's Chinese passengers to get out. The inversion is continued as Verne's protagonists seek safety below the waves, Conrad's above: "Secretly each of them thought that at the last moment he could rush out on deck—and that was a comfort. There is something horribly repugnant in the idea of being drowned under a deck" (80). The moment additionally serves as a reminder that the crew of a steamship—as captured by Greiffenhagen's iconic image of the *Nan-Shan*'s engine room during a wave that rakes the entire ship (Figure 1)—experience the sea not merely from inside a steel vessel but literally while underwater. As the coal-stoker narrator of James Hanley's *Sailor's Song* (1943) reflects upon entering the engine-room: "'Why you're under an ocean, you're under a sea" (45).

A second parallel occurs at each story's climactic moment, when the metal ship is navigated by its reckless captain into an unearthly arena where it must do battle with some ultimate combination of weather and ocean waves. In each case, the author evokes a never-before-encountered space located somewhere within the space of the sea as conventionally imagined:

> Monstrous waves rush in from all points of the horizon. They form a funnel fittingly called the "navel of the ocean," with a power of attraction stretching over a distance of fifteen kilometres. Not only are ships sucked in, but also whales and even polar bears from the Arctic.
>
> It was here that the *Nautilus* had involuntarily—or perhaps voluntarily—been engaged by its captain. It was describing a spiral whose radius was decreasing all the time. The boat, still attached to its side, was also being transported at a dizzying speed. I could feel it. I was experiencing the turning feeling caused by a rotation that goes on for too long. We were in a state of terror! Terror to the highest degree! Our blood was no longer circulating. Our nervous systems were deadened. We were covered with cold sweat, as if on a death-bed. What a noise around our frail boat! (Verne, *Leagues* 379)

> Through a jagged aperture in the dome of clouds the light of a few stars fell upon the black sea, rising and falling confusedly. Sometimes the head of a watery cone would topple on board and mingle with the rolling flurry of foam on the swamped deck; and the *Nan-Shan* wallowed heavily at the bottom of a circular cistern of clouds. This ring of dense vapours, gyrating madly round the calm of the centre, encompassed the ship like a motionless and unbroken wall of an aspect inconceivably sinister. Within, the sea, as if agitated by an internal commotion, leaped in peaked mounds that jostled each other, slapping heavily against her sides; and a low moaning sound, the infinite plaint of the storm's fury, came from beyond the limits of the menacing calm. (Conrad, *Typhoon* 82)

There is an obvious resemblance between the physical properties of these spaces, each of which is circular, rotating, precisely circumscribed, rent by terrifying sounds, and disrupted by unseen currents. Yet where Verne harnesses the resources of realism—scientific precision (the "power of attraction stretching over fifteen kilometres") and local detail ("fittingly called 'the navel of the ocean'")—Conrad performs a peculiarly Modernist defamiliarization of natural phenomena, what Fredric Jameson has defined as an "*aestheticizing strategy*" intended to "authorize and reinforce a new representational space" (218–19). The sky is glimpsed through "a jagged aperture," waves fall "confusedly," clouds are "inconceivably sinister," and a ring of dense vapours manages somehow to be both "gyrating madly" and "motionless." Not least, the eye of the storm is evoked as a "circular cistern," that is to say, as a zone not of air, but water.

In the climax of each novel, too, the means by which the narrator escapes seemingly certain death is withheld, creating a narrative aporia that is immediately followed by the tale's conclusion several days later.[17] Thus the final chapter of *Typhoon* jumps forward to the "bright sunshiny day" (91) when the *Nan-Shan* makes port in Fu-chau, while in *Twenty Thousand Leagues* Professor Aronnax declares: "What happened that night, how the boat escaped from the formidable undertow of the Maelstrom, how Ned, Conseil, and I emerged from the deep, I cannot say" (380).

Rereading *Typhoon* in terms of *Twenty Thousand Leagues*—that is, approaching it as an engagement with the literary sea rather than a fictional adaptation of memories of real people and incidents—involves many such moments of recognition. Without its ever actually sinking, the crew repeatedly imagine the *Nan-Shan* to have become inverted, submerged, or otherwise displaced from the surface of the sea. The second engineer bawls at Jukes, "'Where's the blooming ship? [. . . .] Under water—or what?" (Conrad, *Typhoon* 71). Likewise, the first mate finds himself "suddenly afloat and borne upwards," entertains an "irresistible notion [. . .] that the whole China Sea had climbed on the bridge" (41–2). And when a freakishly large wave strikes the ship, it creates an unthinkable fissure in the surface of the sea which recalls the stuff of sailors' legend:

> With a tearing crash and a swirling, raving tumult, tons of water fell upon the deck, as though the ship had darted under the foot of a cataract.
> Down there they looked at each other, stunned.
> "Swept from end to end, by God!" bawled Jukes.
> She dipped into the hollow straight down, as if going over the edge of the world. (74)

Only by a miracle does the *Nan-Shan* avoid joining the company of "submarined" ships, as Conrad's commanding officer in "The Tale" calls them. Even so, when she finally does make port, it is as an emissary from a maritime nether world:

> She had about her the worn, weary air of ships coming from the far ends of the world—and indeed with truth, for in her short passage she had been very far; sighting, verily, even the coast of the Great Beyond, whence no ship ever returns to give up her crew to the dust of the earth. She was incrusted and gray with salt to the trucks of her masts and to the top of her funnel; as though (as some facetious seaman said) "the crowd on board had fished her out somewhere from the bottom of the sea and brought her in here for salvage." (90)

The *Nan-Shan*'s resemblance to a vessel returned "somewhere from the bottom of the sea" is no mere throwaway on Conrad's part. Like the *Nautilus*, she has been enabled by the unnatural force of mechanized propulsion, coupled with the defiant obstinacy of a taciturn skipper, to escort readers into a space without precedent in the history of maritime fiction. Conrad's greatest sea tale reveals itself as an attempt to make the prosaic space of commercial shipping every bit as alien and enchanted (in Weber's sense) as the watery abyss of Verne's hallucinatory scientific romance.

A special significance thus attaches to Conrad's overlooked epigraph for Heinemann's first English edition of *Typhoon*, a passage from John Keats's *Endymion* (1818) evoking the majestic expanse of the sea-god's royal palace: "Far as the mariner on highest mast / Can see all around upon the calmed vast, / So wide was Neptune's hall . . ." (3.866–68). More than merely an allusion to spaciousness, its full meaning lies in the strategically placed ellipsis which, in Keats's original, are followed by the lines:

> [. . .] and as the blue
>   Doth vault the waters, so the waters drew
> Their doming curtains, high, magnificent,
> Awed from the throne aloof [. . .] (3.866–71)

What Keats here describes is an entire maritime world that has been inverted: the seeming blue of a sky is in fact the submarine dome of the ocean's surface viewed from below. For our part, as we wait with the *Nan-Shan*'s crew in the unearthly silence of the storm's eye, inside a "dark and echoing vault [. . .] a circular cistern of clouds" (Conrad, *Typhoon* 82), we behold for the first time an underwater world—above the waves.

"He and Jukes looked at each other."

Figure 1. *Pall Mall Magazine* (March 1902), 411.

NOTES

1. McFee, "Great Tales", 1; James Montgomery Flagg, "Joseph Conrad" (Johnson 24). The sea, an Australian commentator noted in 1926, was the essential element in Conrad's mass appeal ("Laureates").

2. A fourth title, the exception to this principle, *Victory*, was presumable chosen for its title alone. On the Armed Services Edition series, see Cole, and Burgoyne.

3. On Hugo's influence on "The End of the Tether," see Stape.

4. The sea itself, that is. On the navigation and mapping of islands, reefs, sand-banks, and coastlines in Conrad's fiction, see Hampson, "Passion," especially 41-4.

5. See Mallios 41-107.

6. See Donovan, "Conrad and the Harmsworth Empire."

7. On Conrad's relation to Greiffenhagen, see Jones, and on Whistler, see Meacock.

8. A possible exception is the publicity materials and scientific documentation generated by the vogue for public aquaria around mid-century (see Brunner 89-122). Yet the zoological and paleontological sketches by Philip Henry Gosse, Henry de la Beche, and Ernst Haeckel (see Cohen) were all staged, speculative, or fantastical—as for that matter were the nereids, mermaids, and mythological beings, all of whom were in any case portrayed atop, not below, the waves. On the conceptual challenges posed by underwater space, see Donovan, "What Lies Beneath" 150-52.

9. Thanks to Patricia Pye for this reference.

10. A designation that encompassed not only Verne's memoirs and travel writings but also his long and better-known series of adventure novels, which began with *Cinq semaines en ballon* (1863). Verne is not mentioned in Yves Hervouet's standard account of Conrad's debt to French literature.

11. On the echoes of Verne's *Journey to the Centre of the Earth* in Conrad's *Heart of Darkness*, see Huggan, "Voyages."

12. The *Gazeta Polska* for these years is available via the National Library of Poland's digital archive POLONA (polona.pl).

13. Although Verne drew inspiration from a visit to an aquarium and a transatlantic crossing aboard the *Great Eastern*, his main source was literary, Matthew Fontaine Maury's *Physical Geography of the Sea* (1855) (Rozwadowski 26-7).

14. See Redford 202-43 and Budgen 50-2.

15. For a detailed analysis of this story in relation to submarine warfare, see Hampson, *Conrad's Secrets* 176-204.

16. See Rubery, "Britain's First Talking Book," and *Untold History*.

17. Appropriately, the word aporia, often used of a philosophical or representational impasse, likely originates in the maritime term πόρος, a passage over a body of water.

WORKS CITED

Berrong, Richard M. "'Heart of Darkness' and Pierre Loti's Ramuntcho: Fulcrum for a Masterpiece." *The Conradian*, vol. 35, no. 1, 2010, pp. 28-44.

Brunner, Bernd. *The Ocean at Home: An Illustrated History of the Aquarium*. Princeton Architectural Press, 2005.

Burgoyne, Mary. "'Writing Man to Fighting Man': Conrad Republished for the Armed Services during the World Wars." *The Conradian*, vol. 38, no. 1, 2013, pp. 99–127.

Carabine, Keith, ed. *Lives of Victorian Literary Figures: Volume VII*. Pickering & Chatto, 2009.

Cohen, Margaret. "Seeing Through Water: The Paintings of Zarh Pritchard." *The Sea and Nineteenth-Century Anglophone Literary Culture*, edited by Steve Mentz and Martha Elena Rojas, Routledge, 2017, pp. 103–18.

Cole, John Y., ed. *Books in Action: The Armed Services Editions*. Library of Congress, 1984, http://catdir.loc.gov/catdir/toc/becites/cfb/84600198.html, accessed 1 July 2018.

Conrad, Joseph. *Almayer's Folly*. Dent, 1949.

———. *Lord Jim*. Dent, 1946.

———. "The Secret Sharer." *'Twixt Land and Sea*. Dent, 1947.

———. *Collected Letters of Joseph Conrad*. 9 vols., edited by Fredrick R. Karl and Laurence Davies, Cambridge University Press, 1983–2008.

———. *The Mirror of the Sea*. Dent, 1947.

———. *Nostromo*. Dent, 1947.

———. *Notes on Life and Letters*. Dent, 1949.

———. *A Personal Record*. Dent, 1946.

———. *The Rescue*. Dent, 1946.

———. *Typhoon, Falk and Other Stories*. Dent, 1950.

———. *Victory*. Dent, 1948.

Dasgupta, Swati. "Lost in Translation: Jules Verne and the Indian Rebellion." *Insurgent Sepoys: Europe Views the Revolt of 1857*, edited by Shaswati Mazumdar, Routledge, 2011, pp. 221–36.

Davies, Laurence. "The Dark Side and the Bright: Conrad in *Ridgway's* and *The Metropolitan Magazine*." *Conrad First: The Joseph Conrad Periodical Archive*, 2013, http://www.conradfirst.net/conrad/scholarship/authors/davies, accessed 1 July 2018.

Donovan, Stephen. "Conrad and the Harmsworth Empire: *The Daily Mail*, *London Magazine*, *Times*, *Evening News*, and *Hutchinson's Magazine*." *Conradiana*, vols. 41–2, no. 3, 2009, pp. 153–77.

———. "What Lies Beneath: The Submarine Shipwreck in Anglo-American Culture, 1880–1920." *Shipwreck in Art and Literature: Images and Interpretations from Antiquity to the Present Day*, edited by Carl Thompson, Routledge, 2013, pp. 150–70.

"Famous Stories of My Childhood: A Famous Writers' Symposium." *Teachers World*, 2 March 1923, p. 1126.

Hampson, Robert. *Conrad's Secrets*. Palgrave Macmillan, 2012.

Hanley, James. *Sailor's Song*. Nicholson & Watson, 1943.

Hervouet, Yves. *The French Face of Joseph Conrad*. Cambridge University Press, 1990.

Huggan, Graham. *The Novelist as Geographer: A Comparison of Conrad and Verne*. 1987, University of British Columbia, MA thesis.

———. "Voyages Towards an Absent Centre: Landscape Interpretation and Textual Strategy in Joseph Conrad's *Heart of Darkness* and Jules's Verne's *Voyage au centre de la terre*." *The Conradian*, vol. 14, nos. 1–2, 1989, pp. 19–46.

Jameson, Fredric. *The Political Unconscious: Narrative as a Socially Symbolic Act*. Routledge, 1983.

Johnson, Burgess, ed. *Caricature: The Wit & Humor of a Nation in Picture, Song & Story.* Leslie-Judge, 1915.

Jones, Susan. "Conrad on the Borderlands of Modernism: Maurice Greiffenhagen, Dorothy Richardson and the Case of *Typhoon*." *Conrad in the Twenty-First Century: Contemporary Approaches and Perspectives*, edited by Carola Kaplan, Peter Mallios and Andrea White, Routledge, 2005, pp. 195–212.

"Joseph Conrad Dies, Writer of the Sea." *The New York Times*, 4 August 1924, p. 1.

Keats, John. *Poetical Works*. Edited by William Gabriel Rossetti, Ward, 1879.

"Laureates of the Deep." *Mercury* (Hobart), 18 June 1926, p. 8, https://trove.nla.gov.au/ndp/del/article/29448356, accessed 1 July 2018.

"MacIntyre Day by Day." *Charleston Gazette*, 2 June 1932, p. 8.

Mallios, Peter. *Our Conrad: Constituting American Modernity*. Stanford University Press, 2010.

McFee, William. "Great Tales of a Great Victorian." *The New York Times*, 1 Jan., 1922.

Meacock, Joanna. "London's River: Conrad, Whistler, and *The Metropolitan Magazine*." *Conrad First: The Joseph Conrad Periodical Archive*, 2013, http://conradfirst.net/conrad/scholarship/authors/meacock, accessed 1 July 2018.

Mégroz, R.L. *Joseph Conrad's Mind and Method: A Study of Personality in Art*. Faber and Faber, 1931.

Morf, Gustav. *The Polish Shades and Ghosts of Joseph Conrad*. Astra Books, 1976.

Najder, Zdzisław. *Joseph Conrad: A Chronicle*. Rutgers University Press, 1984.

Niland, Richard, ed. *Joseph Conrad: Contemporary Reviews*. Vol. 3, Cambridge University Press, 2012. [Cited as CR 3]

"Our London Letter." *The Citizen* (Gloucester), 30 Apr. 1903, p. 3.

Peters, John G., ed. *Joseph Conrad: Contemporary Reviews*. Vol. 2, Cambridge University Press, 2012. [Cited as *CR*]

Redford, Duncan. *The Submarine: A Cultural History from the Great War to Nuclear Combat*. I.B. Tauris, 2010.

Rozwadowski, Helen M. *Fathoming the Ocean: The Discovery and Exploration of the Deep Sea*. Harvard University Press, 2005.

Rubery, Matthew. "Britain's First Talking Book." 24 November 2016, https://audiobookhistory.wordpress.com/2016/11/24/britains-first-talking-book/, accessed 1 July 2018.

———. *The Untold History of the Talking Book*. Harvard University Press, 2016.

Simmons, Allan H. ed. *Joseph Conrad: Contemporary Reviews*. Vol. 1, Cambridge University Press, 2012. [Cited as CR 1]

Stape, J.H. "Victor Hugo's *Les Travailleurs de la mer* and 'The End of the Tether.'" *The Conradian*, vol. 30, no. 1, 2005, pp. 71–80.

Stape, J.H., and Owen Knowles, eds. *A Portrait in Letters: Correspondence to and about Conrad*. *The Conradian*, vol. 19, nos. 1–2, 1995, pp. 1–287.

Stauffer, Ruth M. *Joseph Conrad: His Romantic-Realism*. Four Seas, 1922.

Verne, Jules. *Twenty Thousand Leagues Under the Sea*. Translated by William Butcher, Oxford University Press, 1998.

Weber, Max. *The Vocation Lectures*. Edited by David Owen and Tracy B. Strong, translated by Rodney Livingstone, Hackett, 2004.

Geography and Law in *Almayer's Folly*

KATHERINE ISOBEL BAXTER

NORTHUMBRIA UNIVERSITY

ABSTRACT

In his preface to *Almayer's Folly*, written soon after the novel's completion, Conrad takes issue with Alice Meynell's recent article on "decivilization": "I am content to sympathise with common mortals" he writes, "no matter where they live; in houses or in huts, in streets under a fog or in the forests behind the dark line of dismal mangroves that fringe the vast solitude of the sea" (3). At first reading, Conrad seems to peddle the very same prejudices he critiques in Alice Meynell: Jim-Eng, the Chinese opium wreck; Taminah, the impassive oriental woman inured against pain; and Almayer himself, the Indo-European ruined by his fantasies of fortune and unable to return to the European world he reveres. Each are stock characters amongst many more in the novel playing a part little different from those given to them by the popular authors whose works Meynell dismisses. What distinguishes them is their narrative context, whose machinations throw into relief the instability of the rule of law and the "civilizing" mission of colonialism. Conrad's time in South East Asia was one of political and legal transformation for Borneo, the repercussions of which Conrad translates directly into *Almayer's Folly*. This paper argues that his sympathies with the colonized are expressed less through individual characters than through the complexities, frustrations, and indeterminacies that arise out of the colonial enterprise. A key concern for Conrad, therefore, is the problem of justice in an international setting. Long before the publication of "Geography and Some Explorers," Conrad's fiction was already illuminating the inconsistencies that emerge in the process of putting international and transnational law into practice in the indeterminate spaces of colonial geography.

KEYWORDS

Joseph Conrad, *Almayer's Folly*, Dutch East Indies, British North Borneo Company, law

"Kaspar! Makan!"—the opening of Conrad's first novel, is justly famous. It was not the only opening that Conrad wrote for his novel, though. For, "soon after [he received] the first proofs of the English edition" in 1895, Conrad composed a short "Author's Note" to *Almayer's Folly*, in which he staked out his ethical relationship to the material of his fiction (*Folly*, xxxviii). This preface was not, however, used in the first edition; indeed, it did not appear in print until 1921 when the American and British collected editions of his works were published. In preparing these collected editions, Conrad wrote new and sometimes supplementary prefatory statements for each work. These prefaces were often retrospective and autobiographical, reflecting more on the interaction of memory and composition than on the ethical import of writing on particular topics. Thus the context of the collected editions, as much as the intervening years, served to soften the pertinence of the "Author's Note" to *Almayer's Folly*, distancing both Conrad and his readers from the contemporary debates to which it originally referred. In what follows, I want to use the "Author's Note" as a way of thinking about Conrad's early aesthetic and ethical concerns and, in particular, about how Conrad negotiates questions of law and geography in *Almayer's Folly*. In doing so I want to highlight the significance of the "Author's Note," which has previously been little discussed, and at the same time to open up the possibility for a larger exploration of Conrad from a legal perspective.

The opening of the "Author's Note" to *Almayer's Folly* reads thus:

> I am informed that in criticizing that literature which preys on strange people and prowls in far off countries, under the shade of palms, in the unsheltered glare of sun beaten beaches, amongst honest cannibals and the more sophisticated pioneers of our glorious virtues, a lady—distinguished in the world of letters—summed up her aversion from it by saying that the tales it produced were "de-civilized." And in that sentence not only the tales but, I apprehend, the strange people and far-off countries also, are finally condemned in a verdict of contemptuous dislike.
>
> A woman's judgement that: intuitive, clever, expressed with felicitous charm—infallible. A judgement that has nothing to do with justice. (3)

The "distinguished" lady to whom Conrad refers was Alice Meynell, whose essay "Decivilised" had appeared in the *National Observer* on January 24, 1891, and was republished two years later in her essay collection, *The Rhythm of Life*. As Conrad's "Note" suggests, Meynell avoids speaking of the indigenous populations of "far-off countries" overtly, and reserves her words for white colonials and "English" provincialism (Meynell 8). Indeed, Meynell devotes a good half of her article to the kitsch that she associates with the degeneracy of the latter: "In England, too, [the decivilized man] has a literature, an art, a music, all his own—derived from many and various things of price. Trash, in the fullness of its insimplicity and cheapness, is impossible without a beautiful past" (9). Nonetheless, the "verdict of contemptuous dislike" that Conrad apprehends is evident in her characterization of "decivilized man" as "bronzed, with a half conviction of savagery, partly persuaded of his own youthfulness of race" (7). It is to this verdict that Conrad responds in his "Author's Note," defending the colonizers, the colonized, and his own art not simply on the grounds of aesthetics but also along ethical lines: "there is a bond between us and that humanity so far away," Conrad writes (3).

The "Author's Note" is intriguing for several reasons. Firstly, at the start of his career Conrad clearly intended his novel to enter into a contentious conversation about the ethics of colonialism. Yet, the "Author's Note," which makes this intention explicit, was not in the end included when the novel first went to print. As Ian Watt observes, its exclusion "remains something of a mystery" (xli). Conrad shared the "Note" with Edward Garnett in early January 1895 but a letter of January 9 to W.H. Chesson suggested that "it may be dispensed with" (*CL* 1:197, 199). In later years, moreover, Conrad implied it had been "suppressed" (Watt xli). Whether that suppression was Conrad's decision or Chesson's and Garnett's, the redaction of the "Note" muted the novel's contribution to literary debates about ethics and colonialism. Secondly, while Conrad's courtroom metaphor is common enough in the aesthetic debates of the fin de siècle, it also signals his awareness of the legal backdrop to contemporary debates about the ethics of colonialism. This alertness to the legal questions raised by colonialism is reflected in the novel itself, as we shall see. Finally, Conrad's claim of equality for the colonized peoples of the British and Dutch East Indies is strikingly unambiguous, far less ambiguous than later expressions of sympathetic feeling such as we find, say, in "Karain." "I am content to sympathise with common mortals," he writes, "no matter where they live; in houses or in huts, in streets under a fog or in the forests behind the dark line of dismal mangroves that fringe the vast solitude of the sea" (Conrad, *Folly* 3). Is this really the progressive statement of solidarity that I, as a middle-class liberal academic, want to hear? To answer this question in what follows, I pursue Conrad's legal metaphor back to *Almayer's Folly* to examine his presentation of colonialism's legal forms in the Dutch East Indies.

TERRA NULLIUS AND UTI POSSIDETIS

In "Placing International Law: White Spaces on a Map," Vasuki Nesiah examines the importance of *terra nullius* and *uti possidetis* as legal concepts deployed in the International Court of Justice's deliberations on Western Sahara, and the border between Burkino Faso and Mali. To frame this discussion, Nesiah draws on "Geography and Some Explorers," reading comparatively between Conrad's essay and the court's deliberations and drawing specifically on Conrad's three ages of geographical exploration: geography fabulous, geography militant, and geography triumphant. Nesiah characterizes the legal concept of the unclaimed frontier, *terra nullius*, as like the "virgin territory [. . .] as yet unmapped" for which late nineteenth-century Europe longed nostalgically (10). *Terra nullius* here is like the "little island [. . .] an insignificant crumb of dark earth, lonely," by which Conrad takes his bearing as he passes out of the Torres Straits and to which he recalls James Cook had gone ashore "perhaps only to be alone with his thoughts for a moment" ("Geography" 274). Neither Conrad nor Conrad's Cook assume anyone has prior claim to this "crumb," on whose beach one might taste "perfect peace" (274). In the case concerning Western Sahara, the International Court of Justice thus deliberated whether the region could be considered *terra nullius* at the point of Spanish colonization or whether the region's allegiances to Morocco in the North and/or Mauritania in the South and East were coherent enough to constitute a political claim of possession by one or both of those countries.

The related concept of *uti possidetis*, in contrast to *terra nullius*, concerns the political and state allegiance of territories. In international law, geographical possessions remain with the possessor at the end of a war: "as you possess." Proof of allegiance or possession, particularly in regions that are non-contiguous with the state exerting its claim, is thus inevitably and frequently contentious. In deciding the border between Burkino Faso and Mali, for example, the confusion over where that border could be drawn resulted from the lack of clarity regarding the state allegiance of regions that were poorly mapped and whose inhabitants were traditionally nomadic—it is hard to know how much of something you own when you're not even sure of quite what it consists.

In the light of Conrad's extended legal metaphor in his "Author's Note" to *Almayer's Folly*, these two concepts, *terra nullius* and *uti possidetis*, provide useful points of entry into the legal context of Sambir in the novel. From the start we are encouraged to recognize the nostalgic desire for *terra nullius* that Lingard's operation in Sambir represents. On the banks of a barely known river that emerges from a barely explored tropical interior, the importance of Sambir, for the Dutch Kaspar Almayer and the British Tom Lingard alike, is its cartographic elusiveness. As we are reminded by Hudig's cashier, Vinck, in Macassar, Lingard had "discovered" the river (Conrad, *Folly* 8). Furthermore, the ongoing "quarrels" between the Dyaks, who inhabit the interior, and the coastal Malays effectively debar the latter from exerting any prior claim of *uti possidetis* upon the tantalizing interior (31). Nonetheless, Conrad's repeated references to the Dyaks signal to his readers that the notion of this interior region as *terra nullius* is suspect. The fact that Sambir falls explicitly within the territorial remit of the Dutch East Indies re-establishes at the very least a colonial right of *uti possidetis*. Both Lingard and Almayer nonetheless romantically imagine Sambir for themselves as *terra nullius*: a region "green and peaceful looking [. . .] [a] promised land" to be "discovered" (8).

Nonetheless, the space Lingard and Almayer imagine for themselves is not quite the unregulated heroic space of exploration that Nesiah identifies in "Geography and Some Explorers." In this essay, one of the final publications of his lifetime, Conrad eulogizes explorers like Cook and Franklin whose exploits were "the search for truth" and whose accounts in turn "sent me off on the romantic explorations of my inner self" ("Geography" 251, 253).[1] Park and Bruce's expeditions in the Sudan and Abyssinia, likewise, had inspired Conrad, he tells us, to imagine "worthy, adventurous, and devoted men nibbling at the edges, attacking from north, and south and east and west, conquering a bit of truth here and a bit of truth there" (254). By contrast, Lingard and Almayer operate in a post-Romantic age. They hope not so much for the ennoblement of truth, but for the commercial prospects of something like the chartered company status of the British North Borneo Company and its more famous antecedent, the East India Company.

By the time of *Almayer's Folly*, the Dutch chartered company, the VOC (Vereenigde Oostindische Compagnie), was a thing of the past;[2] however, like the United Africa Company in what was soon to become Nigeria, the British North Borneo Company, which was chartered in 1881, maintained primary responsibility for the administration of British North Borneo even after the territory became a British protectorate in 1888.[3] Throughout this time, which coincides with the temporal setting of *Almayer's Folly*, the British North Borneo Company retained its original aim of economic exploitation of the region's natural resources. This program of exploitation is exemplified in the extensive experimental gardens established in Borneo to trial crops, which led rapidly to large-scale plantations of export produce, such as tobacco. Indeed, the former governor, William Hood Treacher, reported in 1891 that 600,000 acres were given over to tobacco plantations and that between 1881 and 1888 (the period in which he was in office) the value of exported goods had more than tripled from $145,444 to $525,879 (Treacher 119, 108). Along with the development of crops, the British North Borneo Company sought to extract as much as it could of the region's natural wealth, which Treacher itemizes in detail:

> bees-wax, camphor, damar, gutta percha [. . .] India rubber [. . .] rattans [. . .] sago, timber, edible birds'-nests, seed-pearls, Mother-o'-pearl shells [. . .] dried fish and dried sharks' fin, trepang [. . .] aga [. . .] pepper, and occasionally elephants' tusks—a list which shews the country to be a rich store house of natural productions. (108)

To these riches Treacher adds "the gold on the Segama River, on the East Coast," which he notes is difficult to access and has eluded European diggers but begun to "repay the labours of Chinese gold diggers" (106).

It is commonly held that alongside the real "Captain William Lingard" (who opened up the Berau river to colonial European trade), Sir James Brooke, Rajah of Sarawak, serves as a prototype for Tom Lingard the "Rajah Laut."[4] While this holds true in some respects, not least Lingard's heroic off-stage exploits in *The Rescue*, in *Almayer's Folly* and *An Outcast of the Islands*, Lingard's territorial aspirations, like Almayer's, are much closer to those of the British North Borneo Company. Brooke's rule was one of legal administration through sovereign authority. By contrast, in *Almayer's Folly* particularly, Lingard's rule, like that of the British North Borneo Company, is governed explicitly by commercial interests. While Lingard may not have georgic aspirations to set up plantations, nevertheless his interest is in trading the resources that lie up the Pantai River in exchange for more or less legal commodities from further along the coast (such as tobacco, gunpowder and opium).[5] His interests are only ever political insofar as politics impinges on this economic relationship to place.

Sambir promises Lingard and Almayer this particular opportunity for commercial exploitation because of its territorial and legal indeterminacy. This indeterminacy is made evident in several ways. First and foremost Sambir, whilst falling within the legal boundaries of the Dutch East Indies, occupies an emphatically insignificant and liminal place in the administration of that colony. Its remoteness is signalled from the start, when Almayer fantasizes about where an uprooted tree floating on the river might end up, whilst he remains trapped upriver and inaccessible: "he began to wonder how far out to sea it would drift? Would the current carry it north or south? South, probably, till it drifted in sight of Celebes, as far as Macassar, perhaps!" (Conrad, *Folly* 6). The remoteness that the tree's imagined journey signals is not only geographical, however. As Almayer's imagination reaches Macassar his "fancy" "quicken[s]," "but his memory lag[s] behind some twenty years or more in point of time" (6). Almayer feels himself here not only displaced to a geographical periphery but a temporal one, too. Conrad's play on words, in which Almayer's lively— "quick"—fancy contrasts with the "lag" of his memory, signals the gap between the Macassar of the past, reached by his memory, and the Macassar of the present, reached by the uprooted tree, that his "quick" fancy attempts and fails to bridge. Sambir is located out of time as well as out of the way.

Legally, the region's indeterminacy is indicated in the novel by a brief but significant reference to the joint Dutch and British commission in the region in 1884, following several years of land disputes between the two in the wake of the British North Borneo Company's charter. At stake in the commission's deliberations, both historically and in the novel, is whether the disputed regions could be determined as *terra nullius* in which case the British North Borneo Company sought to exercise control, or whether the Dutch could claim *uti possidetis*. As Ian Watt suggests, there is, in fact, little evidence from the period that "Britain was ever seriously interested in annexing parts of Eastern Borneo as far south as Tanjung Redeb," the locale which forms the basis for Sambir (xxv). Conrad uses the historical moment of the commission, however, to dramatize in a legal context the temporal and geographical isolation that Almayer feels imaginatively when he watches the uprooted tree float down the river.

Thus we are told at the end of chapter 2 that when the British North Borneo Company is founded there is a stir: "Great changes were expected; annexation was talked of; the Arabs grew civil," and Almayer grows hopeful, for, as he himself explains a few pages later, the English "knew how to develop a rich country" (Conrad, *Folly* 26, 29). The expectation that Almayer shares with the other traders of Sambir is that the region will be declared *terra nullius* and therefore available for British annexation, leading to increased trade and wealth. In the imagined time that lapses between the end of chapter 2 and the start of chapter 3, however, the legal decision is taken to abandon the Company's claim "to that part of the East Coast [. . .] leaving the Pantai river under the nominal power of Holland" (28). The ensuing arrival of a Dutch man-o-war on the coast, delivering a new flag to Lakamba, the Rajah of Sambir, signifies the Dutch authority's exercise of *uti possidetis*, but this happens only once the British drop their own claim. Implicit in this brief episode is Sambir's insignificance and indeterminacy. The apparent contestation over whose rule applies in the region, that of the British or the Dutch, highlights its indeterminate status. That neither government, however, seems eager to exert their claim underlines its inconsequence for their rival colonial projects: the British claim is "abandoned," while the indifference of the Dutch is signalled by the passive inheritance of Sambir; it is left ("leaving") to its "nominal" rule.[6]

The arrival of the Dutch to assert their "nominal power" is marked, as noted above, with the symbols of legal and political authority: the presentation of a flag to the local Rajah. Nonetheless, the rhetorical gesture of the flag, as we later discover, is in fact secondary to an investigation into the illegal gunpowder trading in which the Dutch suspect Almayer is embroiled. This expedient visit is matched by the expediency of the local hosts, who likewise hang flags and hurry their slaves "out of sight into the forest and jungle," in order to present the appearance of conformity to Holland's "nominal power," which included a ban on slavery (28). These bothersome performances of political cordiality belie the mutual mistrust and bad faith that characterize all parties involved. As Ian Black notes, historically the more far-flung possessions of the Dutch East Indies, including the various states in Borneo, were referred to as *lastposten*, that is to say "nuisances" (281).[7]

Sambir is thus cast legally as well as imaginatively as a troublesome, indeterminate space, where claims of possession are made expediently. Sambir's illegal gunpowder trade is one clear "nuisance" to the Dutch, and we might, like them, first assume that this trade is intended to support the long-running war of resistance against the Dutch in Aceh, when the chief of the visiting "Commission" suggests Almayer's involvement (Conrad, *Folly* 29).[8] We learn in the following chapter, however, when Lakamba's license for powder is revoked and a load of one hundred and fifty barrels confiscated, that unbeknownst to the Dutch the powder is also put to use in "the desultory warfare carried on by the Arabs and the Rajah with the up-river Dyak tribes" (38). The "nuisance" of Sambir here is not so much directed at the Dutch as it is an offence that occurs within their purview because the territory falls within their possession.

The Aceh War represented a political dispute over territorial sovereignty, albeit one that was economically motivated.[9] Nonetheless, the officers of the Commission who arrive in ceremony to greet Lakamba, following the British North Borneo Company's abandonment of its claims, make clear their preference for trade with Almayer's Arab rival, Abdulla, rather than legal and administrative support for the lone resident Dutchman. Trade trumps citizenship and statehood for the Dutch officials in Sambir, despite the rhetorical symbolism of their flag-bearing visit. Once again, Sambir's legal status seems ambiguous, making sense only when understood as peripheral: Sambir is not a territory over which the Dutch wish to exercise *uti possedetis*, however, having been "left" it they address the nuisance its existence presents expediently.

The officials disregard Almayer's claims to protection primarily because they suspect him of treason. Of course, as a treasonous subject, Almayer forfeits his right to the protection of the law that he begs. But this dismissal of Almayer is also inflected with a snobbery that Andrew Francis unpacks: in the period in which the novel is set there was a distinct difference drawn between those who went to the Dutch East Indies only for a limited time (*trekkers*) and those who stayed (*blijvers*). The former looked down upon the latter, particularly if they became "too Indies" ("'You always leave us'" 54 and n. 22). Almayer's father, we are told, was a "subordinate government official" working in the Botanical Gardens in Buitenzorg (Conrad, *Folly* 6), an earlier Dutch version of the experimental gardens developed by the British North Borneo Company noted above. As such, Almayer is the son of *blijvers* himself and thus an "Indo-European" in the anxiously precise taxonomy that the Dutch colonies developed to distinguish class and caste. Thus, treasonous or not, the gin-soaked Almayer in his "flowered sarong" represents exactly the type of man who has become "too Indies" for the Dutch officials to pay interest in his claims to their protection. Almayer's "timid hints anent the protection required by the Dutch subject against the wily Arabs" imply that there is a legal relationship akin to *uti possedetis* between them (not so much "one of us" but "one of ours") (29). The Dutch officials' rebuff is as decisive as their departure from the jetties of Sambir.

"NOT ABSOLUTELY PROHIBITED BY LAW"

If the territory of Sambir is treated expediently and indeterminately by the international authorities of the Dutch and British, it also nurtures local legal indeterminacies, not least in marital relations, slaving, and trade. Taking marriage first, it is important to recognize that Almayer's cohabitation with Mrs. Almayer is not unusual as such. Indeed, as Francis notes, prior to the opening of the Suez Canal unofficial unions between Dutch colonials and Indonesian women were common and even encouraged insofar as these unions were understood to limit the demand for prostitution ("'You always leave us'" 54, 49). Likewise, the mode of their union was by no means unheard of. It was not uncommon, as Laura Ann Stoler explains, for Indonesian women to be handed on to a younger friend by a man retiring from the colonies, just as Lingard hands over his young ward to his protégé, Almayer (49). Moreover, Lingard's care for his ward—her education, her marriage to a European, her dowry (she is to be left his estate)—suggests that he hopes that his adoption of her as his "daughter" will ensure she is accepted into European society. As Francis suggests, however, entry into European society seems to have been reserved for the legitimate Eurasian children of European men, with the occasional exception where illegitimate Eurasian children were recognized by their European fathers ("'You always leave us'" 52–3). The dramatic story of Lingard rescuing his ward from Sulu pirates not only puts paid to any suggestion of a biologically paternal relationship, but also removes any opportunity to prove Eurasian rather than straightforwardly Asian ethnicity. His ward thus fails to meet the social criteria by which she might pass acceptably into European society. Moreover, as Stoler notes, "the East Indies Company, like the Dutch, firmly discouraged Euro-Asian marriages" (48). Thus, ironically, it is Almayer's legal relationship to his Asian wife that is out of place, rather than their cohabitation.

The troublesome fact of their Euro-Asian marriage is repeatedly underlined by the use of her legal title—she is emphatically "Mrs." Almayer. Indeed, her legal naming as wife is varied only in her legal and biological relationship to Nina as "mother" (and to Dain as "mother-in-law") and in Lingard's designation of her as "my daughter" (Conrad, *Folly* 111, 52, 8). The Dutch Almayer, who has grown up in the finely stratified society of the Indies, recognizes immediately the transgression of marriage to an Indonesian, feeling a "confused consciousness of shame" (10). Lingard, ever the optimistic businessman, assures Almayer that "Nobody will see the colour of your wife's skin. The dollars are too thick for that" (10). By contrast Almayer, endlessly anxious about his social standing, reconciles his shame to his avarice (for the dowry) by reasoning that "she may mercifully die" or else that it is "easy enough to dispose of a Malay woman" by sending her away (10). Thus, Almayer and Lingard consciously flout the unwritten colonial regulation of civilized conduct and instead use the legal contract of marriage as a proxy for a business deal which both hope will make them rich.

If Sambir permits the privileging of expediency over civilized respectability, signalled in Almayer's marriage, a similar permissiveness is reflected by the presence of slavery.[10] In 1893 Ada Pryer recorded in her memoir, *A Decade in Borneo*, that

> In accordance with the terms of the Royal Charter, slavery is *not yet entirely* abolished, but measures have been taken to modify it, and *its ultimate extinction* is a mere matter of time. All children born of slave parents since 1883 are free, while the importation of any fresh slaves is prohibited, neither are slaves allowed to be bought or sold in the territory. (153; my emphasis)

Returning to the subject towards the end of her account, she uses similarly evasive and contradictory language: "Slavery though *not absolutely* prohibited by law is *largely* restricted and has *almost* died a natural death" (187; my emphasis). She goes on to give a singularly disingenuous account about the carefree lives of those still enslaved, suggesting that "slaves were often as well if not better clothed than their masters and loafed through life in much the same lazy manner [. . .] if hard work was demanded of them they thought themselves very ill-used" (187).

Bulungi's slave girl, Taminah, seems to fulfil Pryer's characterization, mooning about as she does after Dain Maroola and failing to sell the cakes she is sent out with each day. She accepts the violent beatings from Bulungi's jealous wives uncomplainingly, with what Conrad troublingly refers to as "the strange, resigned apathy of half savage womankind" (Conrad, *Folly* 30). But even if her presence reinscribes the stereotypes of gender and race that Pryer unreflectively promotes, she nonetheless highlights the slipperiness of legal jurisdiction alluded to evasively in Pryer's optimistic assessment of slavery in Borneo: "not *absolutely* prohibited by law [. . .] *almost* died a natural death" (187; my emphasis). Indeed Pryer's combination of superlatives "entirely," "ultimate extinction," "absolutely," are tellingly qualified by "not yet," "largely," "almost" in ways that signal the ongoing compromise between statute and practice. Moreover, these passages neatly reveal a pragmatic combination of nominal legal declaration (e.g., "all children [. . .] are free") with an active policy of non-intervention that operates on the rhetorical basis that slavery will die a "natural death" in "a mere matter of time" (Pryer 153, 187).

Although cast in a much rosier hue, Pryer's account differs little from a report about the conditions of Berau, the historical site of Sambir, which appeared in the *Straits Times Overland Journal* a decade earlier in 1883, a year before the Dutch-British Commission, which informs the novel's political backdrop:

> The inhabitants are lazy and unenterprising. Labour is for woman and slaves only. Slaves are met with in [*sic*] almost every house. On the lower river, there is even a large village wholly inhabited by slaves. The authorities allow this, in spite of Art. 115 of the Government reg. whereby slavery in Netherlands India has been abolished. Most of the slaves are fairly well off excepting those who have to work in the mines. (qtd. in Sherry 130)

Taken together, these accounts supply suggestive detail to the early mention of slavery noted above, when the Dutch commission arrives in Sambir. Hurrying the slaves "out of sight," the inhabitants of Sambir go to some effort to present themselves as naturally inclined to the law even though the Dutch authorities are disinclined to enforce it. In this disingenuous performance of the law in which all participate but none believe, we see that expedient combination of statute and non-intervention to which Pryer's account gestures.

Slavery's ambiguous status is complicated further in the Almayer household, where at key moments familial and enslaved relationships are substituted. This propensity is first signalled in Almayer's response to Lingard's suggestion of marriage. In Almayer's mind "a Malay women" is "a slave after all [. . .] convent or no convent, ceremony or no ceremony" (Conrad, *Folly* 10). By contrast, the young Mrs. Almayer reassures herself on their wedding day that "according to white men's laws, she was going to be Almayer's companion and not his slave" (19). Mrs. Almayer's aspirations are soon dashed, though, and in urging on her daughter's relationship with Dain as one that will bring Nina wealth and happiness, she reflects that in fact she has been a "slave all [her] life" (112). The practical misery of Mrs. Almayer's sense of marital enslavement is thrown into relief by the romantic enslavement that Dain and Nina profess for each other towards the end of the book (112, 129, 136). At the same time, Mrs. Almayer's status as wife (not slave) is undermined by Almayer's familial reference to his domestic slaves as "my own people." The inherent ambiguity of "own," signalling both ownership and kinship, muddies the relationship communicated in this phrase. This elision of his Asian family with his Asian slaves echoes the blurring of Asian slave and Asian master implicit in the accounts of slavery we find in Pryer and the *Straits Times Overland Journal* report, where slaves might be "better clothed than their masters" (Pryer 187).

The final example of Sambir's indeterminacy that I want to examine is the figure of Jim-Eng, the Chinese opium smoker who in the last pages of the novel moves into Almayer's Folly with him, supplying him with the opium he had earlier resisted. Like Taminah, the passive slave girl, Jim fulfils a stereotype, this time of the Chinese opium addict. With no immediately apparent employment, Jim-Eng lounges, observes, smokes, representing the trope of indolence that had attached to oriental opium smoking since the end of the eighteenth century. Nonetheless, like Taminah, Jim-Eng's presence begs other questions of geography and law.

Firstly, we might ask whence does Jim-Eng's opium come? In the latter half of the nineteenth century, both the Dutch and the British colonial powers regulated the opium trade in Borneo with profitable taxation. This regulation was managed by the Dutch, as by the British, through opium "farmers." The colonial powers auctioned off the rights to trade opium, supplying successful bidders with the commodity wholesale and thus "farming out" its circulation and retail. As Carl Trocki and others have demonstrated, the opium farming business was rapidly dominated by Chinese merchants, who developed and drew upon large scale and increasingly international networks of finance.[11] These networks were frequently founded on *kongsi*: Chinese communities of trade, finance, and labor, which governed themselves through principles of direct democracy and commercial enterprise. *Kongsi* were often associated with mining as well as the opium trade and, like the Dutch and British chartered companies, exercised direct rule over their territories whilst pursuing commercial profit. By the mid-nineteenth century, the western region of Borneo was controlled to a considerable extent by *kongsi* republics, and the Dutch fought three wars against them in an effort to bring the region under their control. The last of these occurred between 1884–85, that is to say, in the same period in which the novel is set. If Lingard and Almayer had hoped to find a *terra nullius* upriver from Sambir on the east coast, the *kongsi* republics had already successfully established similar claims on the west coast.

The *kongsi* both paid their members for their labor and sold their members/laborers goods and supplies including opium.[12] Indeed, the Chinese remained not only the primary vendors but also the primary consumers of opium in this period. As the opium trade expanded in reach and revenue, increasingly large-scale investment was needed to bid successfully for the opium farms auctioned by the Dutch and British, driving the development of an economy of international trade and investment amongst these Chinese communities that stretched from Burma and Shanghai through the Malay archipelago to Australia (Trocki, "Opium" 311). Although both the Dutch and the British governments and publics expressed regular qualms about the morality of the opium trade, the sheer volume of revenue that it returned drowned out any sustained protest long into the twentieth century.[13] A more pressing concern for the British and Dutch was the regulation of opium sales to increase revenue, and the policing of unregulated opium sales. Thus while the colonial powers sought to drive up competition between *kongsi* for opium farms, *kongsi* syndicates might collude to keep the auction prices down and thereby increase their own opportunity for profit (312). In terms of policing opium sales, responsibility fell to the farmer, and the syndicates rapidly developed their own police forces to protect their territory from smuggling (310). As the financial power and independent security of the Chinese syndicates grew, so did British and Dutch anxieties. This led to contradictory responses, which characterized the Chinese on the one hand as victims of a merciless colonial trade that reduced them to "opium wrecks," and on the other as astute and untrustworthy "foreigners" whose enigmatic networks threatened the financial and physical security of the colonies.

Jim-Eng embodies both these characterizations. As Agnes Yeow points out, in *An Outcast of the Islands* Jim-Eng's background as Straits Chinese is made explicit, suggesting that he represents "one of the very small group [of] affluent Chinese who had made their fortunes and become upwardly mobile" (85). With a wholesale quantity of opium (six cases), "Conrad's Jim-Eng is not simply a private consumer or even an opium shopkeeper, but *the* opium revenue farmer of Sambir with the monopoly" (89). Jim-Eng's social standing is less clear in *Almayer's Folly*, however, where his fondness for the consumption rather than the commercial exploitation of opium is emphasized. The enigma of his trade, married with his interest in the comings and goings of others, keeps the legality of Jim-Eng's operation in question in the earlier novel, an indeterminacy that is erased in *An Outcast*. The possibility left open in *Almayer's Folly* that Jim-Eng might trade opium illegally with impunity once more underscores the novel's suggestion that neither the Dutch nor the British consider Sambir worth their attention. In fact, Jim-Eng's sole appearance in *An Outcast of the Islands* seems likewise designed to highlight his ambiguous relation to both British and Dutch powers. Demanding protection of Almayer, Jim-Eng appears on his doorstep pursued by Willems who demands that he take his hat off before the Dutch flag. Jim-Eng refuses, claiming he is British and will only take his hat off before the Union Jack. As Yeow points out, Jim-Eng's claim is underwritten by his Straits-Chinese identity, which also provides the basis for identification of shared whiteness with Almayer (86). Nonetheless, if Jim-Eng is indeed a legal opium farmer in Sambir, his license must have been bought from the Dutch. Likewise, his claim to Almayer's protection on the basis of shared whiteness fails to acknowledge Almayer's own self-identification as Dutch, not British.

Reading back from this scene of muddled allegiances in the later novel to the ending of *Almayer's Folly*, we can discern a fitness to the befuddled companionship to which Jim-Eng and Almayer finally resort. As Straits Chinese, Jim-Eng represents the second or third generation of Chinese colonialism in the region (85). Like the Dutch and British, he distinguishes himself from the Arabs, Malays, and indigenous tribes as white and, more specifically, as "English." Yet to the novels' British characters, Ford and Lingard, Jim-Eng is emphatically a "Chinaman" (Conrad, *Folly* 154). Similarly, as the Indo-European son of *blijvers*, Almayer's own claims to Dutch identity and protection under Dutch law are swept aside by the officials who visit Sambir. Like Sambir itself, Almayer and Jim-Eng are abandoned by the British and neglected by the Dutch. In such a situation both resort to escapism: Almayer through his incessant day-dreaming, Jim-Eng through his opium pipe.

Their shared dreams are reflected in Jim-Eng's "proud" rechristening of Almayer's folly as the "House of Heavenly Delight" (154). Almayer had intended the building as an architectural correlative to the luxury that his impending wealth would deliver once the British North Borneo Company took over Sambir. It was to be a space of indolence and pleasure, funded by the assured economic boom that British rule would bring. Jim-Eng's name for the unfinished building thus only repeats Almayer's aspiration in a different (Chinese) script. Jim-Eng is a long way from the *kongsi* republics in Sambir but his occupation of Almayer's Folly, the home the Dutchman had built for himself in eager anticipation of success akin to that of the *kongsi* syndicates, suggests a colonization of sorts, not least in the eviction of Almayer's former faithful servant, the Malay Arab, Ali. His claim is not to *terra nullius* but *uti possedetis*. When Ford asks Jim-Eng what the script on the silk wall-hanging means, he replies "that is the name of the house. *All the same like my house*. Very good name" (154; my emphasis). "He smokes. I live here," he tells Ford (153).

"A JUDGEMENT THAT HAS NOTHING TO DO WITH JUSTICE"

So, to what extent are the claims which Conrad makes to sympathy, perhaps even solidarity, with colonial subjects born out by the novel? At first glance Conrad seems to peddle the very same prejudices he critiques in Alice Meynell, the unnamed author of the article with which he takes issue in his "Author's Note": Jim-Eng, the Chinese opium wreck; Taminah, the impassive oriental woman inured against pain; Almayer himself, the Indo-European ruined by his own fantasies of fortune and unable ever to reach the European world he reveres. Each are stock characters amongst many more in the novel playing a part little different from those given to them by the popular authors whose work Meynell dismisses. What distinguishes them is their narrative context, whose machinations throw into relief the instability of the rule of law and of the "civilizing" mission of colonialism, including chartered company colonialism.

It is a commonplace to note that Conrad's time in South East Asia was surprisingly short given the vividness and extent of its influence on his fiction. Nonetheless, his time there and the ensuing years were ones of particular political and legal transformation for Borneo, in particular, the repercussions of which Conrad translates directly into his first novel. I want to argue therefore that the sympathies that he proclaims for "common mortals no matter where they live" are expressed less through his presentation of individual characters than through his dramatization of the complexities, frustrations, and indeterminacies that accompanied the colonial enterprise of the late-nineteenth century. This is why he claims that Meynell's essay expresses a "judgement that is nothing to do with justice." Meynell is, as her essay makes clear, offended by the people themselves. Conrad's concern, or at least one of them in *Almayer's Folly*, is with the problem of justice in an international setting. Attending to this fact enables us to see how, long before the publication of "Geography and Some Explorers," Conrad's fiction was already illuminating the inconsistencies that emerge in the process of putting international and transnational law into practice in the indeterminate spaces of colonial geography.

NOTES

1. See also Nesiah 3.

2. The VOC was established in 1602 and dissolved in 1799 when its holdings were translated into a formal colony by the Dutch Government (see Francis, *Culture* 12–3).

3. The United Africa Company was founded by George Goldie in 1879 through the amalgamation of several trading companies in the region. Goldie's company obtained chartered status in 1886 as the Royal Niger Company. For a discussion of Conrad's literary and personal engagement with colonial chartered companies, primarily in South and Central Africa, see Stephen Donovan.

4. John D. Gordan was one of the earliest to note Conrad's invocation of Brooke in the details of Lingard's life (618). See also Robert Hampson, *Cross-Cultural Encounters* 212, n. 4.

5. In this regard it is interesting to note Treacher's comment on the relative value of Chinese gold diggers: "The Company will probably find that Chinese diggers will not only stand the climate better, but will be more easily governed, be satisfied with smaller returns, and contribute as much or more than the Europeans to the Government Treasury, by their consumption of opium, tobacco and other excisable articles, by fees for gold licenses, and so forth" (106).

6. Tarling suggests that the war between the Dutch and Aceh at this time left the Dutch authority in their "Outer Regions" stretched (139). This suggestion supplies one reason for their apparent lack of interest in Sambir in *Almayer's Folly*.

7. Black cites an 1865 report on Borneo in the records of the former Netherlands Ministry of Colonies in the Rijksarchief, The Hague, K1665, 16/10/65, 15. Andrew Francis draws attention to this fact in relation to Conrad's Asian fiction (*Culture*, 13, n. 26).

8. The wars between Aceh (in Northern Sumatra) and the Dutch ran between 1871–78 and again from 1881–1905. It is this second war which looms in the background of *Almayer's Folly*.

9. The region was home to the highly lucrative production of peppercorn.

10. Robert Hampson provides a useful discussion of the open secret of slavery in *Almayer's Folly* in *Conrad's Secrets* 37–42.

11. See Karl Trocki and J.F. Scheltema.

12. Trocki notes the relationship between opium's analgesic qualities and its high use amongst Chinese mining laborers, such as those attached to *kongsi*, suggesting that "we should consider the possibility that opium was in fact a necessity, that it was a 'work drug'" ("Opium" 302).

13. For an account of the British lobby against the trade, see J.B. Brown, who notes that it

"was not until 1946 that Great Britain halted non-medicinal shipments of opium to her Far Eastern possessions" (110).

WORKS CITED

Black, Ian. "The 'Lastposten': Eastern Kalimantan and the Dutch in the Nineteenth and Early Twentieth Centuries." *Journal of Southeast Asian Studies*, vol. 16, no. 2, 1985, pp. 281-91.

Brown, J.B. "Politics of the Poppy: The Society for the Suppression of the Opium Trade, 1874-1916." *Journal of Contemporary History*, vol. 8, no. 3, 1973, pp. 97-111.

Conrad, Joseph. *Almayer's Folly*. Cambridge University Press, 1994.

———. *Collected Letters of Joseph Conrad*. Vol. 1, edited by Fredrick R. Karl and Laurence Davies, Cambridge University Press, 1983.

———. "Geography and Some Explorers." *National Geographic*, vol. 45, no. 3, 1924, pp. 241-74.

Donovan Stephen. "'Figures, facts, theories'": Conrad and Chartered Company Imperialism." *The Conradian*, vol. 24, no. 2, 1999, pp. 31-60.

Francis, Andrew. "'You always leave us—for your own ends': Marriage and Concubinage in Conrad's Asian Fiction." *The Conradian*, vol. 35, no. 2, 2010, pp. 46-62.

———. *Culture and Commerce in Conrad's Asian Fiction*. Cambridge University Press, 2015.

Gordan, John. "The Rajah Brooke and Joseph Conrad." *Studies in Philology*, vol. 35, no. 4, 1938, pp. 613-34.

Hampson, Robert. *Conrad's Secrets*. Palgrave Macmillan, 2012.

———. *Cross-Cultural Encounters in Joseph Conrad's Malay Fiction*. Palgrave Macmillan, 2000.

Meynell, Alice. "Decivilised." *The Rhythm of Life and Other Essays*, 1891, Elkin Mathews and John Lane, 1893, pp. 7-11.

Nesiah, Vasuki. "Placing International Law: White Spaces on a Map." *Leiden International Law*, vol. 16, 2003, pp. 1-35.

Pryer, Ada. *A Decade in Borneo*. Hutchinson, 1893.

Scheltema, J.F. "The Opium Trade in the Dutch East Indies 1." *American Journal of Sociology*, vol. 13, no. 1, 1907, pp. 79-112.

———. "The Opium Trade in the Dutch East Indies 2." *American Journal of Sociology*, vol. 13, no. 2, 1907, pp. 224-51.

Sherry, Norman. *Conrad's Eastern World*. Cambridge University Press, 1966.

Stoler, Ann Laura. *Carnal Knowledge and Imperial Power: Race and the Intimate in Imperial Rule*. University of California Press, 2002.

Tarling, Nicholas. *Imperialism in South East Asia: "A fleeting, passing phase."* Routledge, 2001.

Treacher, W.H. *British Borneo: Sketches of Brunai, Sarawak, Labuan, and North Borneo*. Government Printing Department, 1891.

Trocki, Carl. *Opium and Empire: Chinese Society in Colonial Singapore, 1800-1910*. Cornell University Press, 1990.

———. "Opium and the Beginnings of Chinese Capitalism in Southeast Asia." *Journal of Southeast Asian Studies*, vol. 33, no. 2, 2002, pp. 297-314.

Watt, Ian. "Introduction." *Almayer's Folly*, Cambridge University Press, 1994, pp. xxi–lxiv.
Yeow, Agnes. "Conrad and The Straits Chinese: The Politics of Chinese Enterprise and Identity in the Colonial State." *The Conradian*, vol. 29, no. 1, 2004, pp. 84–98.

The Spatialization of Moral Judgment: Borders in Conrad's "Amy Foster," *Heart of Darkness,* and *Under Western Eyes*[1]

YAEL LEVIN

THE HEBREW UNIVERSITY OF JERUSALEM

ABSTRACT

This paper utilizes spatial figurations in "Amy Foster," *Heart of Darkness,* and *Under Western Eyes* in bringing Conrad's poetics to bear on the question of modernist borders. The illustration proceeds by tracing thematic and stylistic articulations of a character's situatedness. The first attends to national determinations and spatial figures, the second to diegetic stratification. The purpose of this analysis is to show how all serve as the national, figurative, and narratological limits that facilitate a determination of a character's moral soundness. Two complementary conclusions are offered. First, Conrad's sympathies may be traced by distinguishing between the signposting of national loyalties and their erasure in universal uprootedness. Robert Hampson's distinction between international and transnational activism will be used to show how the difference alerts us to moral considerations in Conrad's poetics. Kurtz, Yanko, and Laspara will serve as test-cases for the analysis, but the distinction will be shown to be no less valuable in its application to a more nuanced reading of Conrad's Jewish characters. Second, the manner in which a character is framed in the fiction, his stylistic situatedness, as it were, serves as a parallel moral gauge. A character's moral worth can be assessed by the manner in which he is circumscribed within the diegesis or outside it, whether his position is fixed or changing.

KEYWORDS

Joseph Conrad, "Amy Foster," *Heart of Darkness, Under Western Eyes,*
international, transnational, borders, Modernism

In her essay "Mr. Bennett and Mrs. Brown," Virginia Woolf pronounces her discontent with the state of early twentieth-century English letters. In doing so, she famously discounts the work of Joseph Conrad: "Mr. Conrad is a Pole; which sets him apart, and makes him, however admirable, not very helpful" (326). More than fifty years later, Terry Eagleton launches a critique of the same canon stemming from the like-minded belief that it fails to represent the ideational and aesthetic shifts attending the historical moment: "Caught within its partial and one-sided attachments," English writing is unable "to 'totalise' the significant movements of its own culture" (15). Eagleton's critique departs from Woolf's in that rather than dismiss Conrad's work, he singles it out: "the seven most significant writers of twentieth-century English literature have been a Pole, three Americans, two Irishmen and an Englishman" (9). As contrary as these two critical impulses might be, both rely on the assumption that aesthetic judgment must be informed by questions of national allegiance and geographical borders. The first does so by way of exclusion, the second, through cross-cultural encounter.[2]

The anchoring of aesthetic critique in national borders might be seen as contrary to the spirit of modernist writing. "To consider modernism," Tim Armstrong suggests, is "to engage with culture defined in terms of an interconnected field of activity in which hierarchy and even causality is problematic; in which agreed boundaries are replaced by permeability and relatedness" (ix). This paper utilizes spatial figurations in "Amy Foster," *Heart of Darkness,* and *Under Western Eyes* in order to bring Conrad's poetics to bear on the tensions underlying the moral and aesthetic articulations of modernist borders. Though the boundaries we encounter in Conrad's fiction are tested and challenged in a way that corresponds with Armstrong's summary, they also survive as the moral yardstick by which readers might judge the characters.

The paper begins by attending to national and spatial articulations of borders in the fiction. My use of the term border will not be limited to national and geographical denotations but will follow the more inclusive connotation of a character's situatedness. The purpose of such a conceptual generalization is to provide an overarching sense of the way in which the proviso of figurative and literal spatial coordinates not only contributes to the fleshing out of character but also serves as scaffolding for moral judgment. This is not a study of the nuances of national belonging and its manifold and often contradictory expressions in Conrad's writing. Where I do wish to intervene in questions of cultural and national identity is in drawing attention to the tendency to overlook a significant difference between two forms of uprootedness or homelessness in Conrad's fiction, a difference that hinges on a spatial metaphor. Robert Hampson's distinction between international and transnational activism serves to challenge the equivalence often drawn by critics between a characterization of national exile and a broader sense of homelessness, between the signposting of borders and their erasure. The first dramatizes the expression of a character's divided loyalties—between the adoptive nation and the nation left behind; the second blurs the matter of national origin altogether. The readings that follow address the thematic separation of spatial and national borders in order to test what is lost in the conceptual slippage between nationally determined and indeterminate conditions of uprootendess. The nuance is particularly significant when considering the modernist topos of alienation as its emphasis on a universally shared sense of exile may be seen to trivialize national and cultural specificities.

The second moral gauge proposed is linked to the spatial coordinates associated with the stratification of narrative levels. A stylistic parallel to the thematic boundaries of national borders and spatial groundedness, the manner in which a character is framed in the fiction, his stylistic situatedness, as it were, contributes to the determination of his moral soundness. A character's moral worth can be assessed by the manner in which he is circumscribed within the diegesis or outside it, whether his position is fixed or changing.

An investigation into borders accrues a double significance when related to Conrad's work. The aesthetic articulation of spatial figures must be shadowed by their literal implications as negotiated in his political writing. In "Conrad, the 'Polish Problem' and Transnational Activism," Hampson outlines the tensions between Conrad's demand for a united Europe and his commitment to Poland's state borders. Addressing "Autocracy and War" and "The Crime of Partition," Hampson notes that Conrad's

> dream of a frontierless Europe is set against a concern with boundaries, the re-drawing of boundaries, and the boundary as a scar, which comes out of an unexpressed identification with Poland. If the Polish State provides Conrad with a model of federalism in "The Crime of Partition," ["Autocracy and War"] is haunted by the erasure of Poland's national boundaries. ("The Polish Question" 31)

This paper is in dialogue with Hampson's multiple treatments of the subject; it sets out to present the tension between strong borders and their erasure metonymically by focusing on the narratological and thematic articulations of borders in Conrad's fiction.³

Kurtz, Julius Laspara, and Yanko Goorall have yet to be grouped together under a single critical lens. Perhaps for good reason. The first is a figure for the voracious narcissism underlying imperialistic desire, the second a minor character associated with extremist political writing, and the third, a Polish exile. Tragic and disarming, Yanko is a man rejected by his adoptive country, a figure for the anxieties of the author who created him. Regardless of the diverging sympathies they might elicit, all three share a unique spatial characterization that is figuratively suggestive of their uprootedness. They are always seen at a remove from the ground, they are not wholly grounded.

Lacking any terms of reference by which to appeal to Kurtz, Marlow reflects that "There was nothing either above or below him—and I knew it. He had kicked himself loose of the earth. Confound the man! He had kicked the very earth to pieces. He was alone—and I before him did not know whether I stood on the ground or floated in the air" (Conrad, *Youth* 144). Such spatial coordinates continue to inform Marlow's efforts to emphasize the difference between them. Where Kurtz steps "over the edge," he himself is said to "draw back [his] hesitating foot" (151). The first falls into a bottomless abyss, the second remains grounded.

Binaries of spatial characterization are even more pronounced in "Amy Foster." Here, groundedness and buoyancy emerge as the leitmotifs that distinguish Yanko from the townspeople. Dr. Kennedy remarks that the latter "cling to the earth." They "are uncouth in body and as leaden of gait as if their very hearts were loaded with chains" ("Amy Foster" 111). The description of Yanko, on the other hand, contains a decidedly different set of figurations:

> But here on this same road you might have seen amongst these heavy men a being lithe, supple and long-limbed, straight like a pine, with something striving upwards in his appearance as though the heart within him had been buoyant. Perhaps it was only the force of the contrast, but when he was passing one of these villagers here, the soles of his feet did not seem to me to touch the dust of the road. (111)

Such striking opposition is not merely the product of Dr. Kennedy's romantic vision. The townspeople repeatedly employ similar markers of difference. Their method of articulating Yanko's freedom is reworded, however, so that it falls into negative stereotypes, the product of parochial thinking. Yanko, a castaway, a poor emigrant in Dr. Kennedy's words, becomes "a hairy sort of gypsy," "a tramp" (118), "a wandering and probably dangerous maniac" (121).

Julius Laspara concludes this procession of ungrounded characters. A "polyglot, of unknown parentage, of indefinite nationality," he is an "anarchist, with a pedantic and ferocious temperament, and an amazingly inflammatory capacity for invective." Unlike Kurtz and Yanko and their place in their respective fictions, Laspara is no more than "a power in the background" (*Western Eyes* 285). But he is given similar spatial markers: "The great but obscure Julius," is always perched, "feet twisted round his three-legged stool." On the rare occasions that he leaves his nest, "it was as though he had descended from the heights of Olympus" (286).

Kurtz, Laspara, and Yanko are all untethered. But the differences issuing from these shared leitmotifs are telling. They allow us to intervene productively in the inevitable generalizations that occur when we view alienation in Conrad's work as an overarching topos rather than the two diverging experiences described above: national exile and homelessness. Hampson's distinction between internationalism and transnationalism is helpful here:

> Transnational activism is to be distinguished from internationalism—a distinction Conrad implicitly makes in 'A Crime of Partition,' when he criticises 'the internationalists' (*NLL*, 121). Where internationalism represents a commitment to world revolution, based on a supra-national class or (more recently) religious affiliation, transnational activism refers to the negotiation of the 'complex loyalty' of living in one country, while also identifying with another as one's place of origin—or, indeed, of living in more than one country. ("Conrad" 34)

To extend this lesson beyond its immediate political articulations is to regard the two prefixes as announcing the difference between an experience of division and unity, between the tensions of competing loyalties and a single idea, religion or value. This is also the difference between the presence or absence of borders as interpretative anchors. In his reading of "Amy Foster," Douglas Kerr notes that "borders are most strictly policed when it comes to overt expression of the immigrant's cultural difference, and the evidence of the basis of his subjectivity in alien cultural practice and tradition. Yanko's simple Catholic piety is an issue here, and is regarded with suspicion by the local folk; but more important is the question of his language" (342). Yanko may be likened to a gypsy, a wanderer, a man whose life testifies to the razing of borders, but the repeated emphasis on allegiance to the country he lost suggests that national borders are not only policed throughout the story but are the necessary hermeneutic center on which we must draw to interpret it. His very clothes testify to his division. He wears both the striped cotton shirt given him by Swaffer, and "the national brown cloth trousers (in which he had been washed ashore)" (Conrad, "Amy Foster" 127). Such division is remarked throughout the description of his attempted absorption. The effort to prepare him for conversion fails to "break him of his habit of crossing himself." Though he takes off "the string with a couple of brass medals the size of a sixpence, a tiny metal cross, and a square sort of scapulary which he wore round his neck," he nevertheless hangs "them on the wall by the side of his bed." Every evening, he continues to recite "the Lord's Prayer, in incomprehensible words and in a slow, fervent tone, as he had heard his old father do at the head of all the kneeling family, big and little, on every evening of his life" (131).

Kurtz and Laspara are not thus divided. Neither may be seen as the fictional counterpart to the author's status as homo duplex. All Europe, we recall, "contributed to the making of Kurtz" (*Youth* 117); Laspara, as quoted above, is "of indefinite nationality" (*Western Eyes* 285). This distinction between Yanko and the former two is morally damning. In "The Crime of Partition" Conrad refers to internationalists as "men who professedly care nothing for race or country" and are associated with "disruption" and a "sinister purpose," with "dark" ways (121). The moral implications of the difference between professing loyalty to a home-state and the disregarding of national borders is apparent in my reading of Kurtz's and Laspara's characters.

In an effort to fathom Kurtz's monstrous devolution, Marlow contemplates:

> I am trying to account to myself for—for—Mr. Kurtz—for the shade of Mr. Kurtz. This initiated wraith from the back of Nowhere honoured me with its amazing confidence before it vanished altogether. This was because it could speak English to me. The original Kurtz had been educated partly in England, and—as he was good enough to say himself—his sympathies were in the right place. His mother was half-English, his father was half-French. All Europe contributed to the making of Kurtz; and by and by I learned that, most appropriately, the International Society for the Suppression of Savage Customs had entrusted him with the making of a report, for its future guidance. (*Youth,* 117)

The passage describes two snapshots of the character, as it were, the before and after of "Kurtz's nerves went wrong" (117). The modifier "original" signals the former. It assigns Kurtz clear national attributes—the English language, and the English/French origin. The metamorphosis from the original to the wraith, however, is signposted by the loss of these markers. The dehumanizing "it" pronoun that follows the ghostly epithet coheres with the notion of complete dislocation. He comes forth from nowhere; he is otherworldly through and through, and is no longer tied to the clear boundaries of national citizenship. The transition is from national allegiance to the supra-national group announced by the claim that "all Europe contributed to the making of Kurtz" (117). Such a group is also associated with the supra-national cause promoted by the *International* Society for the Suppression of Savage Customs. Though, as Hampson notes, Conrad elsewhere extols the virtues attending the idea of a united Europe, particularly a united Western Europe (one that would exclude the Russian menace which he describes in several of his political essays), Kurtz serves as a figure for the dangers of a united cause that would preclude the sovereign or human rights of the individual state in service of a larger scheme or purpose. The brick-maker testifies to the manner in which European division gives way to supra-national cooperation under such an overarching and dangerous ideal. As he remarks, the work in Africa is a "cause entrusted to us by Europe," a cause qualified by a "higher intelligence, wide sympathies, a *singleness* of purpose" (79; my emphasis).

Such singleness of purpose is very often tied to empty rhetoric, to a beautiful but dark eloquence. The report Kurtz writes for the society repeatedly signals the loss of spatial boundaries in such terms:

> "By the simple exercise of our will we can exert a power for good practically *unbounded*," etc., etc. From that point he *soared* and took me with him. The peroration was magnificent, though difficult to remember, you know. It gave me the notion of an exotic Immensity ruled by an august Benevolence. It made me tingle with enthusiasm. This was the *unbounded* power of eloquence—of words—of burning noble words. (118; my emphasis)

The repetition of the word unbounded, on the one hand, and the figure of flight, of soaring, on the other, is indicative of the intermixing of the motifs of borderlessness and ungroundedness explored above. Here it is rhetoric that is seen as unbounded and ungrounded. But Kurtz's uncanny spatial coordinates are also attached to his physical presence. First appearing "above the shoulders of [his] bearers," Kurtz's form is in the likeness of a "disinterred body," a being untethered, ungrounded, unchecked. Self-begot like Milton's Satan, he is a being all his own. What he sees are the extensions of his own ego— "'My Intended, my ivory, my station, my river, my . . .' everything belonged to him" (116). Kurtz's rhetorical and physical ungroundedness may be seen as an allegorical figure for the monstrous expressions of a European solidarity gone wrong.

Laspara's status as émigré renders him closer in characterization to Yanko. Yet where the latter is afforded the sympathy of the implied author, the former accrues the full figurative arsenal of degeneration. Yanko is romantically described as "a woodland creature" ("Amy Foster" 111). Laspara, in contrast, is described thus: "A fine bold nose jutted over a thin mouth hidden in the mass of fine hair. All this, accented features, strong limbs in their relative smallness, appeared delicate without the slightest sign of debility" (*Western Eyes* 285). Hirsute and diminutive, he is reminiscent of such late nineteenth-century monsters as Bram Stoker's Dracula and Robert Louis Stevenson's Mr. Hyde. His diminutive stature is repeated excessively over the course of the passage; he is "picturesque but diminutive, as if seen through the big end of an opera-glass." He is a "tiny man" possessing "a little thin hand with hairy wrists and knuckles," a "diminutive personage" who looks "like a reduction of an ordinary-sized man." His "strong limbs" are so "in their relative smallness" (285). Laspara further cements his role as imperial gothic threat with his frequent dismissal of the significance of language as national marker. Exhibiting Dracula's linguistic dexterity and the power of assimilation that such a talent provides, he speaks Russian "as he [speaks] and [writes] four or five other European languages, without distinction and without force" (287). Katherine Baxter addresses the historical situatedness of the linguistic anxieties evident in the makeup of such multilingual characters. Noting that the fear of "colonial and/or Eastern 'others' who spoke English *too* well" is "evident in both fiction and official documents of the late nineteenth century," Baxter suggests that such fears may be seen "as allegorical of anxieties about more literal border transgressions and so-called reverse colonization" (20). The danger is clearly evident in the making of Laspara's character. If Dracula infects his victims through the contamination of their blood, Laspara does so by demanding they lose their national and personal allegiances through translation. When Razumov objects that he cannot write because he does not speak English, Laspara suggests he write in Russian, reassuring him that they will "have it translated. There can be no difficulty" (Conrad, *Western Eyes* 287). Laspara then makes a similar offer to Nathalie.[4] Testifying to the ease of translation—suggestive figuratively of the ease of border crossing and cultural contamination—Laspara's character once again underlines the threat of an international power's intervention in national contexts. Razumov's and Nathalie's translated words can be used to promote social revolution wherever it is needed.

Laspara's "great pepper-and-salt full beard" (285) indicates that the fault line between international and transnational experience also doubles to signal religious faith. Judaism and Christianity are linked with different modes of national affiliation. The Jewish faith is not dependent on nation-state borders;

the practice of Christianity, on the other hand, is predominately regulated by the sects and denominations of a nation or region, a difference that is well-demonstrated in the distinction between Catholic and Protestant religious practices in "Amy Foster." In the short story, such beards as Laspara's emerge as markers of Judaism, and are associated with an absence of any national allegiance or definitive origin. These men are described as having "been going about through all the little towns in the foothills of [Yanko's] country. They would arrive on market-days driving in a peasant's cart, and would set up an office in an inn or some other Jew's house. There were three of them, of whom one with a long beard looked venerable" ("Amy Foster" 116). Their scheme dispossess Yanko's father of a fine portion of his land, which he sells to "a Jew inn-keeper in order to pay the people of the ship that took men to America to get rich" (117).

The difference between the international razing of borders and their transnational resurgence is thus also relevant to the ongoing critical discussion on Conrad's attitudes to Judaism. Critics holding varied and at-times contradictory views on the subject often meet in the claim that there is an underlying affinity between Conrad's thematization of exile and Jewish experience. Peter Mallios is representative when he suggests that

> There is much about Conrad's fiction that recalls Jewish, and especially Jewish émigré, expression and experiences [...] Conrad's greater thematics of diaspora, marginalized and embattled community, and decentered and thwarted search for a homeland, as well as his conflicted and decentered relation to hegemonic nationalist assertion, his internationalized perspective on question of human politics, and his critical disinterest in Christian morality and metaphysics, all open themselves up to Jewish corollaries (113).[5]

The moral distinction between international and transnational commitment demands we rethink Conrad's attitudes to the Jewish faith, as different forms of decentered experience command different sympathies from the author. The perception of Judaism as "a supra-national" group might explain why it shares in the condemnation afforded to anarchists, capitalists, and other internationalists sporting a "dark" purpose. Though we might believe faith, ideology, and economic praxis merit separate responses from the implied author, the manner in which all eschew nation-state borders and national allegiance might explain the similarity underlying their treatment. Yankel, the Polish patriot in "Prince Roman," is a case in point. His characterization hinges on the same Jewish stereotypes evoked in the description of the wandering Jews in "Amy

Foster." But where the latter are cast in the role of villains, the former elicits sympathy. The difference between the characters is not one of religious faith but of national designation. Yankel is a patriot—he is committed not only to his faith, but also to his country. The wandering Jews are not associated with divided loyalties; they have no respect for national borders.

If borders emerge as a moral yardstick by circumscribing a character within a clear cultural or national sphere, epistemological and rhetorical limits appear to function in a metonymically related way. Andrew Gibson distinguishes between Kurtz and Marlow in terms comparable to those traced above. "The Kurtzian principle," he writes, "is one of grandiose and summary representation which seeks to encompass and articulate the whole" (60). On the other hand, "what pervades 'Marlovian' discourse is a sense of epistemological dead-end, of determinate limits to knowledge and representation, the irreducible mystery of the world encountered by the cognitive intellect" (62). Where Kurtz's discourse is associated with an all-encompassing and unbounded epistemology, Marlow's thought constantly draws awareness to limits, to borders, to the compartmentalization of knowledge. The latter is morally sanctioned; it might be partial, but it is sound. The former is condemned and feared as the product of a voracious narcissism that wishes to comprehend the whole within the one: a single goal, a single master, a single, undivided mind. To follow the extended metaphor attending this paper, it is the difference between partial and universal insight, between a bordered experience and an experience without borders.

Laspara offers an image of the latter as befitting the international determinations of his character. Attending on Nathalie Haldin's visit to Laspara, the language teacher has a glimpse of a room, "with a porcelain shade pulled low down over a big table (with a very large map spread on it)." The only person known to him here is "little Julius Laspara, who seemed to have been poring over the map, his feet twined tightly round the chair-legs." In keeping with a former characterization where he is likened to an Olympian God, Laspara's "elbows [are] propped on the big-scale map" (Conrad, *Western Eyes* 328) as he hatches a military conspiracy in Russia. The narrator notes:

> Later on, much later on, at the time of the newspaper rumours (they were vague and soon died out) of an abortive military conspiracy in Russia, I remembered the glimpse I had of that motionless group with its central figure. No details ever came out, but it was known that the revolutionary parties abroad had given their assistance, had sent emissaries in advance, that even money was found to dispatch a steamer with a cargo of arms and conspirators to invade the Baltic provinces. And while my eyes scanned the

imperfect disclosures (in which the world was not much interested) I thought that the old, settled Europe had been given in my person attending that Russian girl something like a glimpse behind the scenes. A short, strange glimpse on the top floor of a great hotel of all places in the world: the great man himself; the motionless great bulk in the corner of the slayer of spies and gendarmes; Yakovlitch, the veteran of ancient terrorist campaigns; the woman, with her hair as white as mine and the lively black eyes, all in a mysterious half-light, with the strongly lighted map of Russia on the table. (330)

Laspara is here cast as an all-seeing author figure whose privileged perspective, as it were outside the storyworld of his making, allows him to launch military invasions. That the plan is ultimately unsuccessful is indicative of Conrad's condemnation of "world revolution" (Hampson, "Conrad" 34). More broadly, it bespeaks his questioning of the very validity of a detached perspective.[6]

If the universal, detached perspective is here demonized, its polar opposite—knowledge bounded, grounded and contextualized—seems more its binary complement than a redemptive alternative. In "Amy Foster," the figurative collocation of groundedness and limited insight is signaled in the repeated metonymical slippages between spatial coordinates and the description of eyes. In contrast to Dr. Kennedy's "profoundly attentive eyes" (Conrad, "Amy Foster" 106), the townsmen have "downcast eyes, as if the melancholy of an over-burdened earth had weighted their feet, bowed their shoulders, borne down their glances" (110). Attentive eyes are associated with the freedom to move about, with an emancipated existence. Being tied to the land, on the other hand, is repeatedly associated with a form of blindness. Yanko is no exception to the rule. At the start it is as if "the soles of his feet" do not "touch the dust of the road." He possesses "lustrous black eyes" and "freedom of movement" (111). This freedom is brought to an abrupt end when Swaffer offers Yanko "something like an acre of ground" (136) in return for saving his granddaughter. The reward is transformative. Dr. Kennedy reports that Yanko appears to grow "less springy of step, heavier in body, less keen of eye" (137). When he looks out at the sea he does so with "indifferent, unseeing eyes" (137). The patterned coupling of the two motifs throughout the story suggests that the parochial grounding of knowledge is suggestive of blindness. Woolf's nationalist dismissal of Conrad's work thus finds its figurative foreshadowing in the story; "Amy Foster" concludes with the loss of the memory of the Polish émigré, "as a shadow passes away upon a white screen" (142).

It is perhaps the opaqueness of such grounded and myopic knowledge that elicits Marlow's reflection whether "all the wisdom, and all the truth, and all sincerity, are just compressed into that inappreciable moment of time in which we step over the threshold of the invisible" (*Heart* 151). Though Marlow here departs from strictly spatial coordinates and offers a liminal chronotope, the implication is that knowledge and truth lie in an experience of dislocation, a release from social, national and human ties that provide the necessary blinders to a disturbing truth. Marlow, who refuses to take that extra step, remains grounded. In terms comparable to those illustrated by the myopia of the townspeople in "Amy Foster," Marlow's reflections suggest that his work (that which grounds him) is the obstacle to a more comprehensive view of the world. He explains: "when you have to attend to things of that sort, to the mere incidents of the surface, the reality—the reality I tell you—fades. The inner truth is hidden—luckily, luckily" (93).

To compare Marlow's form of myopia to that associated with the townspeople in the short story is nevertheless problematic. Marlow may choose to look away from the hidden truth, but he nevertheless glimpses it in a way that the former cannot. Having "peeped over the edge" himself, Marlow claims he understands "better the meaning of [Kurtz's] stare that could not see the flame of the candle but was wide enough to embrace the whole universe, piercing enough to penetrate all the hearts that beat in the darkness. He had summed up—he had judged" (151).

Marlow is in-between: he is both grounded and ungrounded; loyal to a nation and a life at sea. As such, he is one of a number of corrective models that the three texts provide as counter to the two mirror images of warped knowledge: the unbounded perspective of Kurtz and the revolutionists or the grounded and limited perspective of the townspeople. In contradistinction to the travesty of omniscience, on the one hand, and parochial partiality, on the other, these alternative epistemological models are validated through layering and border-crossing—two separate stylistic measures that are both premised on the signposting of spatial boundaries. Where Kurtz and the townspeople are both oblivious to borders—the first through an all-encompassing narcissism, the latter through parochial blindness, these alternative epistemological models are premised on a recognition of these borders; they constantly call attention to their presence.

Much has been written about the narrative techniques of *Heart of Darkness* and *Under Western Eyes*. Without wishing to rehearse unnecessarily what is already long established, it would suffice to mention the ways in which the stylization of the two novels coheres with the argument traced here. The proliferation of different voices and perspectives in both allows for juxtapositions of limited perspectives that might shed light on one another without falling into the trap of a detached, universal perspective on the one hand, or an unchecked parochial or idiosyncratic point of view, on the other. The first does so by framing Marlow's account with that of an anonymous narrator whose ideological allegiances are markedly different from his own, a voice extolling the abiding virtue of exploration and conquest throughout British history. While Marlow's challenging of imperialist discourse undermines the unchecked hyperbole of he who introduces him, Marlow is himself checked, in turn, by this framing device. His physical attributes show him to be touched by the journey, perhaps morally contaminated by the experience. Undermining the soundness of his account, he is seen both physically and acoustically as a double to Kurtz. Stylistically, then, the narrative method doubles Marlow's unique in-between position; it undermines the soundness of his account by framing him with another's perspective at the same time that it undermines that external frame through its juxtaposition to Marlow's criticism.

Though the later novel is the product of a single narrator, the oscillation between different narrative positions, between heterodiegetic narration (where the story is reported from a vantage point external to the events) and homodiegetic narration (where the narrator is installed into the storyworld and reports as a witness to the events) serves to undermine the reliability of his account. Such a unique narrative position is effectively the articulation of a division of loyalties between one bordered perspective and another—one that is bordered by the storyworld and one that is bordered by the experience of an external focalizer outside it. His positing of disinterest at the outset falls apart when we learn of his involvement with the key figures populating his narrative. The narrator's crossing of the borders of his own narrative, from an external point of view to an internal one, allows us to trace the unreliability of his account and reflect on its intentional and perhaps unintentional deceptions.

"Amy Foster" follows the narrative method employed in *Heart of Darkness*. In keeping with the critical responses to the former, here, too, such narratological stratification elicits suspicious readings aimed at unmasking the various manipulations of the prime narrator. Robert Andreach's claim that Dr. Kennedy's "excess of rhetoric—repetition, questions, negatives—demonstrates that he cannot comprehend what he witnessed," is a claim easily applicable to the narrators of the longer fiction discussed above (262). If Myrtle Hooper suggests Dr. Kennedy "never attempts to represent Amy's point of view" (56), Jürgen Kramer takes the reading further still and argues that it is Dr. Kennedy who is at the heart of this narrative: "In truly Marlovian fashion, the teller dominates the tale: Dr. Kennedy feels prompted by some chance remark to tell this particular story, he tells it in his way, and the story as told serves his self-fashioning more than that of the story's protagonists" (10). Such critical responses to the story cohere with the claim that the diegetic border in Conrad's work serves as a site for the testing of moral and epistemological significances.

The story nevertheless departs from the examples read above. Unlike *Heart of Darkness,* here the multiplication of narrative frames (the framing of Dr. Kennedy's narration by that of an anonymous narrator) does not emerge as a destabilizing device. The two narrative frames provided do not offset one another through contradictory ideological or cultural commitments; the doubling of the frame does not result in the juxtaposition of two competing points of view. Yanko's story is introduced by two narrators that are wonderfully matched. Various critical analyses of Dr. Kennedy's narration show this doubling to be necessary nonetheless; we need to see Dr. Kennedy from the vantage point of another in order to tease out the motivations that might color his version of events and the way they are interpreted. Still, the oddity of the duplication of like frames demands some unpacking.

The story begins with a repetition of a voluntary homecoming. The unnamed narrator introduces Dr. Kennedy as a Navy surgeon who, having travelled the world, has finally decided to return to England. Such a return is repeated in the description of his own relation to the story: "A good many years ago now, on my return from abroad, [Dr. Kennedy] invited me to stay with him" (Conrad, "Amy Foster" 106). The doubling of the narrative frame here appears redundant. It does not pit one ideology against another, but juxtaposes two like-minded individuals who mirror one another's interpretation of the events. When the anonymous narrator comments that Amy Foster seems "a dull creature," Dr. Kennedy answers, "precisely" (107). There is nothing in the select exchanges between the two that contributes to our questioning of either perspective. Kramer points out the implied coordination between the two frames. He describes "an agreement between the two narrators" (7) on Amy's characterization and then adds:

> Responding to some of his visitor's casual questions, [Dr. Kennedy] attempts to tell Yanko and Amy's story as if he were a neutral observer capable of setting the record straight for once and all. And he is supported by his friend, the frame-narrator, who praises not only his wealth of experience, particularly of foreign countries, and his scientific intelligence, but also his "unappeasable curiosity." (8; quoting Conrad, "Amy Foster" 106)

In keeping with this coordination, there is no competing voice to question Dr. Kennedy's concluding remark, wherein Yanko is "cast out mysteriously by the sea to perish in the supreme disaster of loneliness and despair'" (Conrad, "Amy Foster" 142).

Some familiar signposts of difference between the two voices are nevertheless posited at the outset and should be noted. For example, the frame narrator says Dr. Kennedy "discoursed" (108), suggesting the kind of imaginative and ornamented or ideologically motivated language Conrad scholars know to treat with suspicion. In contradistinction, his own speech is modified with "listlessly" (107), an adjective suggestive of a different temperament commanding a different perspective. Such difference is nevertheless undermined when we see the extent of repetition that binds the two accounts. The "Greek tragedy" (107) of Dr. Kennedy's discourse is repeated in the "chariot of giants [. . .] of legendary proportions" in the anonymous narrator's listless account. The latter describes the men he sees as walking past slowly, "unsmiling, with downcast eyes, as if he melancholy of an over-burdened earth had weighted their feet, bowed their shoulders, borne down their glances" (110). Dr. Kennedy then reiterates the self-same image. The men are "as leaden of gait as if their very hearts were loaded with chains" (111). Where the multiplication of diegetic borders in *Under Western Eyes* and *Heart of Darkness* contributes to the destabilization of knowledge, the doubling of the narrative frame in "Amy Foster" establishes coherence.

Two complementary effects ensue. First, the two narrators' sympathy for Yanko and criticism of the people who misunderstand and mistreat him goes unchecked. As readers we are not left to unpack an obscure or convoluted message. Nor are we given the freedom to make of Yanko what we might. The multiplication of narrative frames serves to emphasize the implied author's message rather than obfuscate and muddle it.[7] A second outcome is that the framing device that serves to anchor our sympathies for Yanko is shown to be just as fixed as the parochial myopia of the people who abuse him in the story. Yanko is just as caged and boxed by the sympathetic narrators who assume responsibility for the representation of his muted voice as he is by the people of Colebrook. The sympathy offered Yanko's character is thus itself over-determined. Perhaps because of the stakes involved in the treatment of a Polish exile's encounter with an English community, Conrad here resorts to an embedded narrative technique not to validate the message through obfuscation but rather to clarify it through repetition. The modernist borders that we encounter elsewhere, boundaries that muddle, confuse, and thereby challenge our understanding are here bolstered up as a unifying, anchoring device that is designed to limit our vision. Rather than function on the strength of difference, such borders provide meaning through likeness and repetition. Recalling the Polish borders Conrad is reluctant to forsake in his dream of a united Europe, here, too, the borders of Yanko's experience must remain literal, clear and intact.

If "Amy Foster" is a psychologically motivated exception to the rule, *Heart of Darkness* and *Under Western Eyes* repeatedly demonstrate that the signposting of diegetic borders contributes not to the clarity of the message but to the obfuscations and limitations that demand we note and consider its contradictions. Narrative embedding in the first and the play on the oscillation between homodiegetic and heterodiegetic narration in the latter participate in the effort to sanction morally the greatest foes of reality through the multiplication of narrative frames—not the ridding or weakening of stylistic borders, but rather their proliferative assertion. The stratification of these texts is demanding on their readers; it testifies to the workings of a modernist border that continuously calls attention to itself as a site of frustration and confusion. The texts provide their readers with multiple borders and frames. These serve, in turn, as the signposts that will allow us to evaluate a character's moral mettle and tease out the implied author's message.

In *Heart of Darkness*, Marlow navigates the snags in his journey upriver towards Kurtz. But unlike the oblivious sailor sitting in Nietzsche's weak craft atop a stormy and limitless sea, Marlow is armed with a device that allows him to remain vigilant of the treacherous ground below. As he comments: "In this shadow we steamed up—very slowly, as you may imagine. I sheered her well inshore—the water being deepest near the bank, as the sounding-pole informed me" (Conrad, *Youth* 108). The device allows Marlow to be tethered and untethered at one and the same time; though lost in shadow he still senses his surroundings. Precariously positioned between an anonymous narrator's frame and his own diegetic darkness, Marlow himself becomes something of a sounding pole by which we might navigate the hidden depths of *Heart of Darkness*.

Conrad's texts are full of borders—but they are not very good for purposes of orientation; they obfuscate where we expect them to clarify. To read Conrad morally, soundly, is to submerge in the interstitial darkness while remaining cognizant of those borders that generate knowledge at the same time that they delimit it. We do so by identifying the sounding poles offered along the way and orienting ourselves accordingly. Such poles are not necessarily remarkable; they are not always unique. But, contrary to Woolf's dismissal, they are certainly very helpful.

NOTES

1. The paper is based on a talk given at the symposium "Placing Conrad: Space and Geography in Conrad's Fiction" held on February 17, 2018, at Senate House, London, in

honor of Professor Robert Hampson. The work presented here is part of an ongoing project on Conrad funded by the Israel Science Foundation.

2. Eagleton's assessment may be seen as a late expression of what Kate McInturff identifies as a trend in Conrad's critical reception already evident in comments made by Edward Garnett and John Galsworthy in 1908. As she writes, "The second trend in representations of Conrad's distinctiveness identifies that foreign element as precisely what is needed to reinvigorate an English Literature that has grown too insular" (McInturff 281).

3. It is beyond the scope of this paper to address the full range of expressions of national and cultural affiliation. Matters of language, faith, and geographical context are discussed here only in so far as they serve my analysis of how spatial coordinates correspond with questions of moral judgment.

4. There are many additional similarities between Kurtz and Laspara. To note just two by way of demonstration, like Kurtz, Laspara's eloquence is protean. As he reflects, "any subject could be treated in the right spirit, and for the ends of social revolution." Recalling also Kurtz's association with "The League for the Suppression of Savage Customs," Laspara mentions a friend in London who has gotten in "in touch with a review of advanced ideas" (Conrad, *Western Eyes* 287).

5. Mallios's interpretation of Conrad's excerpted letter in *The New Republic* offers a positive interpretation of Conrad's attitude to the faith, suggesting that the argument he makes in the latter "derives not from any 'criminal' assessment of Jewishness per se [...] but rather from Conrad's sense of the criminal intentions and effects involved in Harris's misidentification of him [...] as such" (112). In contrast, Adam Gillon takes Conrad's anti-Jewish prejudice as a given, the product of his cultural background. Regardless of this significant difference in their respective treatments of the matter, both relate the Jewish character back to the wider theme of exile. As Gillon writes: "that is why his attitude toward the Jews assumes added significance, as the heroes of Conrad's fiction usually 'do not belong' themselves; they are mostly social pariahs, outcasts, men alienated from the society of fellow humans" (42). Needless to say, the deterritorialized perception of Jewish identity is a well-established trope. In his historicist account of German-Jewish identity at the turn of the nineteenth century, Todd S. Presner distinguishes Goethe's desire for the "geographic mooring of a nationally grounded subject" and Kafka's experience, a token to "German/Jewish modernity" as it "emerges in a deterritorialized, non-national space in which mobility is variously mapped in the German language through narratives of travel" (67).

6. Hampson argues that such critique productively challenges an "early stereotype of modernism as the product of detached superior vision" ("Spatial Stories" 64).

7. This effect is complemented by the distinction between Marlow's and Dr. Kennedy's attitude towards the truth value of narrative. A student in one of my undergraduate seminars, Adva Kramer, notes that where Marlow opens his narrative with the comment "if we may believe what we read" (Conrad, *Youth* 49), Dr. Kennedy philosophizes that "there is a particle of a general truth in every mystery" ("Amy Foster" 106). Much like the contrasting effects of the embedded frames, *Heart of Darkness* emphasizes doubt where "Amy Foster" repeatedly calls readers to internalize a well-delivered moral.

WORKS CITED

Andreach, Robert. "The Two Narrators of 'Amy Foster.'" *Studies in Short Fiction*, vol. 2, 1965, pp. 262–69.

Armstrong, Tim. *Modernism: A Cultural History*. Polity, 2005.

Baxter, Katherine. "Speaking Foreign: Conrad and Modernist Multilingualism." *Studia Neophilologica*, vol. 85, no.1, 2013, pp. 17–28.

Conrad, Joseph. "Amy Foster." *The Nigger of the 'Narcissus,' Typhoon and Other Stories*, Dent, 1950, pp. 105–42.

———. "The Crime of Partition." *Notes on Life and Letters*, Dent, 1949, pp. 115–33.

———. *Youth, Heart of Darkness and the End of the Tether*, Dent, 1965.

———. "Prince Roman." *Tales of Hearsay and Last Essays*, Dent, 1955, pp. 29–55.

———. "The Romance of Travel." *Countries of the World*, edited by J.A. Hammerton, vol. 1, February 1924, pp. xviii–xxviii.

———. *Under Western Eyes*. Dent, 1947.

Eagleton, Terry. *Exiles and Émigrés: Studies in Modern Literature*. Chatto and Windus, 1970.

Gillon, Adam. *Joseph Conrad: Comparative Essays*. Edited by Raymond Brebach, Texas Tech University Press, 1994.

Gibson, Andrew. *Postmodernity, Ethics and the Novel: From Leavis to Levinas*. Routledge, 2001.

Hampson, Robert. "Conrad, the 'Polish Problem' and Transnational Activism. *Conradiana*, vol. 46, nos. 1–2, 2014, pp. 21–38.

———. "Spatial Stories: Joseph Conrad and James Joyce." *Geographies of Modernism*, edited by Peter Brooker and Andrew Thacker, Routledge, 2005, pp. 54–64.

Hooper, Myrtle. "'Oh, I hope he won't talk': Narrative and Silence in 'Amy Foster.'" *The Conradian*, vol. 21, no. 1, 1996, pp. 51–64.

Kerr, Douglas. "Conrad and the Immigrant: The Drama of Hospitality." *The Review of English Studies*, vol. 67, no. 279, 2016, pp. 334–48.

Kramer, Jürgen. "What the Country Doctor 'did not see': The Limits of the Imagination in 'Amy Foster.'" *Joseph Conrad: The Short Fiction*, edited by Daphna Erdinast-Vulcan, Allan H. Simmons, and J.H. Stape, Rodopi, 2004, pp. 1–11.

Mallios, Peter Lancelot. *Our Conrad: Constituting American Modernity*. Stanford University Press, 2010.

McInturff, Kate. "'The Heritage of Perception': Nation and Deracination in Early Conrad Criticism." *Conradiana*, vol. 37, no. 3, 2005, pp. 275–92.

Presner, Todd. S. *Mobile Modernity: Germans, Jews, Trains*. Columbia University Press, 2012.

Woolf, Virginia. "Mr. Bennett and Mrs. Brown." *Collected Essays*, vol. 1, Hogarth Press, 1966, pp. 319–41.

The Inheritors, H.G. Wells, and Science Fiction: The Dimensions of the Future

LINDA DRYDEN

NAPIER EDINBURGH UNIVERSITY

ABSTRACT

In 1901 H.G. Wells published *Anticipations*, a provocative speculation on the future course of technology and on how social and political systems might evolve. In the same year, Conrad and Ford published their collaborative novel *The Inheritors*, a fantasy involving a race of individuals from the Fourth Dimension, the Inheritors of the title, who propose to transform society very much along the lines suggested by Wells. This paper examines the similarities between Wells's predictions and the intentions of Conrad and Ford's Inheritors for the future of humanity to argue that *The Inheritors* is the authors' response to conversations they had with Wells in the years prior to his challenging thesis in *Anticipations*. The central argument is that Conrad and Ford wrote their novel as an imaginative rebuttal to Wells's more outrageous predictions.

KEYWORDS

Anticipations, *The Inheritors*, Fourth Dimension, Joseph Conrad, Ford Madox Ford, H.G. Wells, science fiction

On November 20, 1901, Wells wrote to his agent, J.B. Pinker, revealing that "Conrad came along today with *Anticipations* on the train. He doesn't like it in a friendly & respectful way & would like very much to go for it in two or three articles."[1] *Anticipations*, Wells's first non-fiction book, published as a volume earlier that month in *Fortnightly Review*, set out, among other things, his radical ideas for how to secure the future of humanity. Looking back over his career in *Experiment in Autobiography* (1934), Wells writes: "Now *Anticipations* was not only a new start for me, but, it presently became clear, a new thing in general thought" (645). This "new thing" contained such extraordinary and revolutionary proposals that it propelled Wells to Edwardian literary superstardom. The book was an immediate bestseller, and by mid-December 1901 Wells was urging Pinker to bring it out as a cheap paperback.[2]

In June of the same year William Heinemann had published the second collaborative effort of Joseph Conrad and Ford Madox Ford, *The Inheritors: An Extravagant Story*.[3] The novel plays with the Wellsian notion that fantastical events might effect a political and social transformation of Britain's very near future. Yet, unlike their friend Wells, who had begun to promote the potential for humanity to progress and to improve, to evolve into higher beings, Conrad and Ford envisioned an apocalyptic dystopia where humanity would be swept away by a race of people from a fourth dimension, the Inheritors of the title. The world promised by these Inheritors is ruled by a calculating, ascetic political class whose hyper-rational values and beliefs are poised to supersede Victorian sensibility, sensitivity, and what they regard as sentimentality.

As Max Saunders argues, the unnamed Fourth Dimensionist woman in *The Inheritors* is "a personification of very much that new rejection of any traditions of piety, altruism or restraint": "The novel poses its present—the present of the Boer War—as a crisis; the turn-of-the-century as a turning point" ("Empire" 132, 126). Robert Hampson elaborates on this when he asserts that in *The Inheritors* this turning point pivots on "the replacement of 'probity' and 'altruism' of the old-style Toryism by the new Toryism of Joseph Chamberlain, and the replacement of 'old-fashioned small enterprises' by ruthless individualism and the 'gigantic trusts' of monopoly capitalism" (68). *The Inheritors* is thus, in many ways, a "condition of England" novel, a timely, but flawed, meditation on Britain's social and cultural values as the new century dawns. In both fiction and non-fiction respectively, therefore, Conrad and Ford and their close neighbor H.G. Wells explore the direction humanity would take in the twentieth century. It is almost inconceivable that the three authors did not discuss these ideas during their regular visits to each other, but, as Wells's letter to Pinker proves, Conrad was not as enthusiastic as the general public about Wells's propositions.

The impact on *The Inheritors* of Wells's ideas about the future will be the main focus of this paper. Along the way, it will also unearth the traces of Wells's scientific writings inscribed in *The Inheritors*, demonstrating that Conrad and Ford were actively drawing on their friend's extraordinary imagination to create their own tale of a fantastic near future. However, the inevitable conclusion is that Conrad and Ford had a very different idea of what constitutes "progress," and that their novel in many ways represents a critique and rebuttal of some of Wells's more radical utopian visions as expressed in *Anticipations*.[4]

THE FOURTH DIMENSION

The idea of a fourth dimensional space was first articulated by Joseph-Louis Lagrange, an Italian mathematician and astronomer, in the eighteenth century. This idea of an unseen, undetected and undetectable spatial dimension to the universe began to take hold of the literary imagination in the nineteenth century. In his Introduction to *The Inheritors*, David Seed confirms that, following the publication of "Edwin A. Abbott's *Flatland* in 1884 and C. H. Hinton's *Scientific Romances* (1884–86), the term 'fourth dimension' had become sufficiently familiar as not to warrant explanation in itself" (xxii).[5] Nearly a decade later the possibility of a fourth dimension still mesmerized the general public. In 1893 W.T. Stead, journalist and champion of the occult, wrote: "we are on the eve of the Fourth Dimension; that is what it is!"[6] Stead's excitement is evidence of what Will Tattersdill describes as "the suggestion that we are on the verge of achieving some great new understanding about the universe, only previously hinted at" (94–5). And indeed, only three years later came the announcement of the discovery of X-rays, a scientific breakthrough that seemed to promise proof of other dimensions, of hidden worlds and alternative universes.

Saunders observes that the turn of the century was a time "notoriously beset with anxiety about the changes the future might bring," and thus *The Inheritors* was written against the backdrop of a "surge of futurological fiction" from the likes of William Morris and H.G. Wells, both of whom used the idea of dimensional travel to probe possible futures ("Empire" 131).[7] This was also a moment when significant scientific and technological discoveries and advances were being made, and *The Inheritors* displays a keen consciousness of this zeitgeist, most notably in its use of the possibilities unleashed by the discovery of X-rays and discussions about the possibilities of a fourth spatial dimension. The result is a novel that, in the words of Elaine L. Kleiner, "is an early attempt to codify the form one can now safely label 'science fiction'" (26).[8]

The fourth dimension is used in literature to explore the possibility of utopias, of potential futures, and the idea of parallel universes inhabited by beings like ourselves but with differing values and morals. This is made clear very early on in *The Inheritors* when the woman from the Fourth Dimension entraps the central character, Etchingham Granger, and reveals another plane of existence, beyond the very tangible, very visible Bell Harry Tower of Canterbury Cathedral:

> One seemed to see something beyond, something vaster—vaster than cathedrals, vaster than the conception of the gods to whom cathedrals were raised. The tower reeled out of the perpendicular. One saw beyond it, not roofs, or smoke, or hills, but an unrealized, an unrealizable infinity of space.
> It was merely momentary. The tower filled its space again and I looked at her. (8)

The idea of a fourth dimension is absolutely crucial to the central aim of Conrad and Ford's novel: an exploration of the values and beliefs that a humane society must adhere to in the face of progress.

"THE FIRST IDEA": *THE INHERITORS* AND H.G. WELLS

Neither Conrad nor Ford had considered writing scientific fantasies before embarking on *The Inheritors*, but they were both awed by the imaginative audacity of Wells's writing, and Ford confirms that *The Invisible Man* (1897), *The Sea Lady* (1901), "and two short stories called, the one *The Man Who Could Work Miracles* and the other *Fear*, made up at that date all the English writing that, acting as it were as a junta, we absolutely admired" (*Joseph Conrad* 43).[9] Ford's primary consideration in singling out these stories is form and expression but, like Conrad, he was also impressed by Wells's imagination, as were many of their contemporaries.[10] Indeed, Michael Sherborne notes that by the turn of the century Wells had become, despite his relative youth, a kind of figurehead for authors seeking new forms of literary expression:

> The south coast was home to several authors who did not fit naturally into the British Establishment and who found it agreeable to position themselves some distance from London and enjoy each other's mutual support, perhaps even reciprocal altruism. Ford Madox Hueffer later claimed that all the literary artists in England lived in a three-to-five-mile radius of Wells's house, looking up to him because of his "immense sales, and the gift of leadership." (138)[11]

Conrad and Ford were two such authors and Wells's proximity inevitably had an impact on *The Inheritors*, as an early reviewer for the *Daily Mail* on 19 July 1901 confirms: "it is interesting to learn that Mr. Conrad and Mr. Hueffer got the first idea of their book from a striking sentence of Mr. H. G. Wells" (Conrad and Ford, *Inheritors* 158). Writing to his agent, J.B. Pinker, just five days before this review, Conrad reveals, "There's a Daily Mail man coming to see me on Tuesday," confirming Conrad as the source of this account of "the first idea" (*CL* 2:341). Saunders is clear that the fourth dimension element of the book was not there in the original manuscript, speculating that Conrad may have "contributed the scientific notion" of another spatial dimension in *The Inheritors* (*A Dual Life* 118). Saunders notes that by October 6, 1899, "Ford had written enough of *The Inheritors* to try it out on Conrad: he drove over to the Pent 'with the manuscript of the opening chapters of the novel rather shyly in his pocket,'" and confirms that "as with 'Seraphina,' the suggestion of collaborating had come from Conrad" (120).[12] According to Ford, on reading the first chapter, Conrad declared: "What the devil is this? It is très, très, très chic! It is *épatant*. That's magnificent" (*Joseph Conrad* 133). Conrad was instantly struck by the modernity of Ford's subject matter, but he saw further potential in the material he had in hand. As Kleiner says, science fiction "is a 'mythologic' rather than a 'mimetic' literature in the sense that its subject matter involves the confrontation of human imagination with the unknown rather than the known" (26). Adding the concept of a fourth dimension thus transformed Ford's "mimetic" tale into one that was "mythologic" and thus, as Kleiner claims, Conrad was indeed involved in the emergence of the science fiction genre.[13]

Conrad and Ford's concept of beings from a fourth dimension resonates with the scientific advances and spiritualist speculations of the fin-de-siècle that were fuelling scientific fantasies, such as those of Wells. For, as Wells himself says of *The Time Machine* (1895), "the idea of treating time as a fourth dimension was, I think, due to an original impulse; I do not remember picking that up. But I may have picked it up, because it was in the air" (*Autobiography* 645). And of course, Wells was ever alert to futuristic possibilities, stating that in 1899 he "was already beginning to realize there might be better guessing about the trend of things" (645). As a result, he wrote *Anticipations*, a text that predicted the future of politics, society, and technology and "which sold as well as a novel" (646).

Conrad and Ford were also influenced by this zeitgeist dominated by concepts of the future and used these for their first published collaboration. The science fiction credentials of *The Inheritors* lie in its use of the idea of a fourth dimension, clearly a Wellsian influence. In *The Time Machine*, the Traveller asserts: "*there is no difference between Time and any of the three dimensions of Space except that our consciousness moves along it*" (8; original emphasis), and it is possible that this was the sentence that prompted "the first idea." Time, in Wells's sense, constitutes the fourth dimension, after the three dimensions.

However, Kleiner argues that Conrad and Ford conceived of the fourth dimension as different to that of Wells:

> Breaking with Wells's geometric model of the future extended like a line continuous from the present, Conrad and Ford chose to imagine the future somewhat like a kernel contained within the seed of the present, co-existing with the present as an alternative universe on a different plane in time, its inhabitants gradually, over time, attaining dominance over present forms of life. (29)

In fact other Wells tales, like "The Plattner Story" (1896) and "The Crystal Egg" (1897), had previously presented the concept of universes within universes that Kleiner notices in *The Inheritors*. It could be argued that Conrad's and Ford's debt to Wells operates on more than one level: their beings from the fourth dimension are also the "inheritors" of Wells's fertile imagination, early science fiction creations. Thus, while Conrad and Ford lacked Wells's scientific training, his agile stylistic simplicity, and his fearless self-belief, they were genuinely excited by the vivacity and unique subject matter of his writing, and this inspired them to attempt their own fantastic tale, one that Conrad, on receiving the manuscript in early 1900, described to Ford as "remarkably weird as a whole" (*CL* 2:234).[14] However, there are further, possibly even more fascinating correspondences with Wells that can be traced in *The Inheritors*.

X-RAYS, SCIENCE FICTION, AND *THE INVISIBLE MAN*

In the autumn of 1898, worried about financial security, Conrad travelled to Glasgow in search of a ship to command. While there he visited Dr. John Macintyre, an early radiologist, and had an X-ray of his hand. Over dinner the conversation turned to speculation about multiple universes, as he details in a letter to Edward Garnett on September 29, 1898:

> The secret of the universe is in the existence of horizontal waves whose varied vibrations are at the bottom of all states of consciousness. If the waves were vertical the universe would be different. This is a truism. But, don't you see, there is nothing in the world to prevent the simultaneous existence of vertical waves, of waves at any angles; in fact there are mathematical reasons for believing that such waves do exist. Therefore it follows that two universes may exist in the same place and in the same time—and

not only two universes but an infinity of different universes [. . .]. (*CL* 2:94–5)

Conrad's excitement reveals a genuine intellectual engagement and fascination with extra dimensional possibilities—as Wells says, "it was in the air" (*Autobiography* 645). Following Röntgen's discovery of X-rays in November 1895, news spread fast, reaching "the English press in the pages of *Nature* on 23 January, 1896" (Tattersdill 95). Anyone who had read *The Time Machine* would have felt that life was imitating art. X-rays, by making the flesh and viscera transparent, and revealing the body's osseous matter, proved that science could demystify magic. It took no great imaginative leap to move to the possibility of unveiling other dimensions. And, as Tattersdill argues, a "key characteristic of X-rays" for the general public in the immediate aftermath of their discovery was that "they were as well explained by the spiritualists as by the scientists": "to those who had been discussing spirit photography, invisible light, and worlds beyond human perception for years, the discovery would have seemed a valorisation rather than a surprise" (96). Indeed, in 1896, in his journal of psychical research, *Borderland*, Stead had speculated that the discovery of X-rays could actually lead to the possibility of a kind of mind-reading: "the presentation of our bones, or the matter of our brain, or the action of the heart, by the 'X' rays would be far transcended in importance, if it were once established that we could procure a permanent record of our passing moods and fancies."[15] In the midst of such feverish imaginings, the authors of *The Inheritors* must have felt that their fourth dimensionists were very much of the moment.

In his letter to Garnett about X-rays, Conrad describes the Scottish author Neil Munro, who was among their party in Glasgow: "[he] stood in front of the Röntgen machine and on the screen behind we contemplated his backbone and his ribs. The rest of that promising youth was too diaphanous to be visible" (*CL* 2:95). Griffin, Wells's invisible man, describes the process of becoming transparent thus:

I shall never forget that dawn, and the strange horror of seeing that my hands had become as clouded glass, and watching them grow clearer and thinner as the day went by, until at last I could see the sickly disorder of my room through them, though I closed my transparent eyelids. My limbs became glassy, the bones and arteries faded, vanished, and the little white nerves went last. I gritted my teeth and stayed there to the end. At last only the dead tips of the fingernails remained, pallid and white, and the brown stain of some acid upon my fingers. (*Invisible Man* 181–82)

Griffin explicitly denies that his process uses "these Röntgen vibrations," but he does reveal that it involves "two radiating centres of a sort of ethereal vibration," giving the invisibility process a scientific basis (172). Drawing on the X-ray, Wells fabricated a plausible explanation of the science behind this invisibility, exploiting a contemporary sensation to create the imaginatively brilliant scientific fantasy that had so impressed Conrad and Ford. Witnessing the effect of the X-ray on Munro, Conrad could not have failed to draw parallels with *The Invisible Man*, and no doubt reflected on how Wells had used an actual scientific discovery to create a fictional tour de force.

As Wells acknowledged, he had an astonishing ability to conjure stories about ordinary human beings in extraordinary situations: in this respect *The Invisible Man* is one of the most successful of his literary endeavors.[16] This creative facility was central to his narrative strategy, as he explains in respect of *The Time Machine* in *Experiment in Autobiography* (1934): "I had realised that the more impossible the story I had to tell, the more ordinary must be the setting, and the circumstances in which I now set the Time Traveller were all that I could imagine of solid upper-middle-class comfort" (516). The use of "ordinary" settings for extraordinary occurrences is one of Wells's most successful narrative devices, and it is a strategy that Conrad and Ford adopted when they planted their Fourth Dimensionists directly into Edwardian British society. Whether it be on the streets of London, or in the drawing rooms of literary figures, or on the hillsides of Canterbury overlooking the cathedral, their beings from another spatial dimension aim to infiltrate the everyday, and confront the ordinary with the extraordinary.

THE INHERITORS AND H.G. WELLS: TIME PRESENT AND TIME FUTURE

Granger's uncanny vision of Canterbury Cathedral at the beginning of *The Inheritors* involves a metaphorical sweeping away of all the monolithic structures and beliefs that have gone before, including, and perhaps especially, religious faith. As Saunders says, the woman's "ability to make Granger feel she has destabilized Canterbury Cathedral shows the power she represents over feudalism and the church, and faith in either" ("Empire" 133). The choice of Bell Harry Tower is symbolic: as the Dimensionists abolish human history, treating religions as mere totems, a new world order will emerge to eclipse the old.

In this opening sequence the authors directly challenge Wells's vision for the twentieth century as he was laying it out in *Anticipations*. On July 7, 1901, in a letter to Elizabeth Healy, Wells explains his prospectus for the book: it was "designed to undermine and destroy the monarch, monogamy, faith in God & respectability—& the British Empire, all under the guise of a speculation about motor cars & electrical heating" (*Correspondence* 1:379). The impending end of Victoria's reign and the dawn of a new century had caused much uneasy speculation, but for Wells it was an exciting opportunity, as Sherborne argues: "Wells sensed that the new century would be a contrasting age of instability, and he was eager to plunge into the flux" (147). With *The Inheritors*, Conrad and Ford also plunged into the uncertainty presented by a new century, but they countered Wells's optimistic prophesies with the chilling portentousness of the intentions of their Fourth Dimensionists.

The woman tells Granger that she comes from "the Fourth Dimension," a spatial plane once inhabited by his own forbears:

> "Your"—she used the word as signifying, I suppose, the inhabitants of the country, or the populations of the earth—"your ancestors were mine, but long ago you were crowded out of the Dimension as we are to-day, you overran the earth as we shall do to-morrow. But you contracted diseases, as we shall contract them,—beliefs, traditions; fears; ideas of pity . . . of love. You grew luxurious in the worship of your ideals, and sorrowful; you solaced yourself with creeds, with arts—you have forgotten!" (Conrad and Ford, *Inheritors* 10)

The woman's assessment of fin de siècle Britain as having grown "luxurious in the worship" of its ideals is a scornful reprimand to what the Fourth Dimensionists regard as humanity's "weakness" for religions and culture. She insinuates that humanity's decadence and self-indulgence have eclipsed the ascetic, hyper-rational approach to human affairs of their fourth dimensional forbears.

In a similar vein, at the end of the novel the woman explains her purpose to Granger in bald terms: "I had to sound the knell of the old order; of your virtues, of your honours, of your faiths, of . . . of altruism, if you like" (153). Art, human compassion, religious faith, romance: these are the concerns and attributes of the late-Victorians that both Wells in *Anticipations* and Conrad and Ford's Dimensionists seek to obliterate as though to purify or rationalize the world. George Hay speculates that the woman's words "could have come straight from the lips of Ayn Rand" (viii). Yet her words also echo those of Nietzsche and the apocalyptic writings of the Bible, and thus whilst the Fourth Dimensionist woman presents herself as a prophet, Granger is unmoved. For him it is like "listening to a parody of a scientific work recited by a phonograph" (9). The sterile distance invoked by the simile compounds the emotionless logic of the woman making her seem robotic, mechanistic.

By the time Conrad and Ford were writing *The Inheritors* in 1900, apart from *The First Men in the Moon* (1901) and *The Food of the Gods* (1904), the best of Wells's science fiction writing was behind him. In *Experiment in Autobiography* he pinpoints the moment that he turned to discursive works prophesying the future: "Along came the end of the century, just apt to my thoughts, and I arranged [. . .] to publish a series of papers discussing what was likely to happen in the new century" (645). These papers were to become *Anticipations*. Wells's attention now was on how to secure humanity's future, and how to ensure that future generations were biologically and intellectually "fit" for their environment, capable of physically evolving in line with Darwinian theories: later he even imagined the now uncomfortable possibility of the emergence of the Samurais of *A Modern Utopia* (1905). At the very moment that Conrad and Ford were writing an apocalyptic tale in which a super race threatened to eradicate humanity, Wells was arguing in *Anticipations* that humanity's very endurance was reliant upon its biological ability to evolve into just such a super race.

In *The Food of the Gods* Wells envisages the emergence of a race of giants, born out of a spectacularly disastrous attempt to create a "super food." The book ends with the giants' leader, Cossar, striking a heroic and defiant pose, "standing out gigantic with hand upraised against the sky":

> For one instant he shone, looking up fearlessly into the starry deeps, mail-clad, young and strong, resolute and still. Then the light had passed, and he was no more than a great black outline against the starry sky—a great black outline that threatened with one mighty gesture the firmament of heaven and all its multitude of stars. (317)

This recalls an image that Wells had used earlier in what he had hoped was a politically and scientifically visionary lecture, *The Discovery of the Future*, delivered at the Royal Institute in 1902 and published the same year. Wells ends this prophetic work by suggesting that humankind could evolve beyond its physical and earthly boundaries: "All this world is heavy with the promise of greater things, and a day will come [. . .] when beings, beings who are now latent in our thoughts and hidden in our loins, shall stand upon this earth as one stands upon a footstool, and shall laugh, and reach out their hands amid the stars" (94–5). For Wells, the future of humanity involves a search for a new space within which to develop, evolve, and improve. In *Discovery of the Future* and *The Food of the Gods* he argues that we need not be bound to the earth by our current physical form, that in the future we could attain to beings that are transcendent, beings that could defy the laws of gravity and find new and unforseen possibilities in the spaces of the starry heavens. Biologically, this was about as far-fetched an idea as Stead's belief in the possibilities of spiritualism. The last hundred years have nevertheless shown that humanity's endeavor to reach the stars may not be as far-fetched.

By introducing the cold, emotionless, and callously logical Fourth Dimensionists as the beings who will shape our future, Conrad and Ford pose moral questions about whether efficiency and pragmatics should be the primary considerations in terms of progress. Wells's assessment of his present Edwardian times is of a Britain mired in tradition, shackled to its history, and lacking the moral courage and intellectual muscle to challenge assumptions about social, political and religious truths. This, too, is the premise of the Inheritors in Conrad and Ford's novel, but its authors tackle these issues from the opposite moral position: their concern is that the Inheritors *do* have the capacity to challenge the status quo and manipulate the future. In one sense the Inheritors are exactly the beings that Wells imagines in *Anticipations*, a race that will eradicate Britain's long established traditions and culture and install a narrow, sterile populism. It is this prospect that dismays Conrad and Ford: they foresee apocalypse where Wells prophesies progress and transcendence.

The woman from the fourth dimension, with whom Granger becomes infatuated, describes the Inheritors' intentions:

> I heard the nature of the Fourth Dimension—heard that it was an inhabited plane—invisible to our eyes, but omnipresent [. . . .] I heard the Dimensionists described; a race clear-sighted, eminently practical, incredible; with no ideals, prejudices, or remorse; with no feeling for art and no reverence for life; free from any ethical tradition; callous to pain, weakness, suffering and death, as if they had been invulnerable and immortal. (*Inheritors* 9–10)

The inhabitants of the fourth dimension consider themselves superior to common, earthbound mortals. Here, rationality prevails and morality is redundant; all approaches to life in this space are governed by issues of practicality and efficiency. In the new utopia that Wells envisions in *Anticipations*, efficiency is paramount, and progress is dependent upon human evolution. As with the Inheritors, "the men of the new republic will not be squeamish either in facing or inflicting death" (*Anticipations* 324). The humanity of the future "will have an ideal that will make killing worth the while; like Abraham, they will have the faith to kill, and they will have no superstitions about death" (324).[17] As Wells had said to Elizabeth Healy, part of his intention in *Anticipations* was to "undermine and destroy" (*Correspondence* 1:379) faith in God, and thus the approach to life and death of the people of the new order will be without sentiment and without compassion. The attitude of these people will be strictly utilitarian: "they will naturally regard the modest suicide of incurably melancholy or diseased or helpless persons as a high duty rather than a crime" (*Anticipations* 324–25). Capital punishment, Wells argues, will be more expedient and humane than a life in prison. When it comes to non-European peoples, Wells is even more unflinchingly "practical." Of the "swarms of black and brown and dirty-white and yellow people, who do not come into the new needs of efficiency," he says, "I take it they will have to go," because the world is not "a charitable institution" (324–25).

In an uncompromising application of social Darwinism, Wells argues that the fault lies in these peoples' inability to adapt to the emerging new world: "So far as they fail to develop sane, vigorous, and distinctive personalities for the great world of the future, it is their portion to die out and disappear" (342). This is strong, distasteful, and unpalatable stuff. However, as Warren Wager points out, "to Wells's credit, he would soon abandon such thoughts"; and Sherborne confirms that within two years "Wells would be arguing against negative eugenics; within three defending black people against race prejudice; within four advocating the desirability of a multitracial society" (Wagar 90–91; Sherborne 152). For Sherborne, *Anticipations* is "both the starting point and the lowest point in Wells's career as a social thinker" (151–52). Provocative and driven by utilitarian considerations, the book marks a pivotal moment in Wells's career both as a novelist and as an influential public figure.

Anticipations was serialized in the *Fortnightly Review* between April and December 1901 and published in book form in November 1901. *The Inheritors* was published in June 1901. It therefore follows that neither Conrad nor Ford could have written *The Inheritors* as a response to *Anticipations*, but they would have had many discussions with Wells on the ideas contained therein, given that all three met up on a very regular basis in this period.[18] Indeed, it is almost certain that Conrad and Ford were incorporating concepts that they picked up in discussions with Wells, for the Inheritors are, in so many ways, the fictional embodiment of Wells's ideas in *Anticipations*. Wells's response to the challenges and possibilities of his own time are pragmatic, functional and, on the surface of it, rational, replete with an optimism born of his scientific background. His ideas are also a response to the possibilities offered by a new century and a new monarch. Deliberately or not, Conrad and Ford's novel is a rebuttal of some of the more outlandish pronouncements in *Anticipations*, a book that Wells maintains "can be considered as the keystone to the main arch of my work" (*Autobiography* 643). It is not surprising that he later labeled *The Inheritors* a "dead, witless book," and lampooned the novel, Ford, and Conrad mercilessly in *The Bulpington of Blup* (1932), possibly out of an enduring sense of pique at its critique of his own ideas (*Correspondence* 3:38).[19]

The fact that on its publication Conrad took exception to *Anticipations* and wanted to pen an article in response to it is further proof of the conflicting ideas that defined the widening intellectual and philosophical gulf between the two writers. The article was never written, but the previously unpublished letter quoted at the start of this paper adds more weight to the well-known comment by Hugh Walpole that on their last meeting Conrad had said: "the difference between us, Wells, is fundamental. You don't care for humanity but think they are to be improved. I love humanity but know they are not" (Rupert Davies, *Hugh Walpole* 168). And their differences did not just lie in their perceptions of humanity itself: humanity's legacy was a further point of divergence.

THROWING AWAY "THE TREASURE OF [THE] PAST"

The premise of both *The War of the Worlds* and *The Inheritors* is invasion. Conrad and Ford's Fourth Dimensionists will eradicate what they regard as decadent humanity:

> The Dimensionists were to come in swarms, to materialize, to devour like locusts, to be all the more irresistible because indistinguishable. They were to come like snow in the night: in the morning one would look out and find the world white; they were to come as the gray hairs come, to sap the strength of us as the years sap the strength of the muscles. As to methods, we should be treated as we ourselves treat the inferior races. There would be no fighting, no killing; we—our whole social system—would break as a beam snaps, because we were worm-eaten with altruism and ethics. (Conrad and Ford, *Inheritors* 12)

As Kleiner says: "the collaborators hypothesized, much as Bulwer Lytton had in *The Coming Race* (1871), that evolution was to be imagined not as orderly progression but rather as a process of 'weeding out' and exterminating unsuccessful life forms to make way for the dominance of existing stronger ones" (29). Against the voracity of locusts and the muffling pervasiveness of a blizzard, resistance is futile. In the face of such an implacable, determined invasion, humanity would be stripped of its life-affirming attributes, would wither and die in a bloodless, but nonetheless deadly, coup. One is reminded of the Martians' merciless destruction of the Home Counties in *The War of the Worlds*. The Inheritors come like snow in the night, muffling the existing world, while the Martians, similarly, spread their silent, black vapour like a deadly suffocating blanket: "the swiftly spreading coils and bellyings of that blackness advancing headlong, towering heavenward, turning the twilight to a palpable darkness, a strange and horrible antagonist of vapour striding upon its victims [. . .] and the swift broadening out of the opaque cone of smoke" (Wells, *War* 148–49). Like Wells and others before them, Conrad and Ford use the potential future extermination of humanity to challenge the complacency of the present and warn about the future.

Thus, when Granger realizes the enormity of the changes that the Dimensionists are initiating, he has another terrifying visionary moment of a different spatial dimension, this time on the streets of London:

> The sheer faces of the enormous buildings near at hand seemed to topple forwards like cliffs in an earthquake, and for an instant I saw beyond them into unknown depths that I had seen into before. It was as if the shadow of annihilation had passed over them beneath the sunshine. (Conrad and Ford, *Inheritors* 143)

This sense of the rending of the traditional fabric of British life also finds expression in Wells's aspirational ideas and utopian solutions in *Anticipations*, but to very different purpose. Wells believed that revolutionary change was necessary and inevitable: for him it was part of the relentless evolutionary pattern of the universe. By contrast, in conceiving their Fourth Dimensionists, Conrad and Ford warned that tackling the complex problems faced by the citizens of a new century required a respect for, and acknowledgement of, the interwoven fabric of the past, present and future, rather than a wholesale disposal of all that has gone before. For, as Conrad has Marlow say in *Heart of Darkness*: "the mind of man is capable of anything—because everything is in it, all the past as well as all the future" (38). The continuity and contingency that Conrad implies here is exactly what is threatened by the Inheritors.

In his letter to *The New York Times* of August 2, 1901, where he defends *The Inheritors*, Conrad clarifies what he and Ford were trying to do:

> Judge them as we may, the spirit of tradition and the body of achievement are the very spirit and the very body not only of any single race, but of the entire mankind, which, without the vast breadth and colossal form of the past would be resolved into a handful of the dying, struggling feebly in the darkness under an overwhelming multitude of the dead. (*CL* 2:347–48)

In an eloquent acknowledgement of the legacy the future inherits from the past, Conrad continues, "thus our Etchingham Granger, when in the solitude that falls upon his soul, he sees the form of the approaching Nemesis, is made to understand that no man is permitted 'to throw away with impunity the treasure of his past—the past of his kind—whence springs the promise of his future'" (*CL* 2:348). The letter is a long and impassioned expression of Conrad and Ford's vision in *The Inheritors*, and in many ways it is an optimistic affirmation of humanity's essential contradictions, contradictions which, for Conrad, make utopias of the type that Wells was beginning to advocate impossible.[20]

By contrast, as the new century unfolded, Wells advocated dispensing with the Victorian past and embracing a future in which humanity could attain to heights as yet unimagined because unleashed from the fetters of history and tradition. In *A Modern Utopia* (1905), the narrator, a cypher for Wells, is described as "always talking as though you could kick the past to pieces; as though one could get right out from oneself and begin afresh" (359). Dispensing with what Wells viewed as the stranglehold of tradition is a theme common to his speculative works post-*Anticipations*—he felt it was a way of enabling radical change. It was also another symptom of the widening gulf between Wells and Conrad, and the crux of their opposing views of history and the future as laid out in *Anticipations* and *The Inheritors*.

CONCLUSION

The intimate literary relations between Conrad, Ford, and Wells inevitably brings into focus the cross-currents in their respective works. For example, when the woman in *The Inheritors* "prophesied a reign of terror for us," Conrad and Ford deliberately echo Wells's invisible man, Griffin, who, as he becomes increasingly embattled and paranoid, announces his intention to declare war on the small county town of Burdock and "establish a Reign of Terror"; all three authors are, of course, conscious of references to the horrors of the French Revolution to which this phrase refers (*Inheritors* 12; *Invisible Man* 229). Even closer in historical terms, Conrad, in particular, had experienced at first hand the terror and the horrors perpetrated by the Belgians in the Congo.

Possibly, when they wrote *The Inheritors* and invoked and challenged ideas and themes from their discussions with Wells, the collaborators were hopeful that their influential neighbor and friend would be engaged with and stimulated by the debate that they provoked: nothing could have been further from the truth. In a letter to the editor of the *English Review* in the summer of 1920, Wells took the opportunity to outline his objections to Conrad and Ford's collaborations, concluding, "That dead, witless book, 'The Inheritors,' justifies my warnings. That and a second book, of which I forget the title—it was an entirely stagnant 'adventure' story, festering with fine language—were an abominable waste of Conrad's time and energy" (*Correspondence* 2:38).[21] This and his later lampooning of the novel in *The Bulpington of Blup* over ten years later prove that his disdain for *The Inheritors* was enduring.[22]

Conrad and Ford's collaboration on The Inheritors was neither a critical nor a commercial success. Its ironic treatment of political utopianism lacks Wells's deft narrative acuity, and his penetrating satiric touch. In the end, the novel suffers from obtuse arguments, a confusing plot, and frequent wooden and unconvincing dialogue. It does, however, bring to the fore the conflicting responses of authors to the radical changes of the emerging Edwardian age, responses that were to become even more polarized as Europe moved inexorably towards the devastating conflagration of the Great War. Conrad and Ford took their lead from Wells in using the chronotope of the fourth dimension to engage in a debate about the possibilities presented by the new century. For Conrad, Ford, and Wells, potential futures are thus imagined through the concept of another dimensional space where the imagination can have free rein to explore what could be without the limitations imposed by the known physical world.

NOTES

1. This letter is a transcript of an original previously owned by George Lazarus, but now, so far as is known, in other private hands. The only reference available at the time of writing is the following: [HGW to JBP, "20 11 01," typed transcription in folder W-P24b, identified as "Laz II 127"]. I am very grateful indeed to Charles Blair at the University of Illinois for bringing this to my attention and for providing the transcript to the letter and that mentioned in endnote 2 below. I have discussed this letter and several others between Wells and Pinker in a paper forthcoming in a special edition of *Conradiana*.

2. Wells's letter is unpublished and in the H.G. Wells collection at the University of Illinois (Laz II, 117).

3. Their first collaboration was on *Romance* (1903), which had been temporarily abandoned over plot difficulties, and they proceeded to write *The Inheritors* which appeared in print before *Romance*. See Ford, *A Personal Remembrance* 117–18.

4. In "Invading Other People's Territory: *The Inheritors*," Mario Curreli briefly discusses the Wellsian influences on the book and deftly demonstrates its debt to other Conrad tales, but gives no sustained discussion of the scientific fantasy elements of the tale.

5. Laurence Davies has traced the origins of the term "Fourth Dimension" even further back to the mathematical developments of the 1870s, particularly in the work of William Kingdon Clifford (Davies, "Ford's Early Fiction" 187–89).

6. W.T. Stead's "Throughth; Or, on the Eve of the Fourth Dimension" appeared in *Review of Reviews 7* in April 1893, p. 426. It is reprinted in Tattersdill 94.

7. Morris, of course, used the idea in his futurological novel, *News From Nowhere* (1890), and Wells began his literary career in 1895 with *The Time Machine*, perhaps the most influential novel to employ the idea of a fourth dimension in time.

8. Kleiner's article, written in 1973, is an important and seemingly overlooked contribution to the field of Conrad studies. It will feature prominently in this article by way of bringing it to the attention of those interested in Conrad's experimentation with genre, and with *The Inheritors* in particular.

9. Actually, Wells never wrote a story called "Fear." What Ford is referring to is a short story, "The Red Room," also known as "The Ghost of Fear" written in 1894 and published in 1896. It concerns a supposedly haunted room, and ends with the narrator declaring: "There is Fear in that room of hers—black Fear, and there will be—so long as this house of sin endures" (*The Plattner Story and Others* 178). Ford wrote one other tale directly inspired by Wells, his 1908 novel, *Mr. Apollo*, inspired by *The Sea Lady* (1902), but this is a fantasy rather than a tale influenced by science.

10. Cedric Watts is convinced that *The Time Machine* and *The Island of Doctor Moreau* (1896) "have left their mark on various Conradian texts, notably 'Heart of Darkness' and *The Inheritors*'" (62).

11. The comment about Wells's sales and leadership come from Ford Madox Ford, *Mightier than the Sword* 154–55.

12. *Romance* was originally entitled *Seraphina*, but the authors changed its title to signal their intention to offer a Stevensonian adventure-romance.

13. The title of Kleiner's article makes this clear from the start: "Joseph Conrad's Forgotten Role in the Emergence of Science Fiction."

14. Although it is not completely clear that in this letter Conrad is referring to *The Inheritors*, there is no other writing of Ford's, or for that matter Conrad's, at the time that would elicit such a response. I am thus assuming that it is their collaboration that is being referred to, and this is corroborated by Karl and Davies in their footnote to the letter.

15. W.T. Stead, "Psychic Photography," *Borderland* 3, no. 3, July 1896, p. 317. Reprinted in Tattersdill 105.

16. See Dryden 26–32.

17. A rather ironic assertion, since Abraham is traditionally the epitome of religious belief.

18. See Dryden 10–26.

19. See Dryden 262–67, for a full discussion of *The Bulpington of Blup*.

20. This idea of the essential contradictions that lie at the core of humanity is one of Conrad's passionate beliefs, one that defines the ultimate conflict between his view of humanity and that of Wells. See *Joseph Conrad and H.G. Wells*, chapter 5, for a fuller discussion of this debate.

21. The "second" book was, of course, *Romance*.

22. See *Joseph Conrad and H.G. Wells*, chapter 6, "The Shape of War and of Things to Come," for more discussion of Wells's response to *The Inheritors* in *The Bulpington of Blup*. It is also interesting to note that the Bulpington of the title is in some ways a satire on Ford and his views.

WORKS CITED

Conrad, Joseph. *The Collected Letters of Joseph Conrad*. Vol. 2, 1898–1902. Edited by Frederick R. Karl and Laurence Davies, Cambridge University Press, 1986.

———. *Heart of Darkness*. Edited by Robert Kimbrough, W.W. Norton, 1988.

Conrad, Joseph, and Ford Madox, Ford. *The Inheritors; An Extravagant Story*. Foreword by George Hay, and introduction by David Seed, Liverpool University Press, 1999.

Curreli, Mario. "Invading Other People's Territory: *The Inheritors*." *Conradiana*, vol. 37, nos. 1–2, 2005, pp. 79–100.

Davies, Laurence. "Ford's Early Fiction and 'Those Queer Effects of Real Life.'" *The Edwardian Fiction of Ford Madox Ford*, edited by Laura Colombino and Max Saunders, Rodopi, 2013, pp. 185–204.

Davies, Rupert Hart. *Hugh Walpole: A Biography*. Macmillan, 1952.

Dryden, Linda. *Joseph Conrad and H.G. Wells: The Fin de Siècle Literary Scene*. Palgrave, 2015.

Ford, Ford Madox. *Joseph Conrad: A Personal Remembrance*. Duckworth, 1924.

———. *Mightier than the Sword*. George Allen and Unwin, 1938.

Hampson, Robert. *Conrad's Secrets*. Palgrave, 2012.

Kleiner, Elaine L. "Joseph Conrad's Forgotten Role in the Emergence of Science Fiction." *Extrapolation*, vol. 15, 1973, pp. 25–34.

Saunders, Max. *Ford Madox Ford: A Dual Life*. Oxford University Press, 1996.

———. "Empire of the Future: *The Inheritors*, Ford, Liberalism and Imperialism." *The Edwardian Ford Madox Ford*, edited by Laura Colombino and Max Saunders, Rodopi 2013.

Sherborne, Michael, *H.G. Wells: Another Kind of Life*. Peter Owen, 2010.

Tattersdill, Will. *Science, Fiction, and the Fin-de-Siècle Periodical Press*. Cambridge University Press, 2016.

Wagar, W. Warren. *H.G. Wells: Traversing Time*. Wesleyan University Press, 2004.

Watts, Cedric. *Joseph Conrad: A Literary Life*. Palgrave Macmillan, 1989.

Wells, H.G. *An Experiment in Autobiography: Discoveries and Conclusions of a Very Ordinary Brain*, vol. 2, Faber and Faber, 1934.

———. *A Modern Utopia*. Chapman and Hall, 1905.

———. *Correspondence of H.G. Wells*. Vols. 1 and 3, edited by David C. Smith, Pickering & Chatto, 1998.

———. *The Discovery of the Future: A Discourse Delivered to the Royal Institute on January 24, 1902*. T. Fisher Unwin, 1902.

———. *The Food of the Gods, and How It Came to Earth*. Macmillan, 1904.

———. *The Invisible Man: A Grotesque Romance*. Harper & Brothers, 1897.

———. *The Plattner Story and Others*. Methuen & Co., 1897.

———. *The Time Machine: An Invention*. Henry Holt, 1895.

———. *The War of the Worlds*. William Heinemann, 1898.

Conrad and George Eliot: Imagining Time, Space, and Event in *Lord Jim* and *The Lifted Veil*

NIC PANAGOPOULOS

NATIONAL & KAPODISTRIAN UNIVERSITY OF ATHENS

ABSTRACT

This study draws thematic and narratological parallels between *Lord Jim* and *The Lifted Veil*, suggesting that Joseph Conrad's and George Eliot's philosophies and views on art were much closer than has hitherto been thought. In her uncharacteristic foray into gothic fiction, Eliot seems to have anticipated many of the modernist techniques usually associated with Conrad, such as the loss of narrative authority and spatiotemporal coherence on which realist conventions were based. This essay also analyzes Conrad's and Eliot's use of the veil motif to address ontological and epistemological problems raised by idealist philosophy such as the interdependence of object and subject and the impossibility of directly apprehending the world. The anticipated epiphanies resulting from lifting the veil in *Lord Jim* and *The Lifted Veil* are finally indistinguishable from psychological projection since they give access to merely another level of illusion rather than to any underlying truth.

KEYWORDS

Lord Jim, The Lifted Veil, narrative technique, modernism, realism, idealism, Joseph Conrad, George Eliot

Ever since Conrad compared his and George Eliot's "modern" quality in a letter to William Blackwood on May 21, 1902 (*CL* 2:418), a number of similarities have been noted between these two novelists' approaches to fiction. F.R. Leavis's 1948 thesis that Eliot's and Conrad's common preoccupation with form and technical originality placed them in the "great tradition" of the English novel (7) has since been revised by K.M. Newton who observes "significant anticipations of modernism" in Eliot's work (2). Jim Reilly also points to the relative failure of Conrad's and Eliot's forays into historical fiction as evidence for the nineteenth-century novel's "increasing impossibility of representing historical events" (2). The most pertinent comparative study of these novelists' work, however, may be Ridley Beeton's that singles out, amongst other affinities, their skill in deploying the "structural image," which is said to unify the narrative by "unobtrusively predicting ahead" or by "encouraging apprehension and retrospection" (84).

In the present essay, besides tracing thematic affinities between *Lord Jim* (1900) and *The Lifted Veil* (1859), I focus on the common structural image of the veil to suggest not only Conrad's possible indebtedness to Eliot but also the way Eliot's novella anticipates many of the modernist techniques that would become hallmarks of Conrad's fiction. One such proto-modernist element in *The Lifted Veil* is the novella's intrusive self-reflexivity that upsets the transparency of the conventions of realist writing. *The Lifted Veil* and *Lord Jim* are also characterized by a modernist rejection of conventional omniscience expressed by their narrators' unreliability. I am particularly interested in the constructedness of their spatiotemporal setting, the way these two texts locate time, space, and event not in the "real" world of Euclidean space and communal experience, but in the mental/textual space of consciousness. This displacement is justified in modernity by Kant's transcendental idealism as well as by the realization that, in the words of Bertrand Westphal, "even the most realistic map does not truly depict the space, but like literature, figures it forth in a complex skein of imagined relations" (x). In exploring such issues, I also highlight the way the proverbial image of lifting the veil in these two writers' artistic practice is subverted by a realization that the resultant disclosure is indistinguishable from psychological projection, since it gives access to merely another fictive terrain, a further level of illusion, rather than to any transcendent or underlying "truth."

In the mental geography mapped out by German Idealism, the figure of the veil, ubiquitous in nineteenth-century discourse, denotes the conceptual borderline between the physical and metaphysical domains. As Romanticism swept across Europe, metaphorical veils began appearing everywhere, encouraging readers to imagine all kinds of semi-concealed wonders lying just beyond their mental reach.[1] In the words of Simon During, lifting the veil promised "communication between the natural world and a veiled supernatural order separated from everyday life by a barrier which is also a threshold" (37). The *terra incognita* behind the veil was visited during this era using a variety of different cognitive tools—artistic, philosophical, occult, and pseudo-scientific—with the process of unveiling resembling a kind of frenetic colonization of the unknown, akin to the appropriation of unclaimed regions of the globe by the British Empire. In an era when human potentialities seemed unbounded and knowledge was galloping apace in all fields, no space real or imagined could be allowed to remain unexplored, uncharted, and unclassified by the penetrating gaze of *homo rationalis*. At the same time, doubts concerning the moral and epistemological limits of the human mind inherited from the eighteenth century were aggravated by the seemingly irresistible march of scientific progress during the Victorian era, resulting in a feeling of cultural unease, comprised of equal parts excitement and apprehension.

The figure of the veil was first associated with the spatiotemporal and ethical spheres in Immanuel Kant's *Critique of Practical Reason* (1788):

> Two things fill the mind with ever new and increasing admiration and awe, the more often and steadily we reflect upon them: the starry heavens above me and the moral law within me. I do not seek or conjecture either of them as if they were veiled obscurities or extravagances beyond the horizon of my vision; I see them before me and connect them immediately with the consciousness of my existence. (161)

Before writing this passage, which locates the natural and moral order within consciousness, Kant had initiated a momentous paradigm shift in the *Critique of Pure Reason* (1781, 1787) that would subsequently divorce science from metaphysics and set the epistemological grounds for late modernity. In the First Critique, he had argued that time, space, and causality, rather than constituting qualities of the empirical world, were fundamental categories of cognition, effectively concealing the "thing-in-itself" behind a "veil of ignorance" (Limnatis 43). According to Kant, whatever unmediated reality may consist of we cannot know it, since we are unable to penetrate the veil and determine whether objects possess spatial and temporal properties in themselves (*Pure Reason* xxxvi). This new paradigm transformed mathematics—the basis of the natural sciences—into little more than a cerebral map superimposed onto an inaccessible ontological terrain. Henceforth, the only certain knowledge which was available for the human subject was knowledge of the mind and its processes; the physical world itself could only be imagined and speculated upon.

Given Eliot's keen interest in the history of ideas,[2] it should not surprise us that the veil image also features in the work of the thinkers with whom she was most familiar. Friedrich Schleiermacher (1768-1834), one of the forerunners of Higher Criticism and a pivotal figure of German Romanticism whom Eliot mentions in a letter of 1851, characteristically writes that, although "a heavy veil conceals every man's destiny," for a determinist who persists in viewing the self from the outside "Freedom seems to him nothing but an illusion, spread like a veil over a hidden and uncomprehended necessity" (21). David Friedrich Strauss's *The Life of Jesus,* which Eliot translated in 1846, is another case in point. Besides its various references to the temple veil that was rent upon Christ's death, this work also employs the figure of the veil in its metaphorical sense of an illusion-producing mechanism that serves to conceal a deeper reality. Strauss thus outlines the process whereby historical elements in the Bible are "embellished by the creations of the imagination, in which the original fact or idea is almost obscured by the veil which the fancy of the poet has woven around it" (28). Furthermore, in *The Essence of Christianity,* which Eliot translated in 1854, Ludwig Feuerbach describes his aim as the unmasking of erroneous systems of belief with a view to disclose the "unveiled, naked truth" (xxxiv).

If the veil image recurs frequently in the writing of the Higher Critics, for Conrad's favorite philosopher it constituted a crucial metaphor for the entire phenomenal world. In the opening pages of the encyclopedic *World as Will and Representation* (1818, 1848), Arthur Schopenhauer introduces the reader to the Hindu concept of Māyā,

> the veil of deception, which blinds the eyes of mortals, and makes them behold a world of which they cannot say either that it is or that it is not for it is like a dream; it is like the sunshine on the sand which the traveller takes from afar for water, or the stray piece of rope he mistakes for a snake. (8)

The projections which make up the empirical world are deemed equally true and false in this passage because they are spatiotemporally present, but also misconstrued by the subject in the manner of a mirage or a misidentification. As Indu Sarin explains, "since the object is negated, it cannot be real. But it cannot be unreal because it was perceived to be real though by mistake" (145). Schopenhauer's espousal of this concept clearly made a strong impression on Conrad, who writes in a letter to W.L. Courtney in December 1897, "there is joy and sorrow; there is sunshine and darkness—and all are within the same eternal smile of *the inscrutable Maya*" (*CL* 1:421). In accordance with Eastern philosophy, Schopenhauer views the veil as conducive to sensual as well as mental error. Thus, like the philosophers that had influenced Eliot, he considers it an obstacle to a clear understanding of the world and something to be overcome—not through scientific methods, however, but through aesthetic contemplation and renunciation of the will.

Schopenhauer's Orientalism led him to posit a Buddhistic nothingness as lying behind the veil of illusion, an absence of meaning in life. Such a pessimistic worldview is often echoed in Conrad's letters whenever the image of the veil appears. Thus, Conrad wrote to Marguerite Poradowska on November 5, 1893, "you who describe things and men, and consequently have raised a corner of the veil, know very well there are moments when the mind slumbers, the months slip away, when hope itself seems lost" (*CL* 1:131). The references to the veil that are found in Conrad's non-fiction, however, support Nietzsche's contrary thesis outlined in *The Birth of Tragedy Out of the Spirit of Music* (1872). There, rather than facilitating enlightenment through the lifting of the veil of Māyā, art as "the *good* will to appearance" is said to help counteract the disillusioning effects of knowledge and sustain our will to live (Nietzsche, *Reader* 131).[3] Thus, in "An Observer of Malaya" (1898), Conrad writes that "like faith, enthusiasm, or heroism, art veils part of the truth of life to make the rest appear more splendid, inspiring, or sinister" (*Notes* 51). An even more explicitly Nietzschean position can be found in "The Life Beyond" (1910) where Conrad translates the Invocation of the sage, Sar Paladan, from French as follows:

> O Nature, indulgent Mother, forgive! Open your arms to the son, prodigal and weary. I have attempted to tear asunder the veil you have hung to conceal from us the pain of life, and I have been wounded by the mystery. . . . . Oedipus, half way to finding the word of the enigma, young Faust, regretting already the simple life, the life of the heart, I come back to you repentant, reconciled, O gentle deceiver! (*Notes* 59)

This passage is unusually mystical for Conrad, summarizing as it does Nietzsche's anti-rationalist message in *The Birth of Tragedy*, while also echoing the moral of Eliot's *The Lifted Veil* spoken by its protagonist: "I thirsted for the unknown: the thirst is gone. O God, let me stay with the known, and be weary of it: I am content" (6).

In *The Lifted Veil*, Eliot broaches some of the most controversial issues of her day, such as degeneracy, clairvoyance, spiritualism, and vivisection. The veil in the title, together with the related terms "shroud" and "curtain," refers to two different but interrelated barriers or thresholds that are traversed during the course of the story. The first is the Kantian veil of time and space which the protagonist can penetrate on account of his extrasensory perception, while the second is the veil separating the living from the dead which is lifted at the end of the novella when Bertha's maid is momentarily revived using blood-transfusion. However, Latimer's involuntary ability to perceive other people's mundane and petty thoughts as well as foresee his own death isolates him socially and deprives him of what the novella presents as the salutary mystery of existence. Mrs. Archer's revivification, instead of opening up fascinating vistas into the other world, discloses her mistress' very worldly plot to poison her husband. This gloomy tale was written shortly after the death of Eliot's estranged sister, Chrissey, which the author confessed had deprived her of "the possibility of many things towards which [she] looked with some hope and yearning in the future" (Eliot, *George Eliot's Life* 3:214). Just as in *Middlemarch* (1859) we are encouraged to feel "grateful that human beings cannot hear the squirrel's heart beat or the grass grow" (Eliot 226), *The Lifted Veil* suggests that the ability to see beyond the veil, either by scientific or intuitive means, constitutes not a blessing but a curse. This conclusion, however, can be said to conflict not only with the rational positivism of the Higher Critics whom Eliot admired, but also with Eliot's oft-stated belief that moral growth depends on "our ability to imagine and understand another's state of mind" (Anger 80), aligning the author more with Conrad's fin de siècle pessimism than with the optimistic Victorian scientism with which she is usually associated.

Lord Jim can also be read as a story which revolves around the protagonist's disillusionment and isolation. From the training-ship incident to the final debacle in Patusan, Jim gradually discovers in the words of the oracular Stein that he is "not strong" or "clever enough" to make his "dream come true" (Conrad, *Lord Jim* 213). Recalling Nietzsche's critique of the rationalistic tendency in modern culture, it is not mortality and human fallibility themselves which prove the protagonist's undoing in *Lord Jim*, but his awareness of them. The more self-knowledge Jim acquires, the more isolated he becomes, until, finally embracing what he sees as his "fatal destiny" (410), he abandons humankind altogether for "his own world of shades" (416). Jim's penultimate disenchantment is signaled by the realization that "He had retreated from one world, for a small matter of an impulsive jump, and now the other, the work of his own hands, had fallen in ruins upon his head" (409). Recalling the "closed secret" of Bertha's face that is described in *The Lifted Veil* as the "shrine of a doubtfully benignant deity which ruled" Latimer's fate (Eliot 26), the veiled figure in *Lord Jim* symbolizes Jim's heroic opportunity which is said to sit "veiled by his side like an Eastern bride waiting to be uncovered by the hand of the master" (Conrad 244): for both protagonists, nemesis attends the unveiling of these brides' faces. Although Jim's story contains more salutary elements than Latimer's, Eliot's 1878 epigraph to *The Lifted Veil* which emphasizes the dangers of knowledge and the importance of maintaining community, could also apply to Conrad's protagonist:

> Give me no light, great Heaven but such as turns
> To energy of human fellowship;
> No powers beyond the growing heritage
> That makes completer manhood.

Inversely, as the confession of a dying man who has no one but the reader to entrust his secrets to, *The Lifted Veil* also recalls the theme of solidarity affirmed through story-telling implicit in the epigraph to *Lord Jim*.

Besides such thematic links, *The Lifted Veil* also foreshadows many of the modernist techniques that would later be associated with Conrad's work. The narrative of Eliot's novella is confined to Latimer's monological first-person account of his life story—something not unusual for nineteenth-century fiction. What is innovative, however, is the way in which the narrative systematically undermines its own authority, not allowing the reader to decide whether the psychosomatically fragile Latimer is faithfully reporting actual events, unconsciously relating false memories, or telling downright lies. As Jill Galvan writes, "we have much reason to question the real existence of Latimer's occult abilities and hence his reliability as a narrator" (242). Such ambiguity is, of course, integral to fiction itself, but also particularly significant in relation to the novella's occult subject matter which, albeit fashionable at the time, was likely to have been dismissed by the conservative readers of Blackwood's *Edinburgh Magazine* "as matters of self-suggestion in nervously disordered minds" (Galvan 243).[4] The ostensibly objective narrative in *Lord Jim* is limited to the first four chapters of third-person omniscient narration which was meant to form part of the short story based on the *Jeddah* affair that Conrad had initially envisaged writing for *Blackwood's*. The subsequent forty-one chapters consist of a collage of mediated and embedded reports which draw attention to their provisional and highly subjective nature. Conrad juxtaposes the different narrative modes and media through which Jim's story is told—objective, subjective, written, and oral—so as to undermine the authority of the one with the other. Consequently, both *The Lifted Veil* and *Lord Jim* are tales premised on a modernist loss of authority which arises primarily from their narrators' unreliability and subjectivity.

The figure of the veil contributes to the modernist topos of epistemological doubt by featuring in the narratives as a figure of deception rather than truth so that the visions seen by the protagonists when lifting various kinds of veils are often indistinguishable from daydreams or hallucinations. Latimer's clairvoyant intimations may simply be the sickly projections of a jaundiced mind. Terry Eagleton has observed that "Latimer's empathy with other minds isn't easy to distinguish from a mere projection of his own arrogance, anxiety and aggressivity into them" (57). Similarly, Jim's catastrophic previsions regarding the fate of the pilgrims on the *Patna* may be nothing more than products of fear, serving to justify subconsciously his anticipated abandonment of duty: as Marlow relates, "Each time he closed his eyes, a flash of thought showed him that crowd of bodies laid out for death, as plain as daylight" (Conrad, *Lord Jim* 105). It may also not be a coincidence that the dreamy protagonist of Eliot's novella, forced by his father to study scientific subjects which he hates and impeded by his sickly constitution from engaging in conventional masculine pursuits, resorts to imaginative escape. Latimer's unproductive "condition of poetic genius" (Eliot, *Lifted Veil* 24) may thus be the self-justification of a narcissistic personality unwilling to adapt to its surroundings and perform the role expected of it. Furthermore, for both protagonists, seeing visions is often likened to somnambulism, with Latimer asking himself whether he is dreaming (16) and "the line dividing [Jim's] meditation from a surreptitious doze on his feet" on the *Patna* said to be "thinner than a thread on a spider's web" (Conrad, *Lord Jim* 25). Escapist tendencies are clearly indicated, and just as Jim flees physically and mentally further and further into illusion symbolized by the East and the setting sun, Latimer, after Mrs. Archer's revelations about his murderous wife, becomes a wanderer in foreign countries before ending up in Devonshire to finally feature in his long-anticipated death scene (Eliot, *Lifted Veil* 69).

Another proto-modernist element in *The Lifted Veil* is its treatment of time, the consciousness of which is often regarded as one of the distinguishing features of modernity.[5] The flashbacks in Eliot's novella are fairly conventional for gothic fiction. However, Latimer's powers of clairvoyance mean that the flashes forward are part-fictive, part-literal, since the protagonist-narrator of *The Lifted Veil* is able to foresee events before they occur. Thus, if we combine the flashes forward in the tale with the flashes back, the convoluted chronologies which emerge disrupt the readers' ability to construct a cogent linear trajectory. An example of the way time seems to melt in Eliot's novella, as in a Salvador Dali painting, can be seen in the unexpected appearance towards the end of chapter 2 of Latimer's old friend, Charles Meunier, which provokes the following remark from the protagonist: "I too felt as if his presence would be to me like a transient resurrection into a happier pre-existence" (61). Such noteworthy departures from the realist narrative mode break the conventions of nineteenth-century fiction by undermining the distinction between perception and narration, or the conceptualization and the actualization of an event.

A case in point is the proleptic representation of the protagonist's death in the beginning of the novella, which strikes us as temporally ambiguous since the date prophesied for it, "20th of September 1850," is "undecidably past, present, and future at any 'moment' or 'point' in Latimer's narrative" (Redfield 162). The fact that Latimer can narrate his own death with absolute certainty suggests that, like Bertha's maid at the end of the novella, the protagonist-narrator of *The Lifted Veil* is in a manner returning from the dead to tell his tale before finally being consigned to oblivion. Thus, not only is the relative degree to which Latimer is alive or dead brought into question, but if Latimer can offer us an accurate description of an event that has yet to take place, that event must initially be regarded as imaginary, regardless of whether it is subsequently realized or not. Eliot's spectral narrator is able both to relate past experiences retrospectively and mentally to construct future ones prospectively, undermining the distinction between these two kinds of activity.

Conrad's celebrated narratological dislocations in *Lord Jim* can also be said to produce a spatiotemporal *mise en abyme*, with crucial events either not being narrated at all, or appearing shadowy by being narrated through a number of media. Our first view of Jim is as a disgraced water-clerk followed by a flashback to his training in the merchant navy. This leads chronologically to the run-up to the Patna incident which is, however, unnaturally interrupted at the point where the ship hits the submerged obstacle and followed by the flash-forward account of the Official Inquiry, the intervening time being slowly filled in by Jim's evidence in court as well as Marlow's interviews with Jim and the French Lieutenant. As Fredric Jameson points out in *The Political Unconscious*, "the first half of *Lord Jim* [. . .] approaching its narrative presence, its anecdotal center, at once denies the possibility of such presence and spills us over into yet further sentence production and the further frustration of presence affirmed and denied" (211). Indeed, the central (non-)event in the novel, the *Patna*'s staying afloat despite its apparently perilous condition, is only revealed analeptically many chapters after the narration of its abandonment by the crew. Thus, besides a psychological device designed to produce suspense through protracted delayed decoding, the narratological dislocations which characterize *Lord Jim* are also a means of subverting the notion of objective time, space, and causality. It is not only up to the reader to participate in the construction of meaning in the text, but also to perceive the contingent and provisional nature of any meaning thereby produced.

The effect is heightened by the rhetorical strategies employed in the novel. As in *The Lifted Veil*, Conrad's novel begins with the protagonist not quite dead yet: Jim's burial is prefigured in the very first sentence of the novel where he is described as a little "under six feet" (*Lord Jim* 3), an ironic syntactical inversion of the idiomatic "six feet under." This rhetorical device is typical of the way tragic narratives presuppose the death of the protagonist which is often foretold at the beginning in order to heighten the fatefulness of the story. However, although it takes the narrative forty-five chapters from its initial tragic premonition to arrive at Jim's melodramatic death in Patusan, the overwhelming majority of the almost 130,000 words devoted to telling his life story comprises just that: words piled on words in abeyance of reality. Jameson associates this aspect of the novel with *écriture*, identifying it as "an aestheticizing strategy" that "seeks to recode or rewrite the world and its own data in terms of perception as a semi-autonomous activity" (218). Jameson concludes that *Lord Jim* constitutes "a kind of reflexive or meta-text—in that its narrative construes the 'event' [as] the analysis and dissolution of events" (246).

It is not events themselves, but their mental/textual inscription and reproduction that preoccupy Conrad, as they do Eliot in *The Lifted Veil*. The self-reflexive interest of the narrative is signaled in both works by a corresponding emphasis on reading and writing. The first time we see Latimer, he is sitting at his desk preparing to relate his life story to us, while his death is anticipated to take place at the very same writing-desk a month later: his entire life is thus circumscribed by textual inscription and endlessly repeated. As Joy Johnson remarks, "Eliot's construction of a continually looping text in *The Lifted Veil* undercuts the dichotomy between separate spiritual and physical realms. [. . . .] Latimer is a narrator entrapped within his own text" (23). Similarly, Jim's career can be said to begin by his reading of "light holiday literature" and end with his aborted attempt to write a letter after the massacre of Dain Waris' party, which is likened by Marlow to "the aimless startled cry of a solitary man confronted by his fate" (Conrad, *Lord Jim* 409). This biographical detail is itself imparted via Marlow's missive to the privileged man, which also contains a reference to the last letter that Jim received from his father: Jim's whole life is summed up in these three letters within letters. Moreover, like the cyclical narrative of *The Lifted Veil* in which "the same text is repeated within the previsions and the actual occurrence" (Johnson 5), various important scenes are explicitly doubled in *Lord Jim*, while the protagonist himself is endlessly refracted in the extended meta-commentary on the Patna incident, as though in a hall of mirrors. These systematic repetitions/reflections in Conrad's novel, like Latimer's "double consciousness" (Eliot, *Lifted Veil* 35), besides emphasizing the inescapability of character, point to an irreducible plurality in events and their concurrence in physical and psychic space simultaneously.

Recalling the way the modernist *Lord Jim* is obsessed with the mechanics of story-telling, Eliot uses *The Lifted Veil* to explore a variety of narratological issues while touching upon the philosophical problem of free will vs. determinism. Firstly, Latimer's clairvoyance, a figurative enactment of realist omniscience, allows him to transcend the cognitive limitation of a mere protagonist-narrator and entertain the omniscience of an author-figure. In fact, Latimer possesses an extreme version of what Eliot called her "double consciousness" (*George Eliot's Life* 2:241), comprising a heightened sensitivity to external stimuli and an ability to access other minds and dimensions at the same time as being fully immersed in her own. Interesting questions of narrative possibility and foreclosure are thus raised, for, although Latimer has foreknowledge of what the characters of *The Lifted Veil* will do, this does not negate his own freedom to act differently at any point, pushing the tale in any number of alternative directions to the one it finally takes. We are invited thereby to adopt the paradigm of fictive teleology in viewing the protagonist-narrator of *The Lifted Veil* who emerges as simultaneously the author of his own life and a mere character among other characters playing his part to the end. This also recalls the way Jim feels that he goes to "conquer the fatal destiny itself" (Conrad, *Lord Jim* 410) at the end of the novel, when to Jewel he seems to be passively and pointlessly surrendering to Doramin's wrath. While the tension between determinism and indeterminism[6] is played out in the protagonists' illusory foreknowledge, a close reading of the veil image in these two novels shows that its relation to the truth is not only that of deception, but also, as Schopenhauer proposes, one of illumination. Yet in both cases, the result is negative, for Latimer's and Jim's previsions engender either debilitating certainty or dangerous illusion.

Besides his prophetic powers, the protagonist of *The Lifted Veil* also possesses the ability to visualize places he has never been to—what subsequently came to be called "distant viewing"—so that both time and space seem "foldable" to him. At one point in the story, Latimer has vivid images of Prague and later confirms their accuracy by visiting the city bodily. Approaching the end of his life, he recounts having mentally visited dozens of such dreamy locales made up "of strange cities, of sandy plains, of gigantic ruins, of midnight skies with strange bright constellations, of mountain-passes, of grassy nooks" (Eliot 59). This implies that the more disillusioned Latimer became by human nature, the more he resorted to imaginative escape, in the fashion of a Romantic poet. The literalization of the theme of escape appears in *Lord Jim* in the aftermath of the *Patna* incident, when Jim is seen in various Eastern ports "in Bombay, in Calcutta, in Rangoon, in Penang, in Batavia" (Conrad 5) just keeping body and soul together until he can find some opportunity to regain his lost honour. What connects these so-called "halting places" (5) which Jim passes through on his way to Patusan with the Romantic settings that Latimer visualizes is the notion of de-substantiation: like Latimer's Romantic visions, they represent little more than a randomly connected series of exotic impressions of the East without independent significance or ontological status outside the consciousness of the Western protagonist. The same, of course, is true of Patusan which, regardless of its complex socio-political reality, is presented by the narrative as Jim's personal landscape painting and appropriately de-historicized: "The stream of civilisation, as if divided on a headland a hundred miles north of Patusan, branches east and south-east, leaving its plains and valleys, its old trees and its old mankind, neglected and isolated" (226). Thus, setting is self-reflexively presented in *The Lifted Veil* and *Lord Jim* as merely the raw material for art.

The tendency of both narratives to transcend or cancel objective space can be said to find its psychological correlative in their protagonists' unusual powers of visualization that are explicitly associated with the poetic imagination. When the hypervisionary Latimer first becomes aware of his extra sensory perception, he wonders whether it were not due to "the poet's nature" (Eliot, *Lifted Veil* 17) in him, and whether it were not through a similar act of "spontaneous creation" that "Homer saw the plain of Troy, Dante saw the abodes of the departed, Milton saw the earthward flight of the Tempter" (17). Jim, an "imaginative beggar" (Conrad, *Lord Jim* 83) who possessed the "faculty of beholding at a hint the face of his desire and the shape of his dream" (175), is similarly presented as an artist figure in Conrad's novel. Faced with the challenge of politically restructuring Patusan, he is said to have "left his earthly failings behind him, and there were a totally new set of conditions for his 'imaginative faculty' to work upon" (218). However, imagination, "the enemy of men, the father of all terrors" (11) is notoriously dangerous in Conrad's world and, on the *Patna*, Jim's "swift and forestalling vision" (96) resembles Latimer's poetic sensibility without the poet's voice (Eliot, *Lifted Veil* 12), making far-off or non-existent dangers appear dangerously close. The involuntary or uncultivated poetic sensibility, besides being fraught with dangers, is also associated with disease in *The Lifted Veil* and *Lord Jim* and makes its presence felt in the protagonists following a period of convalescence. Thus, it is after recovering from a long illness in Geneva that the nineteen-year-old Latimer first discovers he can distantly view cities to which he has never been. Similarly, it is after recovering from the falling spar incident that Jim is motivated to join the *Patna*, upon which his waking visions begin to impose themselves on his psyche with ever-greater force. The nature of these visions, like the imagination which gives rise to them, are viewed as double-edged in these works, both morally damning and psychologically consoling.

In conclusion, Conrad's writing sometimes implies the existence of an invisible reality underlying the world of the senses which good art has the power to reveal. We see this in Conrad's letter to Helen Watson of January 27, 1897, where he says that in *The Nigger of the "Narcissus"* (1897) he "had tried to get through the veil of details at the essence of life" (*CL* 1:334), a claim also echoed in the Preface to that work. At other times, as in *The Lifted Veil* and *The Birth of Tragedy*, art is seen as vital in maintaining the veil in place and keeping the subject enchanted, in contrast to modernity's tendency of "unveiling [. . .] those heartless secrets which are called the Laws of Nature" (Conrad, *"Narcissus"* 5). At such times, the fiction seems to suggest that behind the veil lies not some deeper, transcendent reality, but the void of uncreated matter, the Buddhist nothingness which Western existentialism also posits as the ultimate ground of being. The implied primordial domain from which all things derive and to which they return is identified in Conrad's fiction with the darkness, and negatively charged. In *The Lifted Veil* too, Latimer's Cassandra-like gift of foreseeing things which he is unable to influence, coupled with a lack of faith in God or the after-life, give him a nauseating premonition of "darkness [. . .] nothing but darkness" (Eliot, *Lifted Veil* 6) lying in wait for mortals beyond the veil. He also has intimations of the universe's motiveless malignity towards the end of his life when, in the midst of his imagined locales, "one presence seemed to weigh on [him] in all these mighty shapes—the presence of something unknown and pitiless" (59). These terrifying moments of metaphysical clarity recall Marlow's glimpses into a malevolent force normally concealed behind the veil of nature in *Heart of Darkness*; Jim experiences something similar in his early career as a merchant sailor:

> There are many shades in the danger of adventures and gales, and it is only now and then that there appears on the face of facts a sinister violence of intention—that indefinable something which forces it upon the mind and the heart of a man, that this complication of accidents or these elemental furies are coming at him with a purpose of malice, with a strength beyond control [. . .] to sweep the whole precious world utterly away from his sight by the simple and appalling act of taking his life. (Conrad, *Lord Jim* 10–11)

Such epiphanies, common in modernist fiction but also in gothic horror, are of ambiguous import since they are meant to reflect genuine revelations of a cosmos deprived of Providence and a nature red in tooth and claw, while simultaneously constituting projections of the viewing subject's mental state, capturing the moment but lacking in universal significance.

Finally, in the work of both Eliot and Conrad the veil image can be seen as a figure for artistic representation itself which promises presence but endlessly defers it, or those "half [. . .] conscious illusions" (*Lifted Veil* 49) vital for provoking desire but not intended to satisfy it. The ambiguity engendered by alternate veiling and unveiling in fiction is perceived by both writers as an antidote to both the barren materialism and the disembodied idealism of modernity. It also fosters what Eliot calls the "honey of probability"[7] which, besides being necessary for the production of "Art and philosophy, literature and science" (48), is viewed as a life-sustaining fiction in *The Lifted Veil* that allows human beings the possibility of hope. Similarly, as J. Hillis Miller observes with regard to *Heart of Darkness* but which could also apply to any work in the oeuvre, Conrad invites the reader to interpret what "either of the narrators sees and names on the first level of narration as a veil or screen hiding something invisible or not yet visible behind it, though when each veil is lifted it uncovers only another veil behind" (118).

NOTES

1. The promised disclosure sometimes extended to the artist him/herself. As Bernard C. Meyer observes, quoting Conrad's famous claim from *A Personal Record* (1912), "it is not every artist whose unseen presence offers so beguiling a temptation for a fuller disclosure of the 'figure behind the veil,' the 'suspected rather than a seen presence'" (3).

2. After Eliot abandoned the evangelical piety of her youth for the Higher Criticism of the Bible, she took advantage of the editorship of *The Westminster Review* to cultivate her passion for contemporary philosophical debate. See Suzy Anger, "George Eliot and Philosophy."

3. This subject is treated at length in Nic Panagopoulos, *The Fiction of Joseph Conrad: The Influence of Schopenhauer and Nietzsche*.

4. For the way some of the themes of *The Lifted Veil* corresponded to specific interests in *Blackwood's* readership, see Kevin Ashby, "The Centre and the Margins in 'The Lifted Veil.'"

5. See the Introduction to Con Coroneos, *Space, Conrad, and Modernity*.

6. For this theme in Conrad, see Ludwig Schnauder's *Free will and Determinism in Joseph Conrad's Major Novels*.

7. This may not be unrelated to Aristotle's claim in the *Poetics* that, in contrast to historiography, poetry represents not the actual, but "what is possible in accordance with probability or necessity" (16).

WORKS CITED

Albrecht, Thomas. "Sympathy and Telepathy: The Problem of Ethics in George Eliot's *The Lifted Veil*." *ELH*, vol. 73, no. 2, 2006, pp. 437–63.

Anger, Suzy. "George Eliot and Philosophy." *The Cambridge Companion to George Eliot*, edited by George Levine, Cambridge University Press, 2001, pp. 76–97.

Aristotle. *Poetics*. Translated by Malcolm Heath, Penguin Books, 1996.

Ashby, Kevin. "The Centre and the Margins in 'The Lifted Veil' and Blackwood's *Edinburgh*

Magazine." George Eliot—George Henry Lewes Studies, vols. 24–25, no. 2, 1993, pp. 132–46.
Beeton, Ridley. "Joseph Conrad and George Eliot: An Indication of the Possibilities." *The Polish Review*, vol. 20, nos. 2–3, 1975, pp. 78–86.
Conrad, Joseph. *A Personal Record: Some Reminiscences*. Dent, 1946.
———. *Collected Letters of Joseph Conrad*. 9 vols., edited by Fredrick R. Karl and Laurence Davies, Cambridge University Press, 1983–2008.
———. *Lord Jim: A Tale*. Dent, 1900.
———. *The Nigger of the "Narcissus."* Dent, 1923.
———. *Notes on Life and Letters*. Edited by J.H. Stape, Cambridge University Press, 2004.
Coroneos, Con. *Space, Conrad, and Modernity*. Oxford University Press, 2002.
During, Simon. *Modern Enchantments: The Cultural Power of Secular Magic*. Harvard University Press, 2002.
Eagleton, Terry. "Power and Knowledge in The Lifted Veil." *Literature and History*, vol. 9, 1983, pp. 52–61.
Eliot, George. *George Eliot's Life as Related in Her Letters and Journals*. 3 vols., edited by J.W. Cross, Jazzybee Verlag, 2018.
———. *The Lifted Veil*. Penguin Random House, 2016.
———. *Middlemarch*. Penguin Books, 1965.
Feuerbach, Ludwig. *The Essence of Christianity*. Translated by George Eliot, Harper & Brothers, 1957.
Galvan, Gill. "The Narrator as Medium in George Eliot's *The Lifted Veil*." *Victorian Studies*, vol. 48 no. 2, 2006, pp. 240–48.
Jameson, Fredric. *The Political Unconscious: Narrative as a Socially Symbolic Act*. Routledge, 2002.
Johnson, Joy. "Print, Image, and the Cycle of Materiality in George Eliot's *The Lifted Veil*." *Nineteenth-Century Gender Studies*, vol. 3, no. 2, 2007, pp. 1–24.
Kant, Immanuel. *Critique of Pure Reason*. Translated by Werner S. Pluhar, Hackett, 1996.
———. *Critique of Practical Reason*. Edited and translated by Mary J. Gregor, Cambridge University Press, 1996.
Leavis, F.R. *The Great Tradition: George Eliot, Henry James, Joseph Conrad*. Chatto & Windus, 1962.
Levine, George, ed. *The Cambridge Companion to George Eliot*. Cambridge University Press, 2001.
Limnatis, Nektarios G. *German Idealism and the Problem of Knowledge: Kant, Fichte, Schelling, and Hegel*. Springer, 2008.
Meyer, Bernard C. *Joseph Conrad: A Psychoanalytic Biography*. Princeton University Press, 1967.
Miller, J. Hillis. "Should We Read 'Heart of Darkness'?" *Joseph Conrad's Heart of Darkness*, edited by Harold Bloom, Infobase Publishing, 2008.
Newton, K.M. *Modernizing George Eliot: The Writer as Artist, Intellectual, Proto-Modernist, Cultural Critic*. Bloomsbury, 2011.
Nietzsche, Friedrich. *A Nietzsche Reader*. Edited and translated by R.J. Hollingdale, Penguin, 1977.

———. *The Birth of Tragedy Out of the Spirit of Music*. Edited by Michael Tanner and translated by Shaun Whiteside, Penguin, 1993.

Panagopoulos, Nic. *The Fiction of Joseph Conrad: The Influence of Schopenhauer and Nietzsche*. Peter Lang, 1998.

Raval, Suresh. "Narrative Authority in Lord Jim: Conrad's Art of Failure." *ELH*, vol. 48, no. 2, 1981, pp. 387–410.

Redfield, Marc. *Phantom Formations: Aesthetic Ideology and the "Bildungsroman."* Cornell University Press, 1996.

Reilly, Jim. *Shadowtime: History and Representation in Hardy, Conrad, and George Eliot*. Routledge, 1993.

Sarin, Indu. "Schopenhauer's Concept of the Will and the Veil of Maya." *Schopenhauer and Indian Philosophy: A Dialogue Between India and Germany*, edited by Arati Barna, Northern Book Centre, 2008, pp. 138–50.

Schleiermacher, Friedrich. *Schleiermacher's Soliloquies: An English Translation of the Monologen with a Critical Introduction and Appendix*. Edited by Horace Leland Fries, Wipf & Stock, 2002.

Schnauder, Ludwig. *Free Will and Determinism in Joseph Conrad's Major Novels*. Rodopi, 2009.

Schopenhauer, Arthur. *The World as Will and Representation*. Translated by E.F.J. Payne, vol. 1, Dover, 1969.

Strauss, David Friedrich. *The Life of Jesus Critically Examined*. Translated by Marian Evans, vol. 1, Calvin Blanchard, 1860.

Westphal, Bertrand. *Geocriticism: Real and Fictional Spaces*. Translated by Robert T. Tally, Jr. Palgrave Macmillan, 2011.

Movement, Gesture, and Space in *Heart of Darkness* and *Lord Jim*

SUSAN JONES

ST HILDA'S COLLEGE, UNIVERSITY OF OXFORD

ABSTRACT

Phenomenological criticism has recently enabled readings of Conrad that consider more closely the writer's reference to the physical body in the text. This essay adds to discussions of Conrad's visual and epistemological strategies the exploration of physical presence, gesture, and movement. By reading Conrad's use of individual gesture and passages of movement in *Heart of Darkness* and *Lord Jim* in the context of contemporary innovations in theatrical dance in the period, the essay examines how Conrad's skepticism about language prompts him to use the silent action of his characters to express moments of affective intensity and to suggest the spatialization of time by the body.

KEYWORDS

phenomenology, kinaesthetics, dance, gesture, narratology, intertextuality, intervisuality, body

INTRODUCTION

Recent criticism of Conrad has revealed the importance of the relationship between the visual, the spatial, and the temporal in his work, emphasizing, for example, the writer's filmic register as an expression of the complexities of his presentation of narrative time and space.[1] Robert Hampson focuses on the new medium of film and introduces the notion of the body into his commentary on the filmic aspect of Conrad's writing in *Lord Jim*: "Conrad describes

Chester and Robinson dodging into view 'with stride and gestures, as if reproduced in the field of some optical toy' [Conrad, *Lord Jim* 133], showing how these new visual technologies increased consciousness of the body, behaviour and movement" (68). In addition, greater attention has been paid to the body, and to reading Conrad through the lens of recent developments in phenomenologically oriented philosophy.[2] This critical turn has illuminated areas of Conrad's writing that generate their extralinguistic elements: affect, performance, embodied mimesis, and intersubjectivity.[3]

In the following essay I shall focus on a related but somewhat under acknowledged aspect of the phenomenological turn in Conrad's dramatization of embodied subjectivity. By comparing two Blackwood's texts, *Heart of Darkness* (1899) and *Lord Jim* (1900), I suggest how movement and gesture in these narratives also respond to the contexts of theatrical dance and theories of contemporary dance in the period. To this end I employ the theories of Gabriele Brandstetter (2015) who, in *The Poetics of Dance*, has shown the ways in which the *pathos* or emotion expressed by the dancer/actor on stage (to some degree compatible with a discussion of Platonic/Dionysian notions of mimesis outlined by Lacoue-Labarthe [92–101]), offers, by using the history of actual gestural representation, a transference of meaning through time. Extending the ways in which Brandstetter relates gesture to the kinaesthetic and to the spatialization of time, I offer a reading of the nonlinguistic and nonvoiced means of communication in these Conradian tales as an often-neglected aspect of their production of affect.

In attending to the phenomenological aspect of Conrad's writing it is important to note initially the extent to which Conrad embeds the language of physical activity in his texts, where image schema metaphors are frequently accompanied by the presentation of expressive gestures lending emphasis to the ambiguity and ambivalence of the language. Narrative voices in *Heart of Darkness* frequently employ a verbal texture in which present participles, accompanied by directional prepositions, convey the experiential quality of action—the *Nellie* "swinging to" her anchor; Marlow "looking into" and "stepping back" from the abyss, the chain gang toiling up the path, the African woman throwing up her hands. Jim's leap from the *Patna*, or over the stockade (mirrored by many other characters' literal and metaphorical leaps throughout the narrative) present us with passages of movement, of indeterminate duration, that frequently act as symbolic textual markers, and often undermine the directions and indirections of narrative. The physicality implied by this linguistic texture provides reflective markers that anticipate or respond to the main events and, more importantly for this discussion, initiate those emotional jolts that accompany the experience of reading Conrad. Who has not felt internally an almost physical response to the complex grammatical juxtaposition of tense: "I had jumped [. . .] it seems" (Conrad, *Lord Jim* 88)? Jim's dislocation of consciousness is so intense in part because we have been set up for it through a system of inexplicably proleptic leaps, such as Brierly's suicide, or the engineer's leap in the throes of *delirium tremens*. The effect of the moment is reinforced as we are reminded of it analeptically when Jim jumps over the stockade to a new life in Patusan.

UNVOICED NARRATIVES AND SILENT GESTURES

While Conrad's linguistic texture holds physical implications, the visual representation of the physical body in Conrad has not always been analyzed as a semiotic structure operating independently of the verbal. Vision in Conrad is often associated with the language of the symbolic, the slippery texture, evasive meaning, and various epistemological problems encountered during the narrative. Ian Watt's *Conrad in the Nineteenth Century* (1980) initiated discussions of the symbolic and metaphorical nature of visual effects in relation to perception in Conrad ("delayed decoding"), where the metaphorical imperative "to make you *see*" posits vision as an aid to understanding (Preface to *The Nigger of the "Narcissus"* 7; original italics). More recently, Philippe Lacoue-Labarthe has extended the exploration of this relationship. Lacoue-Labarthe is particularly insightful in this context because his philosophy builds on phenomenological accounts such as those established by Heidegger, Husserl, Merleau-Ponty, and Ricouer. Nidesh Lawtoo's commentary and collection of essays, *Conrad's "Heart of Darkness" and Contemporary Thought*, on Lacoue-Labarthe's reading of *Heart of Darkness* has opened up important new phenomenological readings of Conrad's text that take into account what Henry Staten, elsewhere in Lawtoo's volume, paraphrases as Lacoue-Labarthe's identification of two voices structuring Marlow's narrative in *Heart of Darkness*: one is the "savage, undifferentiated clamour" of *physis* or nature, and the other is the voice of Kurtz, associated with the voice of art or *techne* (Staten 157). Lacoue-Labarthe's reading is especially pertinent because his understanding of the embodied voice offers the interdisciplinary potential of exploring this novella against other art forms—in this case the aesthetics of music.

However, the implications of emotional affect produced by the physical body require further exploration. The description of movement and gesture in Conrad relates to a variety of emotional responses and narrative functions that do not necessarily fit, for example Lacoue-Labarthe's focus on "voice" (95–7).[4] In this discussion, I turn to the implications of movement and the individual gestures of the body performed without voice or any form of utterance, where continuities in the use of a gestural and physical lexicon help us to understand more fully Conrad's method. The performative nature of gesture not only produces emotional resonance, it emerges as a marker of Conrad's representation of the human experience of time and space. However, following from Watt, we find that Conrad frequently draws attention to the narrative of epistemological process in which the embodied subject gains understanding of what s/he sees or experiences.[5] Thus we can add to such associations between vision and knowledge the importance of embodiment and the kinetic. These phenomena suggest the body's situation in time and space and also cultivate an emotional response in both character and reader.

In his presentation of gesture and movement, Conrad's sensitivity to the relationship between seeing, moving, and acquisition of knowledge often expresses a highly skeptical position. Precisely because physical expression cannot easily be transformed into "meaning" verbally, the physical activity of protagonists reinforces withdrawal of narratorial/authorial judgement and emphasizes communication of the unsayable and the unknowable. One way in which Conrad's textual and narratological techniques communicate spatial and temporal gaps is through the visual representation of the text on the page, through typographical disjunction. Hesitations in understanding, dislocations of conscious thought, gaps in the discourse, are often represented on the page by ellipsis; and the uncertain experience of time combined with the body's passage across geographical space is sometimes conveyed by introducing actual space on the page, as in the temporal leap indicated between chapters in *Typhoon*, between the moment of the typhoon, anticipated at the end of chapter 5, and the moment of the ship limping into harbour at the beginning of the next chapter.

But in order to represent the inadequacy of language itself, Conrad often turns to the specific gestural and kinetic patterns of an individual moving subject to explore the spatial implications of his stories (his protagonists' equivocation frequently expressed by *dis*location of bodily and gestural experience). Felix Ó Murchadha outlined in a recent discussion of a range of post-Kantian positions, "the understanding of space as dynamic," which includes exploring the concept of space as something defined always in relation to the action and perception of the "moving" subject (37). Such philosophical explorations are illustrated in Conrad's writing, not only by denotative verbal expressions of space, but through his visual evocations of kinetic energy, relating gestures and movement in dynamic phrases that in themselves express the spatiality of the text.

In an earlier study of physical and narrative movement in *Heart of Darkness*

I explored the representation of movement phrases throughout Marlow's recounting of his tale. By "movement phrase," I mean the rhythmically choreographed division of physical action, represented verbally in the text by the description of short passages evoking paced activity, as in the passage in *Heart of Darkness* in which the African woman, Kurtz's mistress, runs along the river bank with "measured steps" (Conrad, *Youth* 107), stops, turns, throws up her arms above her head, turns, runs on. With the aid of Paul Ricoeur's famous reading of the intersection of Aristotle and Augustine in *Time and Narrative*, I showed how these physically choreographed phrases contribute to the novella's narratological structure and its focus on the enigmatic gap, the hiatus of representation.[6] Marlow thus structures the narrative space by arresting the teleological progress of our reading, inserting into the text flashes of startling visual impact that may later accrue their full significance as narrative markers. These moments are expressed kinetically in the silent yet evocative movement of the subjects of the tale.[7] I argued that Conrad's description of movement phrases within Marlow's retelling of the tale aids a fundamentally skeptical reception, where the onus of interpretation is never determined by the narrator or author, but is left ultimately with the readers.

However, the current essay extends the argument further to focus on characters' actual kinetic experience and how their gestures and movements relate to one another to produce emotional affect driving mood, tone, and the individual's experience of space and time. By focusing on *Heart of Darkness* and *Lord Jim*, I shift the perspective beyond the narrative properties of the movement phrases of *Heart of Darkness* to that of the experience of the actual body represented in both texts, the she or he who communicates without words. By thinking about Conrad's distinctive use of gesture, I suggest ways in which the physical and kinetic texture of the narrative aids the presentation of his narrators' and his protagonists' equivocation in both texts.

Conrad mobilizes a further significant aspect of corporeal movement, one that emphasizes the individual protagonist's gesture. In this category, we might ask what implications arise from, for example, the pointing of a finger (an empirical indicator characteristic of Stein, for example), the flinging of an arm, the supplication, the wringing of hands? When, where, and why do they occur? What narrative function do these discrete physical actions offer? Although such gestures often accompany a movement phrase of greater duration, I shall argue for the importance of the single physical gesture, which combines a sense of rootedness in the core of the body enacting it, and an often expressive movement of arm or hand directing us (symbolically) beyond the body's current position. Such gestures in part offer an opportunity to consider the performative element of the body in the text. Apparently conventional in their association with stage histrionics, or in some cases with the quotidian movement of "realist" expression, gesture paradoxically gives Conrad access in *Heart of Darkness* and *Lord Jim* to a modernist articulation of the spatialization of time by the body. Unlike the active flow of the movement phrase, rhythmically punctuating the conventionally teleological thrust of the tale, these single gestures signal a kind of Benjaminian *JetztZeit*, often connecting past and future in the presentness of the retelling, but also metaphorically linking geographical spaces in the text.[8] So, for example, the African woman's reaching after Kurtz in the boat is repeated by the Intended, "a tragic and familiar Shade resembling in this gesture another one" (Conrad, *Youth* 125). The Intended also gestures to an absent Kurtz at the window during her interview with Marlow in the "sepulchral city" (125).

The corporeal and the kinetic take precedence in Conrad's fin de siècle texts at moments of profound psychic crisis that belong to a very particular register of ambivalence related to social, racial, gender identification, political and psychological anxiety. In this respect the gestural, however abstract or non-teleological—often appearing as if uninitiated by any obvious temporal logic—provides a form of negotiation of emotional expression, a felt presence that stands in for linguistic absence, across time and space. Moreover, the quality and frequency of gestural language presented in these narratives warrants an unexpected comparison to aspects of the period's protomodernist and modernist dance aesthetics.

A HISTORY OF GESTURE IN PAINTING, PERFORMANCE, AND NARRATIVE

Marlow repeatedly hints at problems of verbal expression in *Lord Jim*, suggesting that such problems may be circumvented most successfully by physical expression and bodily action, and in some cases gesture replaces verbal inexpressibility. For example, Marlow uses a kinetic verb to characterize Marlow's relationship to Jim. In chapter 8 he declares that "He swayed me" (*Lord Jim* 75), while recounting the tale to a group of listeners and outlining the dilemma of storytelling. But his story is not simply communicated through words: "for the success of this yarn I am missing innumerable shades—they were so fine, so difficult to render in colourless words . . . " (76). In fact, we find that gesture frequently aids interpretation of those "shades" of meaning, and while the representation of gesture in Conrad's fiction belongs ultimately to the field of narrative theory, in order to unpack such use of gesture it is helpful to address turn-of-the-century and early-twentieth century innovations in drama and dance. Gesture delivers its own theoretical function—often as an expression of experiential states passed on through a history of representation.

One of the most effective accounts of gestural activity across the arts of the period can be found in the work of dance theorist Gabriele Brandstetter, whose *The Poetics of Dance,* written in German in 1995, was translated into English in 2015, and whose subsequently wide availability has been revolutionary for dance scholars of recent years. Brandstetter also illuminates dance's relationship to other art forms in the period of modernist experimentation. Innovations in performance dance at the turn-of-the-century (such as those of Loïe Fuller or Isadora Duncan) were frequently sceptical of the use of dance in the service of narrative in nineteenth-century ballet (for example, *Lac des cygnes, La Belle au bois dormant*—the big narrative ballets of the Maryinsky Theatre, St. Petersburg). Instead, these innovators focused on the indeterminacy of gesture, drawing attention to dance's potential, not simply as mimetic form, but as an aesthetics in and of itself. Conrad employs such use of apparently abstract, ambivalent, non-narrative gesture to advance his own skeptical attitude to narrative. Thus, as we shall also explore in this essay, recent theorizations of modernism in dance, where the dynamics of gesture provide similarly ambivalent strategies, help us to explore the work of gesture and space in these Conrad stories.

Crucially for this discussion, Brandstetter observes a burgeoning of aesthetic innovation around 1900, where figural representations of dance absorbed into painting and literature are seen as symptomatic of a crisis of perception and of language in the period. Brandstetter draws her theoretical framework from Aby Warburg's *Mnemosyne* project, begun in 1924, which aimed to map pathways of an afterlife of antiquity, reanimated in the art of later times through the reproduction of gestures of great symbolic, intellectual, or emotional power (Brandstetter 15). Using Warburg's categories of gesture in the *Mnemosyne Atlas,* Brandstetter analyzes how such specific figural representations of movement have particular currency in the fin de siècle and early twentieth-century period, when they stand in for a general cultural crisis during the initial period of modernism, revealing "a moment of aporia between the 'now' of movement and the history of representation" (2). Brandstetter outlines her routing of the argument through Warburg, describing his "atlas of emphatic gestures" as one that can tell us how contemporary dance to some degree reanimated the gestures of the "ancient" and the "primitive" and how these gestures were used in art at the turn of the twentieth century to embrace and denote the memory of a "gamut of expressions in the grip of emotions"—recovering an ancient "primal instinct" that is transformed anew in modern art (13). This catalogue of Warburg's "pathos formulae" is a repertoire of the history of gesture, "the mimetic human" in corporeal images belonging to cultural memory or symbolic formulations that are "hidden under and transformed by the self-interpretations of the modern subject" (13).

We cannot completely conflate the aesthetics of literature, painting, or sculpture with dance, but choreographer Siobhan Davies, in an interview with Elli Goldstone, gives us a sense of the individuality of Warburg's ideas and their potential relation to choreographic creation:

> Towards the very end of his life, Warburg worked on what has become, perhaps, his most influential project, the *Mnemosyne Atlas*, named after the Greek goddess of memory. For this he drew out unexpected affinities between photographs, artworks, often separated by centuries and cultures and pinned them onto large, cloth-covered boards, rearranging them in form and content, how a gesture carved upon a classical tomb might reappear, for example, in a Florentine painting. This was not an attempt to trace a lineage between such manifestations, but rather thought-space, in which the images become something to be experienced rather than merely understood. (Davies)[9]

To return to Conrad, we can suggest an analogy between the idea of a *Mnemosyne Atlas* and Conrad's alertness to a common visual lexicon of a whole history of the representation of gesture, especially transmitted through the visual arts. In this respect, Brandstetter establishes how human gestures, throughout the history of painting, sculpture, and visual arts, while apparently denoting single, static moments in time, in fact frequently evoke a far more fluid temporal movement between present, future, past.[10] The effect of the representation of gesture creates a dynamic of movement linking human emotion across space and time. So, for example, to aid interpretation, Conrad has Marlow interpolate into the descriptions of Jim's demeanor a single gesture, drawn from a familiar iconographic lexicon to suggest the experience of uncertainty. At certain points in the narrative Conrad gives Jim a gesture of despair, as Jim holds his head in his hands. Conrad may be alluding to Adam's pose in a painting such as Masaccio's "Expulsion from the Garden of Eden" (c. 1425). Although Masaccio captures within the frame of the painting a single moment of time, Conrad's representation within the tale is created almost in the manner of a *tableau vivant*. We might be reminded that, in fact, Masaccio's painting itself offers a far more extensive history, beyond the two-dimensional frame of the painting, of emotional crisis in human experience that stretches beyond the moment of the Fall narrated in Genesis. Recalling the pose of Masaccio's Adam, Jim "took his head in his hands for a moment, like a man driven to distraction by some unspeakable outrage" (Conrad, *Lord Jim* 83). It is with this outwardly silent theatrical gesture that Marlow understands the significance of an inward struggle undermining more obvious generic markers. Within "the pauses between the words [. . .] there was an element of burlesque in his ordeal—a degradation of funny grimaces in the approach of death or dishonor" (84). Conrad employs the unvoiced gesture to create the equivocal tone of Jim's felt experience throughout the tale.

Thus, when Jim "took his head in his hands for a moment, like a man driven to distraction by some unspeakable outrage" (83), his action provides an example of how meaning emerges from an emotional history supported by a vocabulary of gestures. With Jim's gesture of despair, Conrad's description of Jim's pose here shows how Conrad (in the manner of Warburg) uses gestural language, transmitted visually through time. The pose literally denotes Jim's despair and metaphorically gestures to a history of aesthetic evocations of the Fall (and in Conrad's case the biblical ironies constantly resound throughout the text in Jim's actual and metaphorical "falls" from grace). This particular gesture reminds readers of paintings/sculptures they may have seen in earlier representations, but these are harnessed here in the service of protomodernist fiction to indicate both psychological crisis and the breakdown of linguistic expression. Another example in Conrad might be suggested by his evocation of the Pietà at the end of *Under Western Eyes* (1911), where Tekla cradles the body of the injured Razumov on her lap, providing a mnemonic trace of the iconography of Michaelangelo's famous sculpture and other representations of the pose.

In *Lord Jim*, Conrad explores gestural potential as an important property of the presentation of time and space in the Warburgian manner. For example, Marlow's narrative of his meeting with Jim in chapter 4 includes significant gestural markers, functioning to emphasize moments of emotional and thematic significance. The recounting of the court case precipitating Jim's "disgrace" alludes to the engineer's apparent bravery with a gesture signifying the critique of romance that pervades the novel: "he let go the rail and made ample gestures as if demonstrating in the air the shape and extent of his valour" (25); and Jim's account of the second engineer includes his registering the magistrate's anxiety: "he rested his temple on the palm of his hands" (30). On the next page, Marlow's response to Jim's account as they are seated on the verandah of his hotel room is accessed through his physical posture: "Marlow's body, extended at rest in the seat, would become very still [. . .] as though [. . .] his spirit [. . .] were speaking through his lips from the past" (31). In these cases the gestural either functions to fix the moment in the reader's memory or spatializes time in its allusion to the protagonist's past.

Such Warburgian "pathos formulae" are transferred into the realm of the dramatic, and thence to the narrative voice. This kind of gestural repetition across time has occurred, for example, between images of the classical Maenads—the followers of Dionysus (depicted in many forms from Greek vases to the English artist John Collier's 1886 painting)—and the histrionic upward thrust of the arms of several "orientalist" performances of dance in London at the turn-of-the-century (in the context of "Greek" dances performed by Isadora Duncan). I argue that Conrad's use of gesture, as embodied in the narrative, corresponds to an affective mode of late-nineteenth/early-twentieth century dance, frequently "orientalist" in style (including Loie Fuller's *Serpentine Dance* from 1891; Ruth St Denis's *Tunisienne* [1904]; or Maud Allen's *Salome* [circa 1906][11]) that dramatizes his critique of the subject in crisis. Such dances relive traces of Dionysiac frenzy, or passionate expressions of grief and awe, yet divorced from their ancient contexts these gestures stand alone at their contemporary moment, offering only mnemonic traces of a preceding narrative. Conrad makes no overt reference in either *Heart of Darkness* or *Lord Jim* to the kind of orientalist dance presentations to be seen in the contemporary music hall. The African woman's dramatic gesture and "deliberate progress" nevertheless conveys an exaggerated, performative quality (*Youth* 107), while Jim's histrionic gestures often conflict with the verisimilitude of the dramatized narrator's representation of his experiences elsewhere in the novella.

In fact, Conrad was familiar with the theatrical gesture of dancers of the period. He attended the music hall, and evidence of his attention to the dancers appears in his drawings of 1890s dancers. Frederick Karl noted Conrad's perception of music hall exoticism, reproducing in his biography of Conrad the writer's pen and ink drawings of a "Woman with a Serpent" (1892–94) and "The Three Ballet Dancers" (1896) (Karl 412–13) —a discussion extended very much further in Warodell's essay, "Conrad's Painterly Drawings." In *Heart of Darkness* and *Lord Jim,* Conrad uses such corporeal gestures as part of an affective vocabulary, embodying emotional and psychological states throughout the texts. But as we shall see from Conrad's distinctive representations of expressive physicality, the historicity implicit in the gesture's transference across time also raises questions about the body's radical communication of spatial dimension, as well as underscoring a variety of contemporary crises: of language, of the Western male colonial subject, of race, and gender.

It is worth returning to the African woman's movement and gestures in *Heart of Darkness*, to look more closely at one of the most well-known gestural interventions to draw out their relationship to movement phrase (mentioned earlier in this essay) in Conrad's work—a scene that appears to emerge from an essentially primitivist lexicon:

She walked with measured steps [. . .] treading the earth proudly, with a slight jingle and flash of barbarous ornaments [. . .] savage and superb, wild-eyed and magnificent; there was something ominous and stately in her deliberate progress. [. . . .] She came abreast of the steamer, stood still and faced us [. . .] looked at us all as if her life had depended upon the unswerving steadiness of her glance. Suddenly she opened her bared arms and threw them up rigid above her head, as though in an uncontrollable desire to touch the sky. [. . . .] She turned away slowly, walked on, following the bank, and passed into the bushes to the left. (107–8)

On the one hand, the African woman's dehistoricized gestures contribute to a familiar rhetoric of Western European representations of the Other as mysterious and indecipherable.[12] The description suggests that the woman's gesture does not follow from conceptual thought or reasoning, and we sense in Marlow's understanding of his own vision the continuation of a Western perspective on a split between mind and body. Yet for Marlow the woman's gesture is aestheticized by the narrator (and we might think of how the gesture anticipates popular images of the "natural," as in the photograph [c.1915] of Isadora Duncan in "Greek" costume, arms aloft, captured by Arnold Genthe). But with this movement phrase, Conrad has his narrator associate the presentation of the primitive with the atavistic movement of the body and a gesture of kinetic communication beyond language. The woman's physical confidence and expressivity does not simply inspire anxiety in the Western onlooker, since Marlow declares her to be both savage and superb. As Conrad distances his authorial voice from that of the narrators of this text, he nevertheless sanctions the action of the African woman both as a manifestation of savagery and an expression of grace, illustrating ambivalence running throughout accounts of primitivism in both literature and theater, where readers/viewers are invited, in their encounter with alterity, to experience wonder, awe, erotic desire, but also approbation and fear.

On the later occasion of Marlow's interview with the Intended, Marlow overlays the vision of the African woman's outstretched arm onto the Intended's reaching for Kurtz within the domestic setting of Europe. The "mnemonic trace" of the melodramatic gesture of "that other Shade" creates a "thought space," in Siobhan Davies's terms, where the apparently conventional exoticization of gesture, as in contemporary melodrama, encourages a modernist critique of colonial space and its implications for female identity. As ever, Marlow encourages his listeners to take an equivocal, ambivalent view—even if here the gesture is most obviously racialized and gender specific. In his mode of presentation of the narrative, in the indeterminate utterances and echoing of gestural ambivalence, his recounting of his tale invites a protomodernist interpretation of the sublime, complicating the presentation of any sense of straightforward melodramatic exoticism.

GESTURE AND MOVEMENT: PACING, JUMPING, AND FALLING

Gesture nearly always accompanies movement in Conrad—the gesture providing a kind of emphasis or a form of staccato, or rhythmic syncopation, to the movement phrase. The action of "jumping" in *Lord Jim* acquires a gestural force when Jim's gestures accompany the retelling of his actions. On the one hand, Conrad's presentation of a structural device symbolized by Jim's fundamental leap from the *Patna* creates *prolepsis* and *analepsis* and adds symbolic significance to metaphorical absences/gaps/traumatic hiati in the text. But these proleptic moments structuring the narrative and anticipating this leap are often accentuated by gesture—as in the delusions of the chief engineer, who is suffering from *delirium tremens* and hallucinates the presence of pink toads under his hospital bed: "'what are they doing now down there?' he asked, pointing to the floor with fantastic precautions of voice and gesture, whose meaning, borne upon my mind in a lurid flash, made me very sick of my cleverness" (*Lord Jim* 46)—and the engineer leaps inexplicably down the stairs. Another proleptic leap, in chapter 6, is that of Brierly's suicide—"he jumped overboard at sea barely a week after the end of the inquiry" (50). Again a kinetic gesture (this time of thing rather than body) establishes the self-inflicted violence of this inexplicable death as "the gates of the other world flung open wide for his reception" (50)—and indeed anticipates the end of the novel with Jim's suicidal offering of himself for fatal reception at Doramin's hands. Thus, Jim's leap from the *Patna* (unaccountable to him) constitutes one in a series of such symbolic action, and Jim's account of his leap in chapter 9 is also framed by the anchoring of the confession in expressive bodily gesture:

> [Jim] raised his hand deliberately to his face, and made some picking motions with his fingers as though he had been bothered with cobwebs, and afterwards he looked into the open palm for quite half a second before he blurted out—"I had jumped . . . " He checked himself, averted his gaze . . . "It seems," he added. (88)

This moment is situated at the "absent" center of Jim's story and connects the narrative across time and space. Jim's famous "leap" from the *Patna* also creates an intertextual resonance with Milton's *Paradise Lost*—a text that in itself explores the corporeal experience of banishment from a state of grace. The significance for *Lord Jim* of the intertext arises from Milton's emphasis on free will in "falling"—actively leaping rather than unconsciously falling (as Jim sometimes insinuates). The important aspect of Satan's free will in Milton's poem is that people make themselves fall; there is no "fate" or other force that causes Adam, Eve, Satan, and the rebel angels to fall. Thus, in book 3 God says that he created Adam "Sufficient to have stood, though *free to fall*" (Milton, *Paradise Lost* 3.95). And in book 6, God does not push Satan and his legions out of Heaven. They actually throw themselves out of Heaven: "headlong themselves they threw/Down from the verge of Heav'n" (6.864–65). Milton's emphasis on the angels' agency in "falling" enables us to reflect on Jim's indecision and on Conrad's presentation of him in terms of his own moral skepticism and on a sense of extreme doubt associated with Jim's "fall" from grace.

Jim's inability to remember the jump propels the story of his obsessive failure to come to terms with guilt and go on. The cognitive disjunction is metaphorized by the notion of leaping into an "everlasting hole," but the gap in memory is framed significantly by Jim's gesture of restlessness and anguish when he continues to recount the incident in chapter 10: "He locked his fingers together and tore them apart" (Conrad, *Lord Jim* 89). Thus, at this moment of extreme crisis marked by temporal and emotional dislocation, the body expresses the cognitive gap, communicating silently that which cannot be remembered nor conveyed in words.

MEASURED STEPS

While Miltonic echoes are heard in the kinetic aspects of *Lord Jim*, significantly for Conrad, Dantean intertexts occur in both texts under discussion here. First in *Heart of Darkness* and then in *Lord Jim*, the repetition of "measured steps," appearing as an intertextual motif across both works, suggests an echo of a Dantean theme that attends to the physical action of the body throughout the *Inferno*. We have noted the gestural force of movement, and the significance of individual gesture to indicate the spatial and temporal aspects of narrative. But the African woman's reaching for the sublime does not, for example, appear as an isolated gesture. It is combined with her "measured steps" and her shifts in direction to create a dynamic movement phrase that in the novella contrasts (ironically) with the rhythmic pace of the chain gang's enforced progress, when "the clink kept time with their footsteps" (*Youth* 56) earlier in the novella. The African woman's silent actions in *Heart of Darkness* mean that the movement phrase explicitly opens up a perspective on the transmission of emotion through primitivist gesture throughout the narrative, but in *Lord Jim* Conrad echoes this choreographed phrase to propose a broader gestural vocabulary as an aspect of his description of Jim's internalization of emotion. (Jim often reflects familiar gestures of everyday life that transmit through time his own history of emotional expression). Conrad invokes the African woman's gesture again in chapter 12 of *Lord Jim*, creating a critique, intertextually across his own works, of his earlier physical communication of the African woman's perplexity and awe. When listening to Jim recounting his story, Marlow, invoking his description of the African woman in the earlier novella, remarks that Jim's frenetic hand gestures produced a certain kind of effect: "he clasped and unclasped his fingers without removing his hands from his stomach, and made it infinitely more effective than if he had thrown his arms up to heaven in amazement" (110).

But not all movements and gestures simply echo the "painterly" quality of Warburg's aesthetic catalogue of gestures. The movement phrases also reflect intertextual references to gesture, and an elusive (and allusive) intertextual connection between Conrad's use of gesture and movement across his own texts. The "measured" steps of the African woman, for example, echo Dante's literary invocation of movement, most obviously illustrated in the Third Circle of the *Inferno*, where, in a recent translation by Robert Torrance, Dante's narrator observes the equivocation of the protagonists: "Thus we passed through that foul conglomerate / Of shades and rain, with measured steps and slow, / Touching a little on the future state" (Torrance 89). "Measured steps" turn up in the chapters set in Marlow's hotel, when Jim's wrestle with his memory and guilt begins in earnest with Marlow, and again we are reminded of a kinetic and gestural vocabulary used previously in relation to the African woman:

> He began to walk with measured steps to and fro before my chair, one hand in his trouser pocket, his head bent thoughtfully, and his right arm at long intervals raised for a gesture that seemed to put out of his way an invisible intruder.
> "I suppose you think I was going mad," he began. [. . .] "The sun could not make me mad. . . ." His right arm put aside the idea of madness. . . . "Neither could it kill me. . . ." Again his arm repulsed a shadow. (Conrad, *Lord Jim* 98–9)

Of course, the echo of "measured steps," which curiously reflects Conrad's own physical knowledge of pacing the watch on board ship, also gestures to cantos 6 and 23 (the hypocrites) of Dane's *Inferno*, where the hypocrites are weighed down with leaded cloaks. In terms of Christian morality, the shame of what might be seen as Jim's potentially hypocritical position is one that constantly weighs on the protagonist's conscience. But the body's single gesture helps to emphasize the moral and psychological frameworks of the protagonists. In *Heart of Darkness*, the African woman expresses no such equivocation in her sublime gesture "beyond" the physical body, and her unswerving gaze locks the experience into a fixed moment of time and place in the African location. But Jim's gestural invocation of potential madness transforms his movement into an expression of far greater indeterminacy. Jim's wrestle is fraught with a sense of the dislocation of consciousness, and yet of a memory that haunts him across time and space. Unlike the Miltonic Fall of the Angels, where Satan and his legions throw themselves out of Heaven, Jim claims his fall was not predicated on an active leap but something initiated by a discontinuity of conscious thought.

Throughout the text Jim's physical activity is fraught with ambivalence, as if the pacing and the gesture is a form of recovering consciousness of that fundamental moment. Conrad repeats the African woman's kinetic and gestural intervention of *Heart of Darkness* in *Lord Jim*, not once, but several times across the text as if to mark out visually, spatially, geographically, and psychologically Jim's "leap" from his discussion of the jump right through to his offering up his life to Doramin: "When he came up into the light of torches the wailing of the women ceased suddenly. Doramin did not lift his head, and Jim stood silent before him for a time. Then he looked to the left, and moved in that direction with measured steps" (311). As Jim unflinchingly advances towards Doramin, it is Doramin who this time lifts his right hand for the final gesture activating Jim's annihilation.

The gestures of both the African woman in *Heart of Darkness* and those of Jim in *Lord Jim* bear in common the way in which they express the outsider status of these protagonists. The African woman's ambivalent reaching for the sky (anguish or sublime freedom?) and Jim's evasive and equivocal movement of brushing away an absent antagonist point to spaces beyond the body, but spaces delimited by the gesture that stands in for a continuous absence, and in Jim's case symbolizing his self-imposed exile. Both their gestures express what Ó Murchadha comments on as the exile's revelation of a "fundamental ontological as well as political characteristic of place, namely that all things suffer: in the sense that all things take place, are in place, and place is that which makes them possible as things" (35). As Jim's gestures show how he grapples with finding his place, we might also be reminded of Giorgio Agamben's remarks: "The *outside* is not another space that resides beyond a determinate space, but rather, it is the passage, the exteriority that gives access—in a word, it is its face, its *eidos*. The threshold [. . .] is, so to speak, the experience of the limit itself, the experience of being-within an *outside*" (xvi; original emphases).

Perhaps this concept of the threshold, "the experience of being-within an *outside*" most succinctly defines the function of gestural vocabulary employed by Conrad in his critique of language.

THE SPATIALIZATION OF TIME

While gesture is to some extent an apparently narrative act in time and space, delivered from the "centered" place of the body as the arms indicate a specific direction towards an imagined closure, in both *Heart of Darkness* and *Lord Jim* gestures also point to nothing, de-historicize the text, marking the psychic breaks/fragmentations/gaps in the narrative paradoxically by an aesthetic act that creates a texture of symbolic patterning. In both these two fictions a preponderance of apparently expressivist gestures only emphasizes potential ambivalence. Gestures in these narratives are often uninterpretable, mark ineffability or equivocation, going nowhere, signifying nothing, other than to stand in for the absences they represent. They may seem to *de*-spatialize time, yet they also *define* or mark out the "exile" spaces in and beyond which the physical body exists.

In this respect, Conrad's use of gesture resembles (remarkably) early-twentieth-century experiments in contemporary dance where gesture is used to create and delimit the space in which the body moves. Early experimental choreographers frequently utilized the apparently histrionic dramatic gesture— the flinging up of the arms (of Isadora Duncan); the intense kinetic energy of the outreached arms of expressionist choreographer, Mary Wigman in *Hexantanz II* (1921)—to design the space of representation. These gestures are emphatically abstract, carry no specific meaning (neither symbolic nor literal), no narrative as such, and fundamentally question traditional ballet's presentation within the proscenium arch frame. Wigman's pupil, Hanya Holm, claimed that Wigman deconstructed the "illusion" of depth as she used the body's movements to create the notion of space and its boundaries or limitations, rather than by placing the body into an already articulated framework.[13] The solo dancer's movement, emotionally and dynamically focused on a diagonal between her and an imaginary antagonist, "creates" both the space in which she moves and the narrative form of the movement. In this way, even in the physical absence of an actual "antagonist," a dancer can project onto the viewer, through gesture alone, the sense that the space is occupied by more than one figure.[14]

The effect is reminiscent of the way Conrad constructed visually in his texts the gestures of both the African woman and the Intended, reaching out towards Kurtz across imaginary space. And Jim's psychic crisis in recounting the leap is represented by his body's constant occupation of a space constituted by gestural confrontations with imaginary demons. The "leap" is the great event of *Lord Jim*, but the emotional history of Jim's irreconcilability is recounted not just in words, nor simply through the symbolic repetition of the jump itself, but through the repeated and remembered gestures and movements that fix in the body the experience of equivocation. In fact the gestural commonality of these accounts problematizes postcolonial readings of the African woman's movement as exclusively orientalist and instead proposes Conrad's use of the body to register a more nuanced expression of physical/psychological crisis/exile. Yet, an emphasis on the spatialization of time by the body in Conrad's literary accounts also shows how physical gesture (frequently markers of non-narrative expression in the choreographic innovations at this time), re-embodied in the literary text, may be identified as a corollary for the disruption of narrative closure by the aesthetic act, in so far as the "choreographic" becomes the reeanactment of time in and by space.

NOTES

1. For examples of philosophical (primarily phenomenological) discussions of time, space, and the body, see Maurice Merleau-Ponty, who uses Husserl's terminology to suggest that the *aspect*'s "invitation to perceive beyond it" (233) is a dynamic aid to interpretation, allowing the viewer to uncover potentialities delimited by the horizon of the view; Gaston Bachelard, *The Poetics of Space* (1958); discussions of Virginia Woolf's modernism in Erich Auerbach's *Mimesis* (1946); space and narrative in Michel de Certeau (1984); and Ricoeur in the second volume of *Time and Narrative* (1984). In relation to Conrad see also Jakob Lothe, *Narrative in Fiction and Film*; John G. Peters, *Conrad and Impressionism*; Con Coroneos, *Space, Conrad and Modernity*; Gene Moore, *Conrad on Film*.

2. See, for example, Nidesh Lawtoo (ed.), *Conrad's "Heart of Darkness" and Contemporary Thought*.

3. While phenomenological criticism of Conrad is not entirely new, Lawtoo's and others' use of Lacoue-Larbarthe suggest interesting new ways through which to frame these recent discussions of Conrad's method in *Heart of Darkness*.

4. I would add that the voice of nature is also constructed by the voice of (certainly Marlow's) narrative art.

5. See Johan Warodell who emphasizes the focus on the language of vision in Conrad criticism at the expense of exploring Conrad's experience of drawing as an important aspect of his negotiation of the non-verbal and the visual: "Eloise Knapp Hay, Ian Watt, Bruce Johnson, and John Peters speak exhaustively about the Conradian connection between verbal impressionism and visual impressionism, yet never mention Conrad's own drawings" (45). See Eloise Knapp Hay, "Joseph Conrad and Impressionism"; Bruce Johnson, "Conrad's Impressionism and Watt's 'Delayed Decoding'"; John Peters, *Conrad and Impressionism*; Ian Watt, *Conrad in the Nineteenth Century*.

6. See Susan Jones, "'She walked with measured steps'"; for the theoretical background see Paul Ricoeur (32–7).

7. Other movement phrases include the depiction of the chain gang's hampered progress and the "measured steps" of the African woman running along the river bank, juxtaposed against the Intended's fixed position in her apartment tragically gesturing to the memory of the dead Kurtz (her gesture itself mirroring that of the African woman reaching after her dying lover).

8. See Walter Benjamin, *Illuminations* 261.

9. Davies observed in this interview that "Aby Warburg was an unconventional art historian—actually, he was an unconventional figure in many ways. Born into one of Europe's richest banking families, Aby made a deal with his younger brother, Max, saying that he would forego his birthright if Max agreed to buy him every book for which he might wish. Max readily agreed, unaware of the extent of the private library his elder sibling would eventually create" [n.p.].

10. We might think of Leon Battista Alberti's concept of *istoria* in his treatise, *Della Pittura* (1436), in which he emphasizes the importance of gestures between figures to evoke narrative in painting.

11. See Carter, *Dance and Dancers*.

12. See Schopenhauer, *The World as Will and Representation*, vol. 1, book 4.63, pp. 452–54.

13. Hanya Holm, transcript of interview with Tobi Tobias, 1975, New York Public Library for the Performing Arts, Dance Division, MGZMT 5-1007. Holm admits that this use of space self-consciously in its three-dimensionality is in fact built into the technique of classical ballet (five or six positions of the feet, and three directions, éffacé, croisé, écarté, which often entailed a spiralling of the upper torso), but that it had become lost in transmission through contemporary teaching methods.

14. Wigman, performing Hexentanz (1921), https://www.youtube.com/watch?v=wkYSRKix9Ls [last accessed 03/05/19]. This film of Wigman's famous solo shows a manifestation of Wigman's ideas about the way in which a single dancer generates an "idea" of space. In one version of the piece she is masked and seated on the floor she constructs, without shifting substantially from one place, a powerful "narrative" of internal struggle with imaginary outside forces. Wigman's method is highly suggestive of a use of the body in space that has been adopted and adapted by many later practitioners of modern dance techniques. Wigman's dramatic confrontation with the audience, face on, and the effect of physical angularity and the foreshortening of the limbs as she moves towards the audience/camera, bears reminders of the exploration of the psychological subtext, the visual techniques, and the dramatic use of light and gesture of contemporary theatre directors like Max Reinhardt, and filmmakers like Robert Wiene, Fritz Lang, and Georg Pabst. See also Marcus on expressionist cinema: pp. 220–24 on Wiene's *The Cabinet of Dr. Caligari* (1920); pp. 63–64 on Lang's *Metropolis* (1927); pp. 268–77 on Dr. Mabuse (1922); and pp. 336–37 on Pabst.

WORKS CITED

Agamben, Giorgio. *The Coming Community*. Translated by Michael Hardt, University of Minnesota Press, 1993.

Auerbach, Erich. *Mimesis: The Representation of Reality in Western Literature*. 1946, translated by William Trask, Doubleday, 1957.

Bachelard, Gaston. *The Poetics of Space*. 1958, translated by Maria Jolas, Beacon Press, 1969.

Benjamin, Walter. *Illuminations*. Edited and introduction by Hannah Arendt, translated by Harry Zohn, Schocken Books, 1968.

Brandstetter, Gabriele. *Poetics of Dance: Body, Space, and Image in the Historical Avant-Gardes*. Translated by Elena Polzer, with Mark Franko, Oxford University Press, 2015.

Carter, Alexandra. *Dance and Dancers in the Victorian and Edwardian Music Halls*. Ashgate, 2005.

Certeau, Michel de. *The Practice of Everyday Life*. Translated by Steven Rendall, University of California Press, 1984.

Conrad, Joseph. *Lord Jim*. Cambridge University Press, 2012.

———. *The Nigger of the "Narcissus."* Cambridge University Press, 2017.

———. *Youth, Heart of Darkness, The End of the Tether*. Cambridge University Press, 2010.

Coroneos, Con. *Space, Conrad and Modernity*. Oxford University Press, 2002.

Davies, Siobhan. *Q&A with Elli Goldstone*. http://www.run-riot.com/articles/blogs/qa-siobhan-davies-having-and-being-body, accessed 3 March 2019.

Hampson, Robert. "From Stage to Screen: 'The Return,' *Victory*, *The Secret Agent* and *Chance*." *Joseph Conrad and the Performing Arts*, edited by Katherine Isobel Baxter and Richard J. Hand, Ashgate, 2009, pp. 59–76.

Hay, Eloise Knapp. "Joseph Conrad and Impressionism." *Journal of Aesthetics and Art Criticism*, vol. 34, no. 2, 1975, pp. 137–44.

Johnson, Bruce. "Conrad's Impressionism and Watt's 'Delayed Decoding.'" *Conrad Revisited: Essays for the Eighties*, edited by Ross C. Murfin, The University of Alabama Press, 1985, pp. 51–70.

Jones, Susan. "'She walked with measured steps': Physical and Narrative Movement in *Heart of Darkness*." *Joseph Conrad: Voice, Sequence, History, Genre*, edited by Jakob Lothe, Jeremy Hawthorn, and James Phelan, Ohio State University Press, 2008, pp. 100–17.

Karl, Frederick R. *Joseph Conrad: The Three Lives*. Farrar, Straus and Giroux, 1979.

Lacoue-Labarthe. Philippe. "The Horror of the West." *Conrad's "Heart of Darkness" and Contemporary Thought: Revisiting the Horror with Lacoue-Labarthe*, edited by Nidesh Lawtoo, Bloomsbury, 2012, pp. 92–101.

Lawtoo, Nidesh, ed. *Conrad's "Heart of Darkness" and Contemporary Thought: Revisiting the Horror with Lacoue-Labarthe*. Bloomsbury, 2012.

Lothe, Jacob. *Narrative in Fiction and Film: An Introduction*. Oxford University Press, 2000.

Marcus, Laura. *The Tenth Muse: Writing About Cinema in the Modernist Period*. Oxford University Press, 2007.

Merleau-Ponty, Maurice. *The Phenomenology of Perception*. 1945, translated by Colin Smith, Routledge, 1962.

Milton, John. *Paradise Lost*. Oxford University Press, 2007.

Moore, Gene, ed. *Conrad on Film*. Cambridge University Press, 2006.

Ó Murchadha, Felix. "Space, Time, and the Articulation of Space." *Spatiality and Symbolic Expression: On the Links between Place and Culture*, edited by Bill Richardson, Palgrave Macmillan, 2015, pp. 21–40.

Peters, John G. *Conrad and Impressionism*. Cambridge University Press, 2001.

Ricoeur, Paul. *Time and Narrative*. 2 vols., translated by Kathleen McLaughlin and David Pellauer, University of Chicago Press, 1984.

Schopenhauer, Arthur. *The World as Will and Representation*. 2 vols., translated by E.F.J. Payne, Dover Publications, 1969.

Staten, Henry. "Conrad's Dionysian Elegy." *Conrad's "Heart of Darkness" and Contemporary Thought: Revisiting the Horror with Lacoue-Labarthe*, edited by Nidesh Lawtoo, Bloomsbury, 2012, pp. 156–98.

Torrance, Robert. *Dante's Inferno: A New Translation in Terza Rima*. Xlibris, 2011.

Warodell, Johan Adam. "Conrad's Painterly Drawings." *English: Journal of the English Association*, vol. 66, no. 252, 2017, pp. 45–69.

Watt, Ian. *Conrad in the Nineteenth Century*. Chatto and Windus, 1980.

"Ba! ba! Ba!": Voicing Noise

JOHAN ADAM WARODELL

UNIVERSITY OF LONDON

ABSTRACT

Joseph Conrad studiously introduced the living, unmediated, stammering, wheezing, and grunting voice into the written text. But how do you record the living voice in verbal format? Reading across the entirety of Conrad's fiction, I attempt the first systematic analysis of all of Conrad's seemingly unsystematic interjections and non-lexical expressions, such as the Brrroum, Pinnnng and Phooooo. The aim is to show that these prolific and seemingly trivial noise-effects are signature markers of Conrad's idiolect, and that they play a significant role in characterization, and the development of direct speech and interior monologues.

KEYWORDS

voice, noise, speech, interjection, non-lexical, Joseph Conrad

Although Conrad "prefers on the whole to let it appear that his writings originate in informal conversation or oral tradition" (Greaney 3), pocketbooks, notebooks, letters, labels, diaries, postscripts, pamphlets, leaflets, gazettes, records, telegrams, maps, manuscripts, newspapers, and other written material—such as revolutionary literature served in soup cans in "The Informer" —play a significant part in Conrad's fiction. The main plot of *Under Western*

Eyes, The Arrow of Gold, "Freya of the Seven Isles," and "The Inn of Two Witches" are, according to their respective narrators, based on written documents, such as a discovered manuscript or a posted notebook. And many of Conrad's books are made up of chapter-length excerpts of quoted writing, including Martin Decoud's pocketbook in *Nostromo*, H.C. Jörgenson's letter in *The Rescue*, the unnamed Captain's diary in *The Shadow-Line*, and Marlow's letter to a "privileged reader"—taking up all the ten last chapters of *Lord Jim* (264).

In contrast to the noted presence of letters and other written documents in his fictional writings, Conrad has made sure that voices are heard across his writings. The banter, babble, blubber, and "chitter-chatter" (*The Inheritors* 173) —the swapped yarn, the after-dinner conversation, the testimonial report, and the overheard rumor—are to date well-recognized elements of Conrad's fiction. Using an "extravagant and chatty prose" (Said 4), "Conrad was, if anything, a dialogist" (Fogel 22), "mesmerized by the spoken word" (Greaney 2), and wrote in "a style that is unmistakably a speaking voice" (Guerard 2). "[F]or good or evil mine is the speech that cannot be silenced," as the main first-person monologist of four of Conrad's books, the middle-aged Englishman Charlie Marlow, accurately puts it in *Heart of Darkness* (80).[1]

But have all the idiosyncratic elements of Conrad's vocal writing been explored? Are there defining elements of this written voice *qua* written voice that have not been the subject of discussion? And how do you reconcile the two seemingly opposite poles of Conrad's authorship—the written voice and the explicit presence of letters and other written material in his texts? Seeking to approach all these intertwined questions, I argue that there is a component of Conrad's conversational and monologic prose that has not received sustained attention. When studying Conrad's written voice we have overlooked the signature markers of oral conversation, the frequent occurrence of interjections and non-lexical vocalizations: the Ach, Ah, Aha, Ahem, Aw, Ay, Aye, Bah, Blab, Bosh, Brrroum, Brrrrrr, Er, Eh, He, Ha, Hah, Hm, H'm, Hoo, Ja, Jee, Na, O, Oh, Oho, Ough, Pfui, Pah, Phew, Phoo, Phooooo, Pinnnng, Pooh, Pssst, Pshaw, Ssh, Sssh, Tfui, Tse, Tut, Ugh, Whew, Whoop, Yaas, Yah, Yam, "rat-tat-tat," "tap, tap, tap," "Cht, cht," (Conrad, *Rover* 25), "Sh—ssh, Shssh!" (*Victory* 31), "Ba! ba! ba! brrr ... brr ... ba! ba!" (*"Narcissus"* 62), "Twang, twang, twang, Aouh hoo! Chroo yah!" (*Victory* 134), "Yap! yap! Bow-ow-ow—ow-ow! Yap! Yap!" (*Lord Jim* 93)—to list a few examples of vocalizations taken from across Conrad's works, which appear to stand in direct contrast to "cold, silent, colourless print," as Conrad classifies the medium of writing in "Autocracy and War" (71).[2]

This essay will compile and explore these by-products and/or components of written oral speech that at first sight may appear as inartistic as any non-voluntary vocalization, such as a burp, hiccup or a cough. Reading across Conrad's fiction, I will attempt a systematic analysis of all of Conrad's seemingly unsystematic interjections and non-lexical expressions. This is an odd undertaking. Conrad's skillful employment of these natural, unedited, spontaneous and accidental expressions makes it easy to overlook them—to forget that they are the product of an author sitting in solitude and silence, using time and thought to create the effect of immediacy: studiously introducing the living, spontaneous, stammering, wheezing, and grunting voice into the written text. The point, of course, is that it is anything but a spontaneous and casual exercise to negate the conventions of the written language—as Conrad masterfully did—and write in a manner that mimics oral language. How do you stammer in writing? How do you write a convincing grunt? How do you record the living voice in verbal format?

By exploring the wide-ranging and surprising use to which Conrad put these interjections and non-lexical expressions, this essay shows that there is a logic that guards the role, function, and variety of these seemingly trivial elements of language and voice.

PRELIMINARY DEFINITIONS: THE PHOO, PINNNNG, AND PHOOOOOF

As I have suggested, Conrad's signature markers of oral conversation—the "Bah!" and the "Bosh!" (*Agent* 22); the "Ba! ba! ba! brrr ... brr ... ba! ba!" (*"Narcissus"* 62)—are understudied, not yet comfortably embraced within precise, scholarly discourse. There are, of course, many excellent reasons for ignoring this seemingly esoteric topic, which includes the study of wheezes, whispers, "whoops and yells" ("Falk" 159), a topic which, as it happens, is exceedingly difficult to define. For instance, is "Yap! yap! Bow-ow-ow—ow-ow! Yap! Yap!" (*Lord Jim* 93) a non-lexical expression? Or is it more aptly classified as an onomatopoeic expression? Is it an element of non/sub/half-language? A sound effect? Neologism? Empty filler? And is it meaningful to classify all items in the list of expressions quoted in the third paragraph of this essay under one label? Do they all belong to the same category?

In *Beyond Words: Sobs, Hums, Stutters and Vocalizations*, Steven Connor offers a useful way of exploring those eclectic "features of speech" that "open language up momentarily to the world of sound events beyond articulate speech" (10). Distinguishing between noisy sounds and noise-effects, Connor coins the phrase "noise-events in speech," "at which there seems to be a significant suspension, or at least complication, of signifying intent" (11). As examples he lists expressions such as Ahem, Grrr, Hic, Mmmm, Pprrpffrrppffff, and Zzzz. My concern is similarly with "noise-events in speech," or what in Conradian terms can be called a "noise of voices," to borrow an expression used in *Suspense, Romance,* and *The Informer.* The noises of the voice elicit attention and are opposed to conventional understandings of articulate speech. They draw attention to human language outside words.

In the list of Conrad's "noise-events," "Hm," "Pshaw," "Aha" and the like are interjections: utterances that serve to express a spontaneous feeling or reaction. These expressions can function as one-word phrases and are normally unconjugated. "Phooooo" and "Bow-ow-ow-ow-ow!" and the like do not necessarily function as interjections. For instance, "Aouh hoo! Chroo yah!" (Conrad, *Victory* 134) is an imitation/evocation of music rather than an expression of a spontaneous feeling. Unlike many interjections, these expressions are non-lexical.

On its own, "non-lexical expression" is too vague to work as a useful definition since it includes any expression that cannot be found in a dictionary—such as multiple types of gestures. Gestures occur across Conrad's oeuvre but they are never expressed in the format of a "Brrroum" or a "Brrrrrr," which are included in the list of expressions discussed in the third paragraph of this essay. Silences are also a form of non-lexical expression, especially in Conrad's writing where they take on wide-ranging meanings. In *Nostromo*, for example, Charles Gould's "silences, backed by the power of speech, had as many shades of significance as uttered words in the way of assent, of doubt, of negotiation—even of simple comment" (203). Qualifying the label as non-lexical *vocal* expressions adds precision, but still allows for questionable inclusions. For instance, Willems in *An Outcast of the Islands* bites himself repetitively on his lower arm as a means of avoiding thinking about his new-lost love, Aissa. The bites themselves are, of course, both non-lexical and vocal but they have little in common with more fully articulated expressions such as "Phoo," "Pinnnng," and "Phooooo!" To restrict these expressions to vocalizations also excludes the few examples of vocalizations that exist in quoted writing (rather than speech)—such as in Marlow's letter and "the pages of the story" to the "privileged reader" in *Lord Jim* where Stein is quoted saying "Ach!" and Jewel, "Ah!" (264). Or, as will be discussed, in a few interior monologues in Conrad's fiction.

With an awareness of the complications in finding a coherent, exclusive, and precise definition of these "noise-events in speech," the aim is to build on these preliminary definitions and explore "the crossovers that result between the meaningless and the meaningful in vocal noise, and the particular kinds of meaning-making work done by the noises of the voice" (Connor 10). The following analysis will demonstrate that these hard-to-define vocalizations in Conrad's fiction are strategically important and related to the advancement of the plot and the communication of meaning.

"A NOISE OF VOICES":
MUMBLES, GURGLES, GROANS, COUGHS, HOWLS

During a lengthy dinner, leaning over a "table with his knuckles propped amongst coffee-cups, liqueur-glasses, cigar-ends" (Conrad, *Lord Jim* 90–1), Jim explains to Marlow what happened when he was beckoned, by his two former shipmates in a *Patna* lifeboat, to engage in conversation "for being a half-hearted shirker" (95). "There are no words for the sort of things I wanted to say," (97) he tells Marlow in a conversation punctuated by silences, vacant staring, false starts, inarticulate noises, and "a ghastly muddle of dubious stammers and movements" (119). From this sentence alone it appears that what Jim wanted to say to his former crew-members can be articulated and expressed—but not in words. "If I had opened my lips just then I would have simply howled like an animal" (97), he goes on to explain.

In the context of Conrad's fiction, howling is not always an expression of the limits of human communication. Conrad describes humans howling in many of his books, as well as quailing, squeaking, squealing, barking, bleating, growling, hissing, screeching, snarling and snorting. Conrad himself "howls" in his letters ("my howl of distress" [*CL* 1:300]). By contrast, it is rare to find an animal howling (a notable exception is Flora's dog in *Chance*). Animals are generally shown speaking with a wide register of expressions. For instance, a parrot and an owl can be found using fluent Spanish in *Nostromo*: "Viva Costaguana!" (82), "Ya-acabo! Ya-acabo!" (418).

In Conrad's fiction, to grunt, grumble, howl, and speak with interjections and non-lexical expressions characterize human speech. The lack of these types of expressions, on the other hand, indicates the presence of an impersonal, monotonic, and/or machine-like voice, as in *Lord Jim* when the French lieutenant utters his "own country's pronouncement," "in the passionless and definite phraseology a machine would use, if machines could speak" (122). Or in *The Rescue*, which records "the impersonal ring of a voice without a master" (218). A similar example can be found in *The Inheritors*, a novel Conrad partly co-wrote with Ford Madox Hueffer. In this book, the narrator Arthur encounters an unnamed lady who says she comes from the Fourth Dimension. She belongs to a "superior race" without "ideals, prejudices, or remorse; with no feeling for art and no reverence for life; free from any ethical tradition; callous to pain, weakness, suffering and death" (9). Unlike earthly humans, she is not "worm-eaten with altruism and ethics" (13). Her voice reflects her machine-like being. According to Arthur, she spoke using an "expressionless voice": "I seemed to be listening to a phonograph reciting a technical work." (9).

A phonograph reciting a technical work would likely speak in an even, monotone, fluent voice. A phonograph does not hesitate, sneeze, cough, stammer or use empty fillers—like most of the characters who are given a voice in Conrad's fiction. A phonograph certainly does not have a speech impediment, unlike a "person who lisped" in *The Inheritors* (17) or Guzman Bento in *Nostromo* who, "His front teeth having been knocked out in some accident of his former herdsman's life, his uttering was spluttering and indistinct" (139) and similar to the "venomous spluttering from the old [and toothless] terrorist" Karl Yundt in *The Secret Agent* (44). In addition to these seemingly permanent speech disorders, there are characters in Conrad's fiction who, on occasion, fail to accomplish the physical act of speaking, due to being overwhelmed by a specific situation—as when Jim speaks with Marlow about the *Patna*; when the Russian Harlequin in *Heart of Darkness* finds that his "feelings [on the topic of whether Kurtz's actions] were too much for speech" (*Youth* 105); when Razumov, in *Under Western Eyes*, is overwhelmed by the unexpected presence of Haldin in his room; or when Hirsch—during a forceful interrogation by the robber-bandit Sotillo in *Nostromo*—gets his Spanish "so mixed up with German that the better half of his statements remained incomprehensible" (329). These multiple instances of speech disfluency across Conrad's fiction imply, among many other things, that Conrad's characters are humans rather than phonographs. Hesitating, stammering, and lisping are, just like howling, at the heart of being a relatable and fallible human—or at least a convincing Conradian representation of one.

CHARACTERIZED BY A COUGH

In *Nostromo*, on the lighter filled with silver, Martin Decoud fears that the cowardly Hirsch, a German hide merchant who has sought refuge in the lighter, will make a sound that will reveal their position to a crew of bandits: "What if Hirsch coughed or sneezed?" (284), Decoud worryingly reflects. In this, "the most desperate undertaking of his life" (426), a cough or a sneeze is portrayed and perceived as the difference between life and death. Neither the cough nor the sneeze materialize at the critical moment when the steamer encounters the lighter, but the threat of this non-voluntary vocalization and "idiotic contingency" (284) serves to characterize Hirsch's temperament of "terror and despair" (292) in contrast to the machismo and heroism of Nostromo and Decoud, the latter of whom "had kept complete possession of himself" (292) during the same encounter.

There are other examples of non-voluntary vocalizations in Conrad's fiction that are meaningful for characterization. In *Under Western Eyes*, the lady companion Tekla takes dictation for Peter Ivanovitch, the great feminist. She is terrified of making herself heard during these writing sessions: "The slightest movement you make puts to flight the ideas of Peter Ivanovitch. You hardly dare to breathe. And as to coughing—God forbid!" (118), she explains to Natalia Haldin. The point here is that a cough—by its very insignificance—tells us something very significant about the "great feminist" Peter Ivanovitch, who seemingly cannot cope with being reminded of the physical presence of a female.

A "groan" functions similarly in *Heart of Darkness*, where it signals the malpractice, corruption, and narrow-mindedness of a notable character. Towards the beginning of the novella, the immaculately dressed accountant voices his grievance: "'The groans of this sick person,' he said, 'distract my attention. And without that it is extremely difficult to guard against clerical errors in this climate'" (Conrad, *Youth* 60). His request for sympathy is as absurd as that of a guard in any death camp. Instead of informing his accounting of the situation—the corruption, mismanagement, death, and forced labor—he understands the groans as a distraction from his proper occupation, the making of "correct entries of perfectly correct transactions" (61). As in *Under Western Eyes*, where Tekla fears coughing in the presence of Peter Ivanovitch, the groans of the sick person overheard by the accountant are significant, telling elements of the texts—and the author's own sympathies.

INTERJECTIONS IN MULTILINGUAL PROSE

Interjections and non-lexical expressions are, like other expressions of sound, contingent on language. For instance, the clock says "tick tock" in English; "tic tac" in Spanish; "dī dā" in Mandarin; "katchin katchin" in Japanese; "tik-tik" in Hindi. When Conrad vocalizes the sound of the clock, as in *The Secret Agent*, it correctly follows standardized English and says "tick" rather than "tik-tik" or "katchin katchin." Does Conrad similarly use interjections and non-lexical expressions mimetically to reflect culture-specific articulations? There are many culture-specific articulations for Conrad to consider, given the presence of multiple languages in his texts, including Dutch, Malay, Arabic, Chinese, Italian, German, Spanish, Russian, Latin, French, English (and "pidgin English" [*"Narcissus"* 13]), unidentified African languages (likely including Bantu), "the international language of the sea" (*Youth* 28) spelled out in flags, and references to "one of those impossible languages which sometimes we hear in our dreams" ("Outpost of Progress" 85).[3] A few texts are to be understood as if they were translated from a source language: *Nostromo* and "Gaspar Ruiz," Spanish; *The Arrow of Gold*, *The Rover*, *Heart of Darkness*, "The Duel," and *Suspense*, French; *Under Western Eyes*, Russian (where the teacher of languages' writing in English primarily originates from Razumov's Russian notebook). Conrad also oversaw translations of his work into French. In short, to say that Conrad writes in English is a truth with modification. To take one example of how complex Conrad's use of multiple languages is, let us look at one sentence in *Under Western Eyes*: "'And how is Herr Razumov,' sounded the greeting in German" (219). In this sentence, *German* is spoken to the *Russian* Razumov in *French*-speaking Switzerland, recorded by Razumov in Russian in his notebook, and translated to *English* by the teacher of languages. If the speaker, hearer, place of utterance, and narrator is taken into consideration, the context of the sentence is an admixture of four languages.

This multilingual aspect of Conrad's prose adds complexity. Conrad's own use of non-English interjections is limited to a few expressions: Ach, Na (German), Eh? (Spanish), Tse! (Malay), Aw (Chinese), Aha, Ah!, Eh (French)—some of which are recycled across his texts. These expressions are either part of an entire sentence written out in German, French, or Spanish, or used to indicate that the person is speaking German, French, Spanish, Malay, or Chinese. While French was Conrad's second language (and English his third after Polish), he had very little exposure to German, Spanish, Malay, and Chinese. That said, the native German Stein in *Lord Jim* convincingly uses German sentence constructions when speaking English, which requires more than a rudimentary understanding of the language. And Conrad had taken multiple lessons in Spanish (*CL* 3:408)—albeit in 1907, after the completion of *Nostromo*.

Even when Conrad lacks a detailed awareness of how to reproduce these sounds in a culturally sanctioned manner, however, he still uses multiple interjections. *Nostromo*, whose primary source language is Spanish, uses the following interjections: Ah!, Aha!, Bah!, Bosh!, Eh?, Ha!, He!, H'm!, Tfui, and "br-r-r-r" (51). Conrad lacks an intimate knowledge of its oral discourse and refrains from revealing his ignorance—which he would most likely have done had he attempted to write the dialogue with a high-frequency of *non-lexical* Spanish expressions rather than standardized Anglophone interjections. He could consult books on the history of South America, as he did, but he would have found it virtually impossible to research non-lexical Spanish expressions and how they are used. The "phonetic spelling of the Oxd. Dictionary is a mere phantasy" (*CL* 7:174), Conrad exclaims in a letter on adequately portraying English speech in *The Nigger of the "Narcissus."* Similarly, discussing Conrad's use of different languages in his texts, Amy Houston speculates that perhaps "the author's relative unfamiliarity with Dutch would explain his failure to translate the speech of Dutch characters with a comparable degree of explicitness" (16), as he did with French.

As with *Nostromo*, *The Nigger of the "Narcissus"* uses multiple interjections: Ba!, Brr, Brrr, Brrrr, Brrrrrr, Ah!, Ay, Aye!, Eh?, O!, Ough!, Pah, Pah!, Phoo!, Yah, Yah!, and, to characterize Mr Baker's speech, forty-seven "Ough!"s. It is an atypical book, based on more than a decade of exposure to the multi-national English being spoken on merchant ships. Conrad is fluent in this language. As I discuss elsewhere,[4] there are more quotations per word in *The Nigger of the "Narcissus"* than in any other Conrad story, apart from *The Inheritors* and *Victory* (quotations per word = the total number of quotations in the book divided by the total word count). The Dent edition of *The Nigger of the "Narcissus"* contains more than 900 direct quotations, more than 110 references to "voice" and "voices," and uses about 400 ellipses (all of which are used to mark pauses in speech). Why there are so many direct quotations in *The Nigger of the "Narcissus"* may be related to the fact that this is a language that Conrad is confident in using. *The Nigger of the "Narcissus"* is made up of slang, colloquialisms, interjections, and non-lexical expressions. Using this type of language correctly requires mastery.[5] A nineteenth-century able seaman did not just have an accurate understanding of technical vocabulary—such as belaying pin, bowsprit, capstan, windlass and jib-boom—but also had an understanding of the informal language that is being spoken aboard. Indeed, Conrad's near-contemporary Herman Melville (1819–91) announces in *Moby-Dick: Or, The Whale* (1851)—written about half a century before *The Nigger of the "Narcissus"* — "that certain locutions unique to the whaling industry were not to be found in Johnson's lexicon or in Noah Webster's 'ark'" (Babcock 91). By writing from the perspective of the men in the forecastle rather than the officers in the after-castle, Melville, along with Conrad and writers like Richard Henry Dana, Jr., revolutionized traditional Anglophone sea-writing. Incorporating authentic speech, Melville was lampooned by his contemporaries for his extravagant and eccentric expressions, his use of "'execrable' English and 'drunken' language" (Babcock 91). There are many examples of atypical and original language use in *Moby-Dick,* which contains the following interjections and non-lexical expressions: ah!, ahoy!, arrah, "Blang-whang!," eh, "Fa, la! lirra, skirra!," ha!, halloa, Hark!, "Hem, hem, hem," "Hish! hish!," Ho!, "Ho, ho!," Hoot!, hump!, hurrah!, huzza!, "La!, la," lo!, O, oh!, "oh-he-yo," "—oh! ah!—," "pooh, pooh!," "shirr! shirr!," Tut!, Um-m, "Um, um, um," whew!, and "Caw! caw! caw! caw! caw!" (Melville 475).

As with Melville, Conrad did not make a "speciality of seamanship *en chambre* [armchair sailing]" (*CL* 3:173), but was able to rely on his own intimate lived experiences of *spoken* language.[6] Here we encounter extraordinary expressions, such as this one: "Ba! ba! ba! brrr ... brr ... ba! ba!" (Conrad, *"Narcissus"* 62). It is an expression that in its combination of seventeen letters, five exclamation points and two ellipses only exists once in the history of literature: in *The Nigger of the "Narcissus."*[7] The uniqueness of this expression does not suggest that Conrad fabricated the expression *ex nihilo* anymore than a painter's unique interpretation of a scene would imply that he or she did not work from observation. "Ba! ba! ba! brrr ... brr ... ba! ba!" is too specific to be a direct recording/translation but likely evokes a remembered event, mood, or feeling. That said, the difference between the aural and the verbal medium undermines the notion that this expression is fully mimetic in nature: "Ba! ba! ba! brrr ... brr ... ba! ba!" is not merely an oral expression— meant to be heard—it is also a visual experience. There is a symmetry to the way the letters combine on the page. It cannot be reduced to an auditory expression—it is an expression of sound that is meant to be read, in silence.[8]

As a stand-alone quotation, the meaning of this expression is, of course, not self-evident. It is Belfast who makes this blabbing noise, unconsciously, half-asleep, and freezing. It is an involuntary expression, caused by an insistent cold. It provokes the chief mate Mr Baker to tell him to "Stop that" (62). Belfast successfully manages to stop his string of "Ba! ba! ba!"s, but Conrad continues using a high frequency of interjections throughout the novel.

This extended "Ba! ba!" expression echoes a similar expression in *Nostromo*, published seven years after *The Nigger of the "Narcissus."* When Don Jose Avellanos visits Mrs. Gould for tea time, he shudders and produces an involuntary non-lexical expression, which signals his dislike for tea: "He drank up all the tea at once in one draught. This performance was invariably followed by a slight shudder and a low, involuntary 'br–r–r–r,' which was not covered by the hasty exclamation, 'Excellent!'" (*Nostromo* 51). Had Conrad never written *The Nigger of the "Narcissus,"* it is doubtful that Don Jose Avellanos would have shuddered in this manner: "br–r–r–r," where the dashes extend a more traditional way of verbalizing a shudder (brrrr) into a staccato shudder, similar to the blabbing noise Belfast made in *The Nigger of the "Narcissus."*

"'AHA!' THOUGHT CARTER":
INTERJECTIONS IN INTERIOR MONOLOGUE

One of the most striking features of Conrad's use of interjections is in interior monologue: "that inner voice that speaks in all of us at times" (*Rover* 321). Or, to use the expression twice employed in *Under Western Eyes* to describe Razumov's interior monologue: "mental soliloquy" (218, 222). In *The Rescue*, D'Alcacer's inner voice is spelled out with an interjection: "'Pah! I shall be probably speared through the back in the beastliest possible fashion,' he thought with an inward shudder" (364). The structure of the sentence echoes Carter's internal thought process, a few chapters later: "'Aha!' thought Carter" (380). In *Nostromo*, Sotillo's interior voice speculates that Hirsch is difficult to interrogate: "the man might have gone mad with fear. A lunatic is a hopeless subject. Bah! A pretence" (446). In the same novel, Linda, outraged by Nostromo's preference for her sister, Giselle, tells herself that he can break her heart, but not her spirit: "Aha! He could not break that" (549). In *Lord Jim*, Egström narrates his initial and internal thought process to Marlow about why his former employee decided to leave, speculating that he wanted a pay rise: "Thinks I to myself: 'Oho! a rise in the screw—that's the trouble—is it?'" (147).

Is this usage of interjections realistic? Do spontaneous vocalizations such as "Pah!," "Bah!," "Aha!," and "Oho!" have a place in interior monologue? Most can relate to some form of non-vocal, verbal expressions such as "aha moments." And many other writers of Conrad's era, notably Virginia Woolf, frequently use interjections in interior monologues. But verbal thought processes may, primarily, be a convention of fiction. After all, a large segment of the history of philosophy is about the relationship between language and thought—and whether language is necessary for thought. To this day there are many unresolved questions.[9]

When interjections are used in interior monologues, one's private sensations, thoughts, and ideas appear to overlap with verbal language, to a surprising extent. This is a peculiar linkage, given that Conrad routinely laments the lack of a seamless transition between sensation, thought and expression: in private letters and public texts, he writes eloquently and repeatedly about his search for the right word (the *mot juste*), on why not everything can be described, and the frustration of being "able to think and unable to express" (*CL* 1:288). Many of his characters—such as Jim, Marlow, and the young narrator in *The Arrow of Gold*—articulate similar views about language's limited ability to express interior thoughts, feelings, and impressions.

Conrad sparingly uses interjections in interior monologue, but these echo his occasional use of interjections in fictional letters. Indeed, Marlow in *Lord Jim*, Decoud in *Nostromo*, and the unnamed Captain in *The Shadow-Line* all write in a style that is formally indistinguishable from the voice that explains how these fictional characters think and speak. Thus, when a fictional letter is included in one of Conrad's texts it is not, as one would expect, marked with trite metaphors and a limited range of expressions. Instead, these fictional letters are remarkably articulate and carry every mark of the modernist author, such as the inclusion of interjections. Thus, while one would not necessarily expect that Marlow, Decoud and the Captain in "The Shadow-Line" were as gifted with the pen as Conrad, the letters they write indicate that they could have had alternative careers as modernist novelists. I am not here implying that Conrad only had one register as fictional writer, the voice. Notable exceptions to the written voice are Carter's letter to Lingard in *The Rescue*, two quoted letters in "The Arrow of Gold," as well as a lengthy letter from "a friend" at the beginning of "The Informer." These letters use more formal language and are written without interjections and non-lexical expressions.

Conrad's use of interjections in speech, writing, and thought is not necessarily unrealistic—in its small way, it communicates the predominance of oral discourse in Conrad's fiction and how it crosses over into thought and writing. Just as a light bulb in a thought bubble in a comic magazine symbolizes that a character has an eureka moment (rather than is thinking about a light bulb), representing interior monologue in verbal thought should not literally be interpreted to mean that the character's thought process can be accurately portrayed in words.

"VOICES CAME TO ME": CONCLUSION

Enclosed within quotation marks, punctuated by ellipses of non-standardized length, marked by accent, and spelled out alongside abbreviated words, interjections and non-lexical expressions are prevalent in Conrad's fiction. Just because Conrad uses interjections and non-lexical expressions with high frequency does not automatically make them worthy of discussion, however. And what characters say is arguably more important than whether they gurgle and mumble when saying something. Yet Conrad's fiction demonstrates that the meaning of these expressions is far from phonetically self-evident; they are used to illustrate a range of diverse happenings, from spitting, singing, freezing, drinking tea, to the sound of a typhoon, and *tristes* ("Twang, twang, twang, Aouh hoo! Chroo yah!" [*Victory* 134]). Conrad's use of interjections and non-lexical expressions in high frequency may of course appear to be as artless as a burp or cough—or as artless as the coffee, wax and ink stains in his manuscripts. It is quite the reverse. These noise-effects can add nuance and nuisance, meaning and confusion, and are important for characterization, the development of direct speech, and interior monologues.

His prose cannot function without these interjections and non-lexical elements—the nuts and bolts of informal oral speech—anymore than the steamer in *Heart of Darkness* can progress without rivets. From *Almayer's Folly* to *Sus-*

pense, Conrad's idiolect is to a varying extent characterized by idiosyncratic interjections and non-lexical expressions. Although a few of these expressions lack a meaning in a dictionary, Conrad's fiction demonstrates that they are sometimes the most telling elements of speech and revealing of the author's own sympathies. These seemingly insignificant noise-events demonstrate Conrad's radical recordings of the living voice in written format: his ability to represent not only that which can be expressed in language, but also a range of human emotion and impressions that cannot be summed up in words.

NOTES

1. There are many notable book-length studies on Conrad and language, including *Language and Being: Joseph Conrad and the Literature of Personality* (1976) by Peter J. Glassman; *Joseph Conrad: Language and Fictional Self-consciousness* (1979), by Jeremy Hawthorn; *Conrad, Language, and Narrative* (2001), by Michael Greaney; and *Conrad and Language* (2016), edited by Katherine Isobel Baxter and Robert Hampson.

2. There are elements of Conrad's non-verbal language that have received sustained attention. In the essay, "'No need of words': Joseph Conrad's Use of the Typographical Ellipsis in *Under Western Eyes* and 'The Secret Sharer,'" Jeremy Hawthorn explores how ellipses and dashes function not only as "silence transcriptions," "gaps at the micro-level of writing" but also as "something in themselves, a sign to draw attention to and comment interpretatively upon some aspect of a spoken or written text or utterance" (6).

3. See Robert Hampson's informative chapter "Conrad and Nautical Language: Flying Moors and Crimson Barometers" in *Conrad and Language* (2016).

4. See Johan, Warodell "The Heroism of Serving Coffee: Joseph Conrad and *The Nigger of the 'Narcissus.'" Partial Answers*, vol. 18, no. 1, 2020, pp. 51-66.

5. This is not to promote the myth of life at sea as a wholly uneducated existence. In Conrad's *The Rover*, Peyrol had during many years at sea "learned to speak intelligibly and think connectedly and even to read and write after a fashion" (8). Helen Chambers has a chapter on Conrad's own extensive shipboard reading in *Conrad's Reading: Space, Time, Networks*. She also notes the "collective reading, writing, and musical performances on board" the *Torrens*, in an article titled "'The first mate is a Polish count, a very quiet fellow': Some New Torrens Documents" (3). Also consider Herman Melville's sailors, who are described reading everything from Adam Smith's *Wealth of Nations* to Plutarch's *Lives* in the forecastle.

6. Despite an intimate experience of the spoken language used by merchant mariners, he is not exempt from making mistakes when writing dialogue. Responding to an inquisitive reader (C.S. Evans), Conrad points out that Donkin's speech in the novel is not in agreement with his cockney designation: "All the phonetics of Donkin's speech are wrong, alas! A real cockney drops his aspirates—but he *never* adds one. Its [sic] the country people who do that [. . .]. What I ought to have done was to take out *every* initial *h* out of his speeches, since I called him a cockney. But God only knows what Donkin is!" (*CL* 7:174).

7. Up until the year 2017 with the publication of the Cambridge Edition, the expression

only existed in manuscript form, all other book-length publications used the non-Conrad edited expression: "Ba-ba-ba-brr-ba-ba."

8. Conrad frequently uses visual simile to evoke sound. To take a few examples from *Lord Jim*: at one point, the skipper's voice resembles "the rasping sound of wood-file on the edge of a plank" (22). And, when hearing that his chief engineer is laid up drunk in bed, his thick throat produces a rumble, "on which the sound of the word *Schwein* fluttered high and low like a capricious feather in a faint stir of air" (23). In the same novel, a teaspoon falling on "the tessellated floor of the verandah rang out like a tiny and silvery scream" (80) and Jewel, holding a torch to light the way for Lord Jim, "seemed to glide without touching the earth; the only sound was the silky swish and rustle of the long grass" (228).

9. For a recent contribution, consider Jose Luis Bermudez's meticulously argued "theory of nonlinguistic thought" (ix) in *Thinking Without Words* (2003). The book spans cognitive ethology, developmental psychology, and cognitive archeology, maintaining that "the capacity for thought is not in any way tied to language possession" (vii). By intertwining evidence of thought processes in pre-linguistic infants, non-language-using creatures and "evidence of thinking behaviors long before even the earliest plausible dates for the emergence of language" (4), Bermudez shows that "the domain of the cognitive far outstrips the domain of the linguistic" (5), that "language is not necessary for thought" (5).

WORKS CITED

Babcock, Merton. "The Vocabulary of Moby Dick." *American Speech*, vol. 27, no. 2, 1952, pp. 91–101.
Chambers, Helen. "'The first mate is a Polish count, a very quiet fellow': Some New *Torrens* Documents." *The Conradian*, vol. 42, no. 2, 2017, pp. 69–87.
Conrad, Joseph. *Almayer's Folly*. Cambridge University Press, 1994.
———. "Autocracy and War." *Notes on Life and Letters*. Cambridge University Press, 2004.
———. *The Collected Letters of Joseph Conrad*. Edited by Frederick R. Karl and Laurence Davies, Cambridge University Press, 1983.
———. "Falk." *The Nigger of the "Narcissus" and Typhoon & Other Stories*. Dent, 1950.
———. "The Informer." *A Set of Six*. Dent, 1954.
———. *Lord Jim*. Cambridge University Press, 2012.
———. *An Outcast of the Islands*. Cambridge University Press, 2016.
———. *The Nigger of the "Narcissus."* Cambridge University Press, 2017.
———. *Nostromo: A Tale of the Seaboard*. Dent, 1950.
———. "An Outpost of Progress." *Tales of Unrest*, Cambridge University Press, 2012.
———. *The Secret Agent: A Simple Tale*. Cambridge University Press, 1990.
———. *The Rescue: A Romance of the Shallows*. Dent, 1920.
———. *Romance*. Dent, 1941.
———. *The Rover*. Oxford University Press, 1992.
———. *The Nigger of the "Narcissus" and Typhoon & Other Stories*. Dent, 1950.
———. *Under Western Eyes*. Cambridge University Press, 2013.
———. *Victory*. Cambridge University Press, 2016.
———. *Youth, Heart of Darkness, The End of the Tether*. Cambridge University Press, 2010.
Conrad, Joseph and Ford Madox Hueffer. *The Inheritors*. Dent, 1941.

Fogel, Aaron. *Coercion to Speak: Conrad's Poetics of Dialogue*. Harvard University Press, 1985.

Greaney, Michael. *Conrad, Language, and Narrative*. Cambridge University Press, 2002.

Guerard. Albert J. *Conrad the Novelist*. Harvard University Press, 1958.

Hampson, Robert. "Conrad and Nautical Language: Flying Moors and Crimson Barometers." *Conrad and Language*, edited by Katherine Baxter and Robert Hampson, Edinburgh University Press, 2016, pp. 10-27.

Hawthorn, Jeremy. "'No need of words': Joseph Conrad's Use of the Typographical Ellipsis in *Under Western Eyes* and 'The Secret Sharer.'" *Conradiana*, vol. 43, nos. 2-3, 2011, pp. 5-23.

Melville, Herman. *Moby-Dick: Or, The Whale*. Penguin, 2013.

Said, Edward. *Joseph Conrad and the Fiction of Autobiography*. Columbia University Press, 2008.

Ward, Nigel. "Non-lexical conversational sounds in American English." *Pragmatics & Cognition*, vol. 14, no. 1, 2006, pp. 41-50.

Warodell, Johan. "The Heroism of Serving Coffee: Joseph Conrad and *The Nigger of the 'Narcissus.'*" *Partial Answers*, vol. 18, no. 1, 2020, pp. 51-66.

A "Modern" Amongst the "Standards": Conrad in the Classroom

PATRICIA PYE

BUCKS NEW UNIVERSITY

ABSTRACT

Conrad's modernity had a significant but overlooked educational dimension. Though school editions of his fiction have received little critical attention, these were instrumental in promoting his work amongst teachers and educationalists. This article opens with a consideration of the "Newbolt Report" (1921), a document testifying to Conrad's significance in the classroom in a progressive period for the teaching of English literature. Focusing on the publication of *Youth and Gaspar Ruiz* in Dent's "Kings Treasuries" series, the article also explores Conrad's misgivings about "school books," and his aversion to the use of literature for pedagogic purposes. Despite this, and as his 1922 interview for the *Teachers World* reveals, Conrad was championed as a modern writer for the modern classroom, ensuring his place in an educational, as well as literary, canon.

KEYWORDS

education, school editions, The Newbolt Report, Dent's "Kings Treasuries," *Youth and Gaspar Ruiz*, *Teachers World*, Joseph Conrad

There is something bewitching in thinking that you can touch the same piece of wood that your ancestor touched a hundred years ago. Even when you come back after having left the school your initials stand out among others as happy remembrances of bygone days, as the oasis will stand out of the desert hastening the footsteps and gladdening the heart

> of the weary traveller. When childhood is past the initials seem to form links in a never-forgotten chain of the happiness of "Youth."
>
> "'Youth" inspired Joseph Conrad in one of his finest works. J.P.F. really stands for "Youth," and so also for happiness. No one can forget his childhood; how eager some boys are to get out into the world and earn their own living —and only too late try to turn back.
> —D. Jackson, Form IVa, Oswestry School[1]

This school-boy's account serves to remind us that Conrad was a familiar name in British classrooms in the 1920s. And "Youth," in particular, was a popular story, thanks to its relevant theme and more pragmatically to the availability of cheap editions produced for schools. The story had an especial interest for the pupils of Oswestry School, due to its mention of *Ride to Khiva*, by Frederick Burnaby, who was a former pupil. A letter from Conrad responding to requests for information about Burnaby was published in the school's magazine *The Oswestrian* in December 1922. The same issue of the magazine includes this reflective piece about the nature of childhood, written by a boy who had been intrigued by some initials (J.P.F.) and a date (1860) carved into a classroom desk. He was also clearly engaged by "Youth," perhaps encountering the full story in Dent's "The Kings Treasuries of Literature" series, or the extracts in *Cambridge Readings in English Literature*. "Glad your boys like my prose," Conrad had responded to George Sampson (a headmaster and the *Cambridge Readings* editor) when asked for permission to publish the extracts (*CL* 9:179). Sampson was amongst the progressive educationalists who helped to promote Conrad's fiction to a new audience. However, as we will see, Conrad had misgivings about "school books" and more generally about the mediation of his fiction for educational purposes.

A TEACHER'S WRITER

As John Stape has noted, Conrad had become a "writer's writer" towards the end of his career, famously being fêted by the likes of William Faulkner and F. Scott Fitzgerald when he visited the Long Island home of his American publisher Frank Doubleday in 1923 (271). But it should not be forgotten that Conrad had also become a "teacher's writer" by this time, achieving status and recognition in the rather more prosaic world of classrooms, textbooks, and examinations. Conrad's fiction was already appearing on examination papers by the time of his death in 1924, and a review of the syllabi for the following years reveals the extent to which he was regarded as a worthy modern addition to the established classics. For example, *Youth and Gaspar Ruiz* was included as prescribed reading in the JMB Matriculation English Literature syllabus for 1926. Meanwhile, in the University of London Matriculation syllabus for the same year, Conrad was an optional "subject for essay" in the English paper, as an alternative to Arnold Bennett.[2]

It is well known that Conrad's popularity had grown since the publication of *Chance* in 1914, but the significance of the educational market in this success has gone largely unnoticed until now. Yet, by 1915, school textbooks were already including him amongst the modern novelists whose works "should certainly be read" (see, for example, Sparks 288). As I will argue in this article, the classroom is a crucial space for the reading, reception, and interpretation of Conrad's work. Conrad's modernity has typically been explored in literary terms, but it should not be forgotten that this had a significant educational dimension. In the years following the First World War, the teaching of English Literature was being reformed, and it is especially productive to explore the consolidation of Conrad's literary reputation in this context. In particular, we witness how perceptions of Conrad's modernity were nuanced by his identity as a "foreign" writer. It is also apparent how influential figures in educational circles helped smooth his path into the "canon," promoting his work to a wider audience and ensuring his future legacy.

However, this popularity with teachers posed a dilemma for Conrad. Unlike some of his literary contemporaries, perhaps most notably H.G. Wells, he was not active in educational circles, nor did he seek to educate through his fiction. And Conrad was especially averse to his work being mined for pedagogic or moral instruction. He makes this plain in a letter to John Dent in 1920:

> On returning home yesterday I found an absurd wire from the Evening Standard asking me to say whether that forthcoming book of mine [*The Rescue*] had in it any "message for the young." Could anything be more silly than such an inquiry and, especially, to a man like me who had never flapped any "messages" in the face of the world? I was sorely tempted to answer that it all depended whether the "young" in question was an ass or not. (*CL* 7:116)

In addition to this kind of journalistic interest in the educational potential of his fiction, however, Conrad had to accept that this was now being adapted for a classroom readership, with all the associated risks of simplification and misinterpretation that this entailed. In later sections of this article, I will discuss the "Kings Treasuries" edition of *Youth and Gaspar Ruiz*, and Conrad's interview with the *Teachers World*, both of which reveal new insights into the mediation of his work for educational purposes. Firstly, it is useful to identify some of the factors informing Conrad's popularity with progressive educationalists in the 1920s.

A CONRADIAN PERSPECTIVE ON THE NEWBOLT REPORT

Since the 1890s, pressure had been increasing in the United Kingdom to assert the study of English Literature over the Latin and Greek classics, and furthermore to teach it on more creative principles. English Literature was not regarded as "the expression of art and genius," rather, as one commentator complained, a *modus operandi* for "exercises in grammar, syntax, and etymology" (Collins 21–2, Shayer 7). Such conflicts between traditionalist and progressive approaches towards language and literature emerge in the debates about Conrad's use of grammar in his early fiction in the late 1890s. As Mary Burgoyne has discussed, some reviewers of *Tales of Unrest* took issue with his use of "like" instead of "as," leading the philologist and lecturer F.J. Furnivall to defend Conrad's use of English and to suggest in the journal *Outlook* that his critics "go back to school and learn grammar" (125).

Furnivall's defence of Conrad was echoed by progressive educationalists over subsequent years, who argued for less focus on the rules of language, and more on creative expression. Ironically, given that he had once famously railed to Cunninghame Graham about being perceived as a "bloody foreigner," the fact that Conrad was a non-native speaker of English was now being promoted as an advantage in educational circles. He clearly had no personal experience of learning English in a British classroom, a space that became associated with outdated rote learning. It was felt by some, therefore, that Conrad had a distinctive style, unfettered by the "soulless" teaching of grammatical rules. As a representative of the English Association asserted in 1920:

> Conrad, coming fresh to the language, can trust the native character of it with far less disturbance from memories of how it has been defaced by soulless repetitions [. . .]. The slight slips that can be detected in his earlier work do not affect the essential truth of this: they are only amusing as showing the difference between school-master's accuracy and the grasp of genius. (Melion Stawell 89)

In a similar vein, the teacher/educational writer Guy Pocock suggested in a note to the 1924 edition of *Youth and Gaspar Ruiz* that Conrad's words were "chosen with the meticulous care of a foreigner, a master indeed of our tongue, but not a native of it." Pocock concluded that Conrad's words had a "somewhat un-English atmosphere," a rather vague statement which can nevertheless be located within the educational discourse of its time (Pocock 182–83).[3] Like the statement above, it alludes to the idea that Conrad's artistry defied linguistic analysis of the type that had characterized traditional literary study. And in a period when progressive English teachers were calling for a greater focus on writers' aesthetics (their "art and genius"), this was a persuasive idea, ascribing to Conrad's fiction a sense of freshness and modernity. Pocock, an assistant master at the Royal Naval College in Dartmouth, Devon, also contributed to the influential government report *The Teaching of English in England* (the Newbolt Report) which was published in 1921. Like other figures who promoted Conrad's fiction in the 1920s, Pocock was at the vanguard of the reformist movement in literature teaching. Indeed, his innovative and "experimental" teaching practices at the Royal Naval College were singled out for praise in this report (Board of Education 103).

The adoption of Conrad's fiction into the educational curriculum can undoubtably be associated with the influence of figures like Pocock and more generally from the publication of the Newbolt Report, not least because there were notable "Conradians" on its committee who helped to promote his work to schools. These included the afore-mentioned headmaster George Sampson, whose *English for the English* (also published in 1921) was a seminal text in progressive educational circles, arguing for a less "arithmetical" (e.g., grammatical) and more creative approach to the teaching of literature (Shayer 76–9). Then there was Sir Arthur Quiller-Couch ("Q"), a prestigious public figure in educational and political circles, who had admired *The Nigger of the "Narcissus"* on its publication in 1897.

The Newbolt Report was instrumental in foregrounding the wider potential of English Literature as a "universal, reasonable, and liberal" means of improving the nation's education (Board of Education 348). Such terms are consistent with the wider social changes that had occurred since the First World War: here the concept of "universality" acknowledges the value of educating everyone for "life," rather than for a "livelihood," as had typically been the fate of the working classes in the Victorian era.[4] As the title of George Sampson's book *English for the English* suggests, this project was underpinned and limited by patriotic aspirations for the enhanced status of England's national literature, which was still symbolized by a prescribed set of pre-twentieth century English writers. However, the Newbolt Report helped establish a climate more conducive to the study of contemporary authors. It also promoted a more artistic and holistic approach to literary study, which shifted attention away from the mechanics of prose to an author's aesthetics and wider themes. There was also greater focus on individual and silent reading (as opposed to the whole class reading aloud, often together), and on encouraging children's creative self-expression. As Shayer has discussed, this reflected the coming together of various modernizing influences in education, including the child-centred psychological theories of Maria Montessori.

According to the terms of the Newbolt Report, "universal" was not synonymous with "global." However, Conrad's fiction clearly had a particular appeal as it offered a varied range of historical periods and geographical locations, opening up opportunities for a more thematic approach to literary study. But there were also more pragmatic reasons behind Conrad's popularity in the classroom. As the Newbolt Report put it: "nothing is more vital for the spread of good literature than the supply of good editions of standard authors at a moderate cost" (Board of Education 359). As we will see, Conrad was well served by his publishers in this regard, especially as the classroom editions of his fiction reflected the new initiatives in literary study.

YOUTH AND GASPAR RUIZ IN DENT'S "THE KINGS TREASURIES OF LITERATURE": "AIDS TO DELIGHT AND LEARNING"

John Dent had high ideals for the "Kings Treasuries" series. This was a junior version of the successful Everyman list, and Dent aimed to "put into school children's hands a series of books which they would love, not task-books or text-books, but real aids to delight and learning" (Dent 236). Such terms were clearly in the spirit of new educational practice, particularly as they foregrounded the notion of "delight" in reading. The list encompassed a rich range of literature, including Shakespeare's plays, collections of poetry, prose, short stories, essays and letters.

As an advertisement for the series in the *Teachers World* (Figure 1) indicates, there were 103 titles by 1924, broadly divided into "modern" and "standard." *Youth and Gaspar Ruiz* was one of the "best moderns," and at a later date it was joined by *Four Stories by Joseph Conrad* ("The Secret Sharer," "The Partner," "The Inn of the Two Witches," and "Freya of the Seven Isles").

In a period when the "classics" suggested Latin and Greek literature, "standard" was often the preferred term for familiar works from previous centuries. An examination question from 1908 provides a helpful summary of the standard authors still being widely studied in schools by the 1920s. This instructs students to write about the names inscribed around the dome of the Reading Room in the British Museum, from Addison to Wordsworth, including Chaucer, Macaulay, Scott, Shakespeare, et al. (Shayer 58). The term "modern" defies a similar list, although at this time it related more to the concept of "universality" and popularity (as foregrounded in the Newbolt Report) than to the still-evolving terms of literary modernism and to the eventual framework (via Leavis) of a new "canon." In the "Kings Treasuries" series there are also collections of modern prose, and the writers represented there include Chesterton, Galsworthy, and Wells, all of whom, like Conrad, had achieved popularity and commercial success with the general public. As the names in the Dent advert suggest, modern could encompass an eclectic range, from well-regarded literary figures like Conrad and Hardy, to more populist writers. Sewell's *Black Beauty* was a widely-studied novel in schools at the time, while the inclusion of Quiller-Couch owes more to his position as overall series editor.

Conrad enjoyed a cordial relationship with both John Dent and his son Hugh, and the latter recalled his visits to their offices: "On Conrad's few visits to London he always came to see the pater. As my office was then alongside my father's I often heard all the sounds of an exciting talk, usually on literature, but later about the war and the many aspects of it which affected them both" (Dent 228). However, Conrad had misgivings about their plans for educational editions of his work. Early in 1920, Hugh Dent had visited him at Oswalds to discuss the "Kings Treasuries" edition, and in correspondence to Pinker Conrad later commented:

> As I anticipated H[ugh] Dent talked about a school book or rather two school books. Without giving up the idea of the Mirror of the Sea selection he has another in his mind composed of Youth and Gaspar Ruiz. He wanted to know if I object. I don't object. [. . .] Apart from mentioning that speaking generally I did not like the idea of school books and that you were aware of my views I made no reply to his argument. (*CL* 7:18-19)

School books were improving in this period, in line with more creative teaching practices, but no doubt Conrad shared the concerns of his literary peers like H.G. Wells that older-style "horrible annotated editions" and "still more horrible text-books of literature," could ruin the enjoyment of reading (45). He would also have had some familiarity with English textbooks through his sons Borys and John.

Aside from this, as we have seen, Conrad had a particular dislike of his fiction being used to "teach." Little is known about Conrad's own schooldays in Poland, but studies of his early reading experiences suggest the greatest influence came from his parents and personal motivation, not from teachers in a classroom. And so the idea of a teacher-led discovery of literature was somewhat alien for him. As Helen Chambers has explored, Conrad "created his own real and virtual reading spaces" in his various childhood homes, and during his career at sea he experienced how ships functioned as "mobile libraries," where literature was encountered by chance rather than design (35, 68). To extend this description, the ship also provided a "mobile classroom," where in due course Conrad's own fiction was to be enjoyed; as Robert Hampson has noted, a survey of crews' reading habits was published in *The Blue Peter* magazine in 1926, and the records of the Seafarers Education Service reveal that the books borrowed included *A Set of Six* and *Chance* (99). On board ship, literature could be enjoyed without the constraints of questions, exercises and forthcoming examinations, and so for Conrad the packaging of his stories into school books may have represented a particularly unappealing feature of shore-life.

The school book thereby signified the type of scholarly and "systematic" approach to literature from which Conrad wanted to distance himself. And his identity as a non-English writer proved helpful when trying to deter teachers from consulting him as a literary/educational sage. Conrad's educational experiences were very different from his literary peers, as he highlighted to the *Teachers World* in 1923, when invited to share his "Favourite Stories of My Childhood":

> Perhaps you have not realised that my childhood was not passed in this country, and that the names of books I read up to the age of 12 in Polish and French would mean nothing to teachers and pupils of to-day. I was a voracious reader; but the fact that I had read as a child "La Legende des Siècles," the tales of Mme. de Ségur, a lot of Polish poets and certain of the novels of Dickens, Walter Scott, and Cooper (also bits of Byron), in Polish and French translations does not seem very helpful from the point of view of the systematic development of a child's intelligence.[5] (1126, 1128)

Fortunately for Conrad, the "Kings Treasuries" edition of *Youth and Gaspar Ruiz* was conceived in the spirit of contemporary educational pedagogy and, although a school book, it avoided the problems associated with the genre. Conrad was particularly pleased with the section of "questions and exercises" at the back of the book, later urging the publisher Doubleday to do something similar for the American market. In 1923, having arranged for Doubleday to be sent a copy, he wrote:

> the book has been furnished with a set of rather intelligently conceived questions. I call your attention to this feature in view of your plans for getting my work read in schools … I am really impressed by the skill and

judgement displayed in arousing and guiding literary appreciation in the mind of a schoolboy or girl. Even if the child did not attempt to answer the questions they are bound to make him think. (*CL* 8:127-8)

The questions were written by Dr. Richard Wilson, who was Dent's educational adviser from 1915–23, working for Quiller-Couch from 1920 (Dent 198). Like Sampson and Pocock, Wilson was among the more innovative and progressive teacher-editors of the time, writing textbooks such as *Spoken and Written English* (1925) and *Reading and Thinking* (1926–27). These foregrounded the value of sensitive reading, and the latter book included paintings, to encourage understanding of an author's visual effects (Shayer 79). Wilson's range of questions on Conrad's stories reflect this creative approach, as does his note that these "were approved by the author in the spring of 1920" (*Youth* 69). This detail might suggest a measure of editorial "back covering" to pre-empt future authorial complaints, but it serves to emphasize that Conrad was a "living author" on Dent's list, at a time when this status would have conferred a sense of currency for pupils and their teachers. It is also consistent with an increased foregrounding of modern authors as real, creative, people, with whom pupils could engage.

There are twenty-nine questions for "Youth" and twenty-four for "Gaspar Ruiz," entitled "A Conrad Catechism." This suggests Victorian-style rote learning, but the content is actually quite wide-ranging, even encompassing some exercises that today might be regarded as "cross-curricular." Students are encouraged, for example, to explore the stories' historical and geographical associations by dating the events described and looking up locations in an encyclopaedia. Reference is also made to the First World War: a question for "Gaspar Ruiz" suggests locating sentences "which might have been spoken by Nurse Cavell."[6] Some exercises are more traditional, including reading aloud and memorizing specific passages, which remained popular classroom activities at the time.

What is most striking about the questions, however, is their highlighting of Conrad's aesthetics, particularly his visual impressionism, through, for example, the location of "word pictures." This reflects the increasingly creative approaches towards teaching English literature: a contemporary guide for English teachers suggests that children "should be trained to look for pictures in both prose and verse" (Tomkinson 201). Such an activity clearly had a particular relevance for teachers and pupils in the 1920s, given the ubiquity of illustrated magazines (including serial versions of Conrad's stories), and the rapid development of early cinema. Futhermore, associations with the cinematic and pictorial effects of stories provided teachers with a means of engaging their pupils, as in this question for "Youth": "From the words 'They loaded us at last' to 'that fool of a steamer smashed' there is a series of pictures which pass with the speed of film. Study the manner in which this effect is produced." Similarly, questions for "Gaspar Ruiz" draw attention to the "grim pictorial quality" of the execution scene and suggest that the story be considered "from the point of view of a drama."

The nature of these questions and exercises reveals the influence of new initiatives in teaching, which encouraged a focus on an author's stylistic artistry rather than a text's linguistic mechanics. Conrad's literary superiority is asserted throughout, by highlighting his skills in language ("The Author uses words carefully"), and encouraging attentiveness to his style ("The description is worthy of more than ordinary attention"). Conrad is thereby distinguished from more populist writers, and it is easy to see how such an approach would have enhanced his literary reputation amongst young pupils. As a question for "Youth" posits, "The sinking of the ship is impressive. How would a melodramatic writer have described the last glimpse of her 'creed and name?'" (*Youth* 169–74)

Together, these questions and exercises help reveal the usefulness of Conrad's fiction in the classroom. Here was a modern author for modern schools, whose fiction was aesthetically superior to more populist writers, yet revealed the influence of popular entertainments. Furthermore, it was a worthy literary competitor to such entertainments, as C.S. Evans (Conrad's former editor at Heinemann) reminded teachers in an appreciation written for the *Teachers World* in 1924: "A popular artist could illustrate any one of Conrad's narratives in such a way that to skim through the pages would give one the idea of a story as breathlessly adventurous as any that enthral the spectators of a cinema film" (975).

Conrad clearly had little input into the questions for *Youth and Gaspar Ruiz*; he noted in the above cited letter to Doubleday, "As to the catechism at the end intended to assist and guide the teachers I wouldn't know how to compose it." However, he did some additional work on the "Author's Note" for this school edition. The content for "Youth" is a straightforward reprint from the Dent Uniform Edition, but Conrad wrote some material especially for "Gaspar Ruiz." He sent the manuscript for this to Thomas Wise in May 1920, referring to it as "A Short Introduction written especially for a School-book which Dent is publishing, and relating to Gaspar Ruiz" (*CL* 7:98-9).[7] This differs slightly from the "adult" version, which eventually appeared in Heinemann's Collected Edition of *A Set of Six* in 1921. There is an element of crafting which suggests that Conrad had the interests of teachers and their pupils in mind. For example, the "Author's Note" for the school edition is characterized by its more self-conscious musings about the nature of fiction, which would have been instructive for teachers and pupils studying literary form. Unlike "Youth," Conrad explains, "Gaspar Ruiz" is "truly fiction, by which I do not mean it is merely invented, but that it is truly imagined from hints of things that have really happened and of people that have really existed at that time, in that locality and under those special conditions of life" (*Youth* 167).

Conrad also describes how "reading and mental assimilation" about the actuality of historic events had been combined to create a "general picture," an explication which would also have assisted pupils' understanding of his techniques (167). There is also some additional information in the school version: for example, he names "Benavides" as the man who inspired the story, a detail which may have appealed to younger readers tasked with studying characterization. The additional detail (missing in the Collected Edition) about gunpowder being a "comparatively mild explosive" (168) may also have been included as an appeal to the stereotypical schoolboy's imagination. This suggests that, towards the end of his career, Conrad began to engage with the specific interests of his educational audience, despite his initial reluctance to publish editions for schools. However, he continued to resist attempts to become a literary sage for the young at a time when journalistic interest in his work included educational publications like the *Teachers World*.

CONRAD AND THE *TEACHERS WORLD*

On November 2, 1922, Conrad was interviewed for the *Teachers World* by the prolific literary journalist and critic R.L. Mégroz. This interview was published later that month (November 15) in the series "Talks with Famous Writers," then duly incorporated by Mégroz into A *Talk with Joseph Conrad* (1926), and *Joseph Conrad's Mind and Method* (1931). The interview took place at the Curzon Hotel in London on the opening night of the play of *The Secret Agent* at the Ambassadors Theatre. Despite being produced in a limited edition, *A Talk with Joseph Conrad* attracted many press reviews on its publication in 1926, many of which focused on Conrad's calm behavior on the first night of his play, rather than the content of the interview itself; the *Daily Mirror*, for example, dubbed him "Cool Conrad." These reviews reveal the intense interest in Conrad during this period, and how it extended to such speculations about the nature of his "personality," a journalistic interest that Mégroz shared. Such was the risk of fame: as the *Daily Telegraph* put it, Conrad seemed "likely to follow Stevenson into the Valhalla of legend, a very perilous refuge for any reputation."[8]

Conrad had initially been reluctant to undertake the interview; famously wary of the press, he had always objected to journalistic interest in his personal life and character rather than his literary craft. In a letter responding to the request from Mégroz, he writes in appreciative terms about teachers' interest in his "personality," but asserts that his fiction is not "practical, improving, enlightening or even revealing" (*CL* 7:560-61). Conrad's aside about his "certain gift for writing prose" may be read as a polite reminder that this is where the interest should be focused.

The published interview includes details likely to appeal to the readership of the *Teachers World*, such as how Conrad had first learned English, his "favourite prose writers," and his views on grammar, which he describes as a "dreadful grind." With English teachers clearly in mind, Mégroz had also ensured that Conrad's responses spanned the literary forms of prose, poetry, and plays. Conrad's responses were the familiar ones, that he had mainly learned English from hearing it spoken by his fellow sailors, and that he admired Dickens and Keats, but "could not write a line of verse to save my life." In the context of the recent staging of *The Secret Agent*, Conrad also describes his struggles with this form: "I do not know if I shall write another play." He notes his "greatest respect for the writers of the 16th and 17th century—not so much for those of the 18th." Given that the eighteenth-century *Sir Roger de Coverley* was a well established "standard" in the 1920s classroom, teachers may have been amused to read that "Men like Addison leave me cold." The study of Bible passages was another established feature of contemporary English teaching, and so Conrad's comments about that would also be of interest. Conrad describes how Ford Madox Ford gave him a "15th or 16th century Bible, and it had an introduction. I cannot remember the name of the writer. The introduction was in translation, and it was a most admirable piece of prose."

Elsewhere in the *Teachers World* interview, Conrad's evident disregard for formal grammar would have stuck a chord with teachers advocating more liberal approaches to teaching English and less focus on the traditional "rules" of language. "After all," he asserts, "Grammar is so arbitrary, why bother about it?" This is the confident response of a successful author, whose wayward grammar had once been criticized, but whose artistry in the English language was now recognized. Indeed, towards the end of the interview, Mégroz urges teachers to re-read Conrad's work with "an eye upon the descriptive effects," as it is "quite an education in the art of English prose."

The *Teachers World* interview helped to consolidate Conrad's reputation in the classroom, whilst asserting his status as a modern writer whose attitudes towards literature and language reflected the new educational spirit of the times. Conrad's response to Mégroz that it was difficult to name "favourites," because "literature comes into different compartments of intellect" echoes the statements about universality in *The Teaching of English in England* and the potential of literature to promote learning across the curriculum. Furthermore, his personal experience of learning English on board ship exemplified how language could be successfully acquired in the "real world" rather than in a classroom. This provided progressive educationalists with a helpful case study when arguing for more pragmatic and realistic approaches to learning the English language.

CONCLUSION

As we have seen, the teaching of English Literature was undergoing a modernization process in the early 1920s. While the terms of literary modernism had yet to have an impact on the school curriculum, it is clear that—to adapt Susan Jones's term—Conrad benefited from an educational "canon of influence" (206). Indeed, when Virginia Woolf included *Typhoon* amongst the "classics" of literature in *The Common Reader* in 1925, it was already on the JMB Matriculation syllabus.[9] This is, perhaps, not so surprising. The classroom and the literary "salon" were worlds apart, but both were influenced by the progress of modernity. The foregrounding of artistic self-expression, more liberal approaches to language, a greater emphasis on individual creativity and psychology: these ideas informed the teaching of literature just as they influenced literature itself. In this context, Conrad's identity as a "writer's writer" and a "teacher's writer" coincides. Both characterizations suggest a readership paying particularly close attention to the stylistics of his prose, whether for artistic or pedagogic purposes. For teachers, perceptions of Conrad's modernity were nuanced by their identification of a uniquely "foreign/English" style, and an artistry which lent itelf to new and more creative approaches to exploring literature. They did not define him as a literary "modernist," but they did discern something intrinsically "new" in his writing.

In *The Common Reader*, Woolf suggests that Conrad might have been more popular with the general reading public had his writing been less highly stylized and prone to being displayed out of context "among other cut flowers of English prose" (283). Yet it was the stylistic intricacies of Conrad's prose which helped to enhance his popularity with school teachers and educationalists, and it was their influence in the classroom that helped to ensure his fiction reached Woolf's "common readers." We tend to overlook the classroom's influence in this regard, and forget how it provides an important public arena for the reception and interpretation of any author's work. More attention should be paid to this when considering how a text acquires "classic" status and enters the literary canon. The adoption of a text onto the syllabus of an examination board for schools is especially significant, as this indicates that recognition of its artistic value has extended into the public realm, far beyond the scholarly world of universities, and rarified literary circles. Such was the case with texts like "Youth" and *Typhoon*, and it is important to remember that, in the years before Leavis emerged as his champion, Conrad had informed and attentive admirers in a less well-charted, but equally influential, sphere.

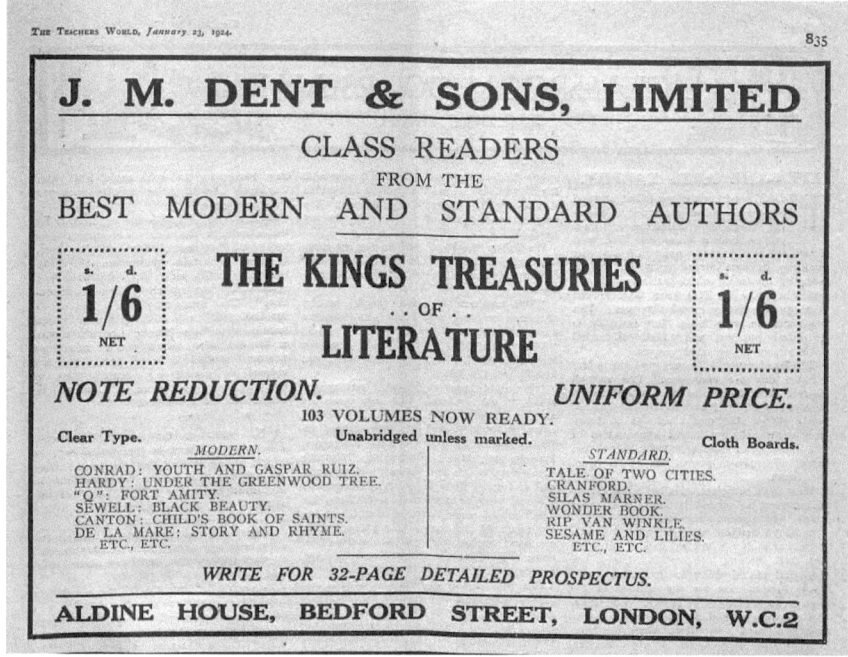

Figure 1. Advertisement for Dent's "The Kings Treasuries of Literature" series, in the *Teachers World*, 23 January 1924, p. 835. ©British Library Board (LOU. LON 405)

NOTES

1. A facsimile of the cited issue of *The Oswestrian* is included in "Conrad First: The Joseph Conrad Periodical Archive," http://conradfirstnet/view/periodicals, last accessed 28 March 2019. I am grateful to Dr. Stephen Donovan for alerting me to this publication.

2. JMB refers to the Joint Board of the Universities of Manchester, Liverpool, Leeds, Sheffield and Birmingham. See *JMB Syllabus and Regulations 1907–1931*, and *University of Lon-*

don Matriculation Papers, January 1924, The University of London Press, Ltd. These are held at the Institute of Education, London.

3. The first edition (1920) of *Youth and Gaspar Ruiz* did not include this note by Pocock, which was added in later reprints, after Conrad's death in 1924.

4. Shayer (1972) provides a useful survey of English teaching in this period, together with a detailed discussion of the Newbolt Report.

5. The other writers included are John Buchan, G.K. Chesterton, John Galsworthy, and Rebecca West.

6. Reflecting the tight budgets and low production costs of such educational editions, these questions were not updated in later reprints.

7. The manuscript for the "Author's Note" to Dent's "Kings Treasuries" edition of *Youth and Gaspar Ruiz* is now held at the Fales Library at New York University.

8. *The Daily Mirror*, and *Daily Telegraph*. Sources are from review cuttings of *A Talk with Joseph Conrad*, held in the archive of R. L. Mégroz, at the University of Reading.

9. See JMB Matriculation syllabus for English Literature, 1924. Typhoon was first included that year, as an alternative to Sir Walter Scott's *Quentin Durward*. Records indicate that it stayed on this syllabus until at least 1929.

WORKS CITED

Board of Education. *The Teaching of English in England*. HMSO, 1921.
Burgoyne, Mary. "'These ignorant and bumptitious reviewers': F.J. Furnivall in Defence of Conrad." *The Conradian*, vol. 35, no. 2, 2010, pp. 121–26.
Chambers, Helen. *Conrad's Reading: Space, Time, Networks*. Palgrave Macmillan, 2018.
Conrad, Joseph. *Youth and Gaspar Ruiz*, The Kings Treasuries of Literature series, Dent, 1920 (rpt. 1924 and 1950).
———. *Collected Letters* of Joseph Conrad, 9 vols., edited by Laurence Davies and J.H. Stape, Cambridge University Press, 1983–2008.
———. "Favourite Stories of My Childhood: A Famous Writers' Symposium." *Teachers World*, 2 March 1923, p. 1126.
Collins, John Churton. *The Study of English Literature*. Macmillan, 1891, pp. 21–2.
Daily Mirror. 6 Nov. 1926, n.p.
Daily Telegraph. 2 Nov. 1926, n.p.
Dent, Hugh R. *The House of Dent, 1888–1938*. Dent, 1938.
Evans, C.S. "Joseph Conrad—by C.S.E." *Teachers World*. 20 August 1924, pp. 973–75.
"Favourite Stories of My Childhood: A Famous Writers' Symposium." *Teachers World*. 2 Mar. 1923, pp. 1126, 1128.
Hampson, Robert. "Conrad, Curle and *The Blue Peter*." *Modernist Writers and the Marketplace*., edited by Ian Willison, Warwick Gould and Warren Chernaik, Palgrave, 1996, pp. 89–104.
Jackson, D. [Form IVa, Oswestry School]. "On Seeing J.P.F., 1860, on a vth Form Desk, *The Oswestrian*, Dec. 1922, p. 22.
Jones, Susan. "Conrad on the Borderlands of Modernism: Maurice Greiffenhagen, Dorothy Richardson and the Case of *Typhoon*." *Conrad in the Twenty-first Century: Contempo-*

rary Approaches and Perspectives, edited by Carola M. Kaplan, Peter Lancelot Mallios, and Andrea White, Routledge, 2005, pp. 195–211.

Joint Board of the Universities of Manchester, Liverpool, Leeds, Sheffield, and Birmingham. (JMB). *The Syllabus of Matriculation Examination, 1907–1931.*

Mégroz, R.L. "Talks with Famous Writers: Mr Joseph Conrad." *Teachers World.* 15 Nov. 1922, pp. 367–68.

Melion Stawell, F. "Conrad." *Essays and Studies by Members of the English Association.* Vol. 6, collected by A.C. Bradley, Clarendon Press, 1920, pp. 83–111.

Pocock, Guy. "A Note on Joseph Conrad." *Youth and Gaspar Ruiz,* The Kings Treasuries of Literature series, Dent, 1924 and 1926.

Shayer, D. *The Teaching of English Literature in Schools 1900–1970.* Routledge, 1972.

Sparks, B.J. *A Matriculation English Course.* University of London Press, 1915.

Stape, John. *The Several Lives of Joseph Conrad.* Heinemann, 2007.

Tomkinson, W.S. *The Teaching of English: A New Approach.* Oxford University Press, 1921.

University of London Matriculation Papers. University of London Press, January 1924.

Wells, H.G. *The Story of a Great Schoolmaster—Being a Plain Account of the Life and Ideas of Sanderson of Oundle.* Chatto & Windus, 1926.

Woolf, Virginia. *The Common Reader.* Hogarth Press, 1924.

Review

Katherine Isobel Baxter and Robert Hampson, eds.
Conrad and Language.
Edinburgh: Edinburgh University Press, 2016. 219 pp.
ISBN: 9781474403764 (hardback); 9781474403788 (e-book).

Katherine Isobel Baxter and Robert Hampson's *Conrad and Language* is a wide-ranging and comprehensive treatment of a central topic in Conrad studies—that of Conrad's understanding of, and wrestling with, language, both as a symbolic system and as a national or regional tongue. With eleven chapters, an introduction, and an afterword, it approaches this subject from divergent and yet complementary methodologies—from affect studies (Josiane Paccaud-Huguet) to disability studies (Baxter) to critical terrorism studies (Andrew Glazzard). The collection might rightly be divided into two sections, with the first six chapters addressing Conrad's exploration of the relationship between word and thing—of the ability (or inability) of language to accurately represent experience—and the next five chapters focusing on Conrad's multilingualism. Thus, although the editors claim in their introduction that the chapters in this volume follow in the tradition of Jeremy Hawthorn and Martin Ray by "approach[ing] the topic of 'Conrad and Language' not from the perspective of comparative linguistics or stylistics, but rather in terms of that 'more than commonly developed consciousness of language', which produced 'an awakened philosophical curiosity about language,'" only the first six chapters really do so (6). The final five chapters follow more closely the trajectory established by the pioneering work of René Rapin, Irmina Pulc, and other scholars who mapped Conrad's negotiation between the various languages he spoke or had in his consciousness. To be sure, these chapters extend beyond the domain of pure linguistic analysis, as they establish telling connections between Conrad's "macaronic" tendencies (his habit of oscillating between languages while writing) and larger concerns of cosmopolitanism, transnationalism, and colonialism, and they are quite valuable in the new angles they adopt in examining "Conrad's existence within and between multiple languages" (Baxter and Hampson 8). Taken together, the chapters in this volume offer a well-rounded and innovative study of Conrad's personal and artistic preoccupation with language.

In his afterword, Laurence Davies identifies two common threads that run throughout the essays: first, he notes an attention to ethics—either the ethics of speech and writing or the ethics of interpretation; second, he detects an awareness "not so much of absence as of incompleteness, loss and imperfection" with regard to language (206, 208). To these I would like to add the following three themes: double voicings in Conrad's texts, Conrad's self-consciousness about his readers, and Conrad's struggle between desiring rigorous linguistic precision and his mistrust of language. These topics are certainly not new to Conrad studies, but they are approached with innovative methodologies that render the content and form of analysis very unique indeed.

Many of the authors correctly discern a linguistic doubleness in Conrad's works. In his examination of Conrad's use of nautical language, Hampson argues that by using mild swear words, substitutes, blanks, and inventive language to represent less palatable swear words, Conrad "offers a double-voiced text: an irreproachable text for the delicate or juvenile reader and a readily translatable text for those with stronger nerves" (19). For his part, John Attridge locates a dualism within Conrad's stylistic imagination between a desire to represent concrete sensory experiences and an interest in more abstract concerns, a dualism that creates a slippage between material and metaphysical worlds (53, 61). Yael Levin also notices a doubling at the narrative level with a dichotomy consistently drawn between the character who acts and the character who remembers and narrates (68). According to Levin, this doubling—and concomitant collapsing of the distance between subject and object—demonstrates Conrad's refashioning of subjectivity along modernist lines, where the subject is no longer cohesive and impregnable but instead is perpetually open to invasion by the language of the other (70). One of the most original pieces is Christopher GoGwilt's chapter on how Conrad probes the transcription, transliteration, and translation of Malay into the Romanized print form of English, which exposes a rivalry between Arabic and Roman alphabets, in order to demonstrate the way in which English is a "site of multiple, discrepant and conflicting histories of language, script and culture" (119). Extending his argument in "The Voice of Darkness" about how "the presence of the French language within statements in English" evidences the object voice at work—the voice of alterity that "splits the enunciation, and consequently the authorial voice"—Claude Maisonnat locates a double voicing created by Conrad's negotiation between French and English, evident in his incorporation—whether unconscious or conscious—of gallicisms, which demonstrate the integrality of French to Conrad's creative impulse and "give a spectral dimension to the narrative as they conjure up another text that remains silent but is mostly present in the mode of absence" ("The Voice" 170; *Conrad and Language* 165). Although approaching the subject from quite different angles, these chapters all attest to the depth and power of the multilayered textuality found in Conrad's fiction.

As all Conrad scholars are almost certainly aware, Conrad was intensely preoccupied with his authorial persona and his reception by the British reading public, a notion to which many of the authors in this volume speak. Hampson's piece, already mentioned, proposes that Conrad manages to attain verisimilitude while representing seafaring terminology for a general readership by using focalization, thereby providing spatial context for the technical language (26). Andrew Purssell explores Conrad's "construction of a mythology of cultural affiliation" in his autobiography, *A Personal Record* (174). Andrew Francis analyzes the incorporation of the languages of the Malay Archipelago into Conrad's fiction in order to show how the colonial enterprise linguistically dispossesses not only the colonized, but also the colonizer—a linguistic displacement surely felt by Conrad (145). Finally, in her keen analysis of the 2012 Russian translations of *The Secret Agent* and *Under Western Eyes*, Ludmilla Voitkovska demonstrates how in his political novels, Conrad cultivated an image of Russia akin to that already circulating in the British imaginary, although doing so caused his rightful place in the Russian canon of British literature to be withheld for quite some time. These studies illustrate the heightened sensitivity of Conrad to his British readers. Situating Conrad's literary production in the context of debates about linguistic purification, immigration, and colonialism, Hampson, Purssell, Francis, and Voitkovska shed new light on Conrad's linguistic sensitivity and his careful construction of both his authorial persona and his reading audience.

The third and most common subject addressed in this volume is the tension Conrad evidently felt between wanting to narrow the gap between signifier and signified and his deep-seated skepticism about language. As already noted, Hampson touches on the problem of technical precision with nautical language. Glazzard similarly attends to the difficulties engendered by technical language in his exploration of Conrad's use of the term "terrorism," revealing how in returning it to the original sense of the psychological and physical violence of state terror in *The Rover* and demonstrating the bodily trauma exacted through "creat[ing] terror with words" in *The Secret Agent* and *Under Western Eyes*, Conrad illustrates the very real, material effects of political language (35,

37). According to Glazzard, political language as used in these novels demonstrates that a stable relationship between word and thing is impossible and that there is "a need for scepticism, vigilance, and an awareness of context and contingency, underpinned by an acceptance that if language has power, that power may be used for a variety of purposes" (41). Attridge's central argument is Conrad's response to G. E. Moore's critique of Absolute Idealism and his engagement with "the New Realism," partly in response to a dislike of journalism's untrustworthy uses of language (45). Attridge contends that while attempting to enact a "rigorous linguistic regimen" to renovate the language of fiction so that it more directly accesses physical reality, Conrad was also aware that literature could not attain to "Perfect Accuracy" because "ideals in all their treacherous vagueness form part of the subject matter of literary representation" (50, 62). In her critical disability studies reading of Conrad's political novels, Baxter challenges Lennard Davis's early readings of Conrad that show disability being used to shore up the hegemony of normalcy, instead asserting that the excess of disability, in its disruptive textual manifestations, functions to reveal how political violence causes linguistic and communicative displacement and to mark ideological discourse as prosthetic in nature (114). Francis too attends to linguistic impairment; however, as with Baxter, linguistic disability serves the ends of ideological critique—this time one targeting the "linguistic decay, inadequacy or compromise to which colonialism contributed" (145). In a volume focused on Conrad's sensitivity to his linguistic otherness, it would have been very welcome for a piece employing a disability studies methodology to do so wholly in order to make a statement about his construction of disability, rather than making disability a prosthetic for another argument. Like David T. Mitchell and Sharon L. Snyder argue in *Narrative Prosthesis*, literary works that use disability as a "narrative prosthesis" make it an "opportunistic metaphorical device" and fail to "take [it] up . . . as an experience of social or political dimensions" (47, 48). Josiane Paccaud-Huguet's study of speech acts in Conrad underscores the tension between written and spoken language, uncovering how Conrad employs the perlocutionary effects of the textual voice—the literary equivalent of the object voice first theorized by Maisonnat in "The Voice of Darkness"—to "awaken the reader to a memory or a truth not accessible to understanding or judgement" (84, 85). Joining affect studies with psychoanalytic and poststructuralist theories of language and the voice, Paccaud-Huguet powerfully illustrates how the materiality of the vocal object in Conrad's writings confronts the reader's body directly with its "pure speechless intensity" (84). Maisonnat also weighs in on Conrad's skepticism about language by suggesting that Conrad's search for the *mot juste* is always already doomed because language is not transparent and, as such, there is always a remainder to signification (161). What emerges from these essays is a multifaceted perspective on Conrad's struggle with the language and medium in which he chose to write.

Given that language can have spoken as well as written aspects, I found it interesting that more pieces did not attend to the aurality of Conrad's fiction—especially when Davies closes the afterword by affirming that "Conrad needs to be heard as well as read" (210). The only one that gestures in the direction of a sonically attuned argument is Paccaud-Huguet's chapter, which explores the silent soundings of the textual voice that demand an ethical response. As such, my only real criticism of this edited collection is that it could have incorporated at least one sustained reading of the phonemic texture of Conrad's works, which, owing to his difficulties mastering the English language noted by so many of the authors, required an intentionality worth meditating upon. In focusing on the graphic components of language, the collection seems to situate itself in the debate as to whether Conrad privileges sight over hearing (a focal point of which is his famous line in the preface to *The Nigger of the "Narcissus"* about using "the power of the written word to make you hear, to make you feel...before all, to make you *see*," with the last word's emphasis interpreted differently by three authors in this collection [14]) as favoring a visual bias in Conrad's oeuvre. All in all, *Conrad and Language* is an inventive, engaging read that is accessible enough for undergraduate English students; that will have a wide appeal for linguists, literary scholars, scholars of transnational studies and migrant studies, and many more; and that is sure to offer many new directions for future studies of Conrad's lifelong investment in the epistemological and ontological concerns of language and the political and ethical dilemmas wrapped up in the negotiations between individual languages.

WORKS CITED

Conrad, Joseph. *The Nigger of the "Narcissus."* Doubleday, 1897, *Internet Archive*, http://archive.org/details/niggernarcissus00conrgoog, accessed 11 December 2013.

Maisonnat, Claude. "The Voice of Darkness." *Conrad's Heart of Darkness and Contemporary Thought: Revisiting the Horror with Lacoue-Labarthe*, edited by Nidesh Lawtoo, Bloomsbury, 2012, pp. 164–80.

Snyder, Sharon L,. and David T. Mitchell. *Narrative Prosthesis: Disability and the Dependencies of Discourse*. University of Michigan Press, 2000.

JENNIFER JANECHEK
University of Iowa

Notes on Contributors

KATHERINE ISOBEL BAXTER is Professor in English Literature at Northumbria University. She has published widely on Conrad including *Conrad and the Performing Arts* (edited with Richard Hand, 2009), *Joseph Conrad and the Swan Song of Romance* (2010), *Joseph Conrad: Contemporary Reviews, Vol. 4* (edited with Mary Burgoyne, 2012), and *Conrad and Language* (edited with Robert Hampson, 2016). She has also published on colonial and postcolonial literature including, most recently, *Imagined States: Law and Literature in Nigeria, 1900–1966* (2019).

STEPHEN DONOVAN is Senior Lecturer in English at Uppsala University, Sweden. His research interests include Modernist and Victorian literature, periodicals history, and empire writing. He is the creator of *Conrad First: The Joseph Conrad Periodical Archive* and is currently working on a study of Victorian investigative journalism and a digital resource on the landmark magazine *Tit-Bits from all the Interesting Books, Periodicals, and Newspapers of the World* (1881–1984).

LINDA DRYDEN is Professor of English Literature and Research Director in the School of Arts and Creative Industries at Edinburgh Napier University. She is the author of *Joseph Conrad and the Imperial Romance* (2000), *The Modern Gothic and Literary Doubles: Stevenson, Wilde and Wells* (2003), and *Joseph Conrad and H. G. Wells: The Fin de Siècle Literary Scene* (2015). She is co-editor of the *Journal of Stevenson Studies* and is responsible for the Stevenson website: www.robert-louis-stevenson.org.

BEN FELDERHOF teaches history at Holland Park School in London. He was awarded a Ph.D. for his thesis "The Tropical forest as symbol and setting in the fiction of Joseph Conrad and his British contemporaries," by Royal Holloway, University of London, in 2018.

JEREMY HAWTHORN is Emeritus Professor at the Norwegian University of

Science and Technology, Trondheim. He has published three monographs and several articles on Joseph Conrad. His *The Reader as Peeping Tom: Nonreciprocal Gazing in Narrative Fiction and Film* was published by Ohio State University Press in 2014, and the seventh edition of *Studying the Novel* by Bloomsbury Academic in 2017. He is currently editing *The Inheritors* and "The Nature of a Crime" for the Cambridge Edition of the Works of Joseph Conrad.

JENNIFER JANECHEK is a Lecturer in Rhetoric at the University of Iowa, where she teaches courses on the rhetoric of disability. Her work has appeared in *Texas Studies in Literature and Language*, *The Conradian*, *Dickens Studies Annual*, *The Victorian*, *Literature & Film Quarterly*, and *The Mailer Review*. She is the winner of the 2016 Bruce Harkness Young Conrad Scholar Award. She is currently working on her book project, "Telephonic Modernism: Engineering the Pure Voice in Modern British Literature."

SUSAN JONES is Professor of English Literature and Fellow of St. Hilda's College. She has published widely on Joseph Conrad (including *Conrad and Women* for Oxford University Press), nineteenth- and twentieth-century women's writing, the periodical press, and modernism. Formerly a soloist with the Scottish Ballet, Glasgow, she also writes on the history and aesthetics of dance. She is founder and director of Dance Scholarship Oxford (http://www.torch.ox.ac.uk/dansox) and author of *Literature, Modernism, and Dance* (Oxford University Press, 2013). She was awarded a Leverhulme Fellowship 2017–18 to write a book on Samuel Beckett and choreography.

YAEL LEVIN is Associate Professor at the Hebrew University English Department and Second Vice President of the Joseph Conrad Society of America. She is author of *Tracing the Aesthetic Principle in Conrad's Novels* (2008) as well as *Joseph Conrad: Slow Modernism* (2020). She has also published on Samuel Beckett and other modernist writers in a number of journals including *Journal of Beckett Studies*, *Journal of Modern Literature*, *Partial Answers*, *Estudios Irlandeses*, and *Twentieth-Century Literature*.

NIC PANAGOPOULOS is Assistant Professor of English Literature & Culture at the National and Kapodistrian University of Athens, Greece. He is the author of *The Fiction of Joseph Conrad: The Influence of Schopenhauer and Nietzsche* (1998), and *Heart of Darkness and The Birth of Tragedy: A Comparative Study* (2002). In addition to his work on Joseph Conrad, he has published on a wide range of canonical writers, including Shakespeare, Swift, Byron, Dickens, Huxley, and Beckett.

JOHN G. PETERS, a University Distinguished Research Professor at the University of North Texas, is past President of the Joseph Conrad Society of America and current Editor of *Conradiana*. His books include *Joseph Conrad's Critical Reception* (2013), *The Cambridge Introduction to Joseph Conrad* (2006), *Conrad and Impressionism* (2001), *A Historical Guide to Joseph Conrad* (2010), *Joseph Conrad: Contemporary Reviews, Vol. 2* (2012), and the Norton critical edition *of Conrad's The Secret Sharer and Other Stories* (2015).

JOHAN ADAM WARODELL was most recently a Postdoctoral Research Fellow at the Institute of English Studies, University of London. He has contributed articles on Conrad to *The Cambridge Quarterly*, *Conradiana*, *The Conradian*, *English*, *ILS*, *Notes & Queries*, and *Partial Answers*. His writing has won prizes from the Joseph Conrad Society, UK, and the Joseph Conrad Society, USA. His first monograph, *Conrad's Decentered Fiction*, is forthcoming with Cambridge University Press.

PATRICIA PYE is a former Senior Lecturer at Bucks New University (UK). She received her PhD in 2013 from Royal Holloway College, University of London, for her thesis "Sound and Modernity in Joseph Conrad's London Fiction." Her publications include *Sound and Modernity in the Literature of London, 1880–1918* (Palgrave, 2017) and articles in *The Conradian*. In addition to sound studies, she is interested in the history of publishing, and is currently researching the educational editions of Conrad's work.

CONRADIANA
A Journal of Joseph Conrad Studies

John G. Peters, Editor
Jana M. Giles, Managing Editor
Editorial Interns: Taylor Barclay, Destinique Fulgence, Caitlyn Hilliard, Eva Hosking, Casey Howard, Bailey Lambeth, Danielle Shepherd, Sachin Shrestha, Ashten Taylor, and Sarah Treadway

Conradiana, an international journal devoted to and welcoming essays on all aspects and periods of the life and works of Joseph Conrad, is published three times yearly in the spring, summer, and fall.

If possible, essays should cite Conrad's works within the text. Except in unusual circumstances, the Conrad texts-cites should adhere to The Cambridge University Press Edition of the Works of Joseph Conrad (if available) or the Uniform edition (Doubleday or Dent).

Submissions should be double-spaced throughout and follow the *MLA Manual of Style*. Manuscripts may be submitted electronically (preferred) as a Microsoft Word file (or in a compatible format) to John G. Peters, Editor, at jgpeters@unt.edu. Authors preferring to submit a hard copy may do so by sending their work to the Editor at 1155 Union Circle, #311307, Department of English, University of North Texas, Denton, TX 76203-5017.

Correspondence should be directed to the Editor, except in the case of subscriptions and other business matters, which should be addressed to Texas Tech University Press sales office, Lubbock, TX 79409-1037. Books for review should be sent to Ellen Burton Harrington, Book Review Editor, Department of English, University of South Alabama, 5991 USA Drive, N., Room 240, Mobile, AL 36588 (eharrington@southalabama.edu).

Subscriptions are $64.00 for individuals and $120.00 for institutions.

Conradiana is indexed in *Abstracts in English Studies, American Humanities Index, Index to Book Reviews in the Humanities, MLA International Bibliography,* and *Twentieth-Century Literature.*

COVER: Detail from "Joseph Conrad Listening to Music," etching by Walter Tittle, courtesy of the Rare Book Room, Southwest Collection/Special Collections Library, Texas Tech University.

This journal is a member of CELJ, the Council of Editors of Learned Journals.

Conradiana—ISSN 0010-6356
Summer–Fall 2017, Volume 49, Numbers 2–3
(published three times a year)
Texas Tech University
Copyright © 2017 Texas Tech University Press
Box 41037
Lubbock, Texas

Printed by Libri Plureos GmbH in Hamburg, Germany